Mark E. Smith and T
Art, Music and Po......

Edited by

MICHAEL GODDARD and BENJAMIN HALLIGAN
University of Salford, UK

ASHGATE

Published by
Ashgate Publishing Limited
Wey Court East
Union Road
Farnham
Surrey, GU9 7PT
England

Ashgate Publishing Company
Suite 420
101 Cherry Street
Burlington
VT 05401-4405
USA

www.ashgate.com

British Library Cataloguing in Publication Data
Mark E. Smith and The Fall : art, music and politics. –
   (Ashgate popular and folk music series)
   1. Smith, Mark E. – Criticism and interpretation. 2. Fall (Musical group)
   I. Series II. Goddard, Michael, 1965– III. Halligan, Benjamin, 1971–.
   782.4'2166'0922–dc22

Library of Congress Cataloging-in-Publication Data
   Mark E. Smith and The Fall : art, music and politics / [edited by] Michael Goddard and Benjamin Halligan.
         p. cm.—(Ashgate popular and folk music series)
      Includes bibliographical references and index.
         ISBN 978-0-7546-6862-6 (hardcover : alk. paper)—ISBN 978-0-7546-6867-1 (pbk. : alk. paper)
      1. Smith, Mark E., 1957 Mar. 5—Criticism and interpretation. 2. Rock music—England—History and criticism. 3. Fall (Musical group) I. Goddard, Michael, 1965–II. Halligan, Benjamin, 1971–.

   ML420.S6716M37 2009
   782.42166092'2—dc22

                                                                2009046894

ISBN 9780754668626 (hbk)
ISBN 9780754668671 (pbk)
ISBN 9781409403920 (ebk)

Printed and bound in Great Britain by
MPG Books Group, UK

MARK E. SMITH AND THE FALL:
ART, MUSIC AND POLITICS

Contents

PART III   THE AESTHETICS OF THE FALL

PART IV   THE FALL, THE MEDIA AND CULTURAL POLITICS

List of Figures and Tables

Figures

Tables

Notes on Contributors

Chris Atton: Professor of Media and Culture in the School of Arts and Creative Industries at Edinburgh Napier University. His long-standing research into alternative media is interdisciplinary, drawing on sociology, journalism, cultural studies, politics and studies in popular music. He is the author of four books, has published numerous papers and is a frequent contributor to edited collections. He has edited special issues on alternative media for *Journalism: Theory, Practice and Criticism* and *Media, Culture and Society*. He is currently researching British post-punk fanzines.

Mark Fisher: Regular contributor to *The Wire*, *Sight and Sound*, *Fact* magazine and *Frieze* and a founding member of the Cybernetic Culture Research Unit but best known for his Weblog, http://k-punk.abstractdynamics.org. Currently he is a visiting fellow at the Centre for Cultural Studies, Goldsmiths College, University of London.

Michael Goddard: Lecturer in Media Studies, University of Salford. His current research centres on East European cinema and visual culture. He has done research into Deleuze's aesthetic and film theories, which has resulted in a number of publications. He is now researching a book on the cinema of the Chilean-born filmmaker Raúl Ruiz. Another strand of his research concerns Italian post-autonomist political thought and media theory, particularly the work of Franco Berardi (Bifo). He is also pursuing research into the fringes of popular music in the 1970s and 1980s, particularly groups such as The Fall, Throbbing Gristle and Laibach.

Mark Goodall: Lecturer in media communications at the University of Bradford. He is the author of *Sweet and Savage: The World through the Shockumentary Film Lens* (Headpress) and is a founder member of The Firminists, an experimental writing group. He is the lead singer/guitarist in the beat group Rudolf Rocker whose song 'Voodoo Lady' was written for *The League of Gentlemen*'s imaginary rock group Crème Brûlée.

Benjamin Halligan: Director of the Graduate School of Media, Music and Performance at the University of Salford. His critical biography *Michael Reeves* (Manchester University Press) was published in 2003. Other areas of recent publication include Andrei Tarkovsky's aesthetics, Socialist Realism, the influence of disco on 1970s sci-fi, new questions of theatre etiquette and the Sarajevo Documentary School. He is currently preparing a study of the militant European films of 1968 and an edited collection *Sights and Sounds: Interrogating the Music Documentary* (Edinburgh University Press), with David Sanjek.

Katie Hannon: A Fall enthusiast, a Pisces and holds a Masters in American Cultural Studies from the University of Manchester. She lives in Chicago with her partner, two cats and a lot of records.

Owen Hatherley: A researcher in political aesthetics at Birkbeck College, London, and a contributor to *Blueprint*, the *New Statesman* and *The Wire*.

Janice Kearns: Senior Lecturer in Media Production at the University of Lincoln, England. A fan of The Fall, she teaches video production and scriptwriting and has a background in broadcast documentaries. Janice has more recently come to media theory and has just completed an MA in Media and Cultural Studies. In her postgraduate studies, she became concerned with the difficulties and debates around the critical analysis of popular cultural artefacts. Her research interests relate to popular television in particular.

Dean Lockwood: Senior Lecturer in Media Theory in the School of Media at the University of Lincoln, England. Seeing The Fall in 1979 was a formative experience. He co-ordinates and teaches theory modules on Media Production and Audio Production degree programmes and MA programmes in Media and Cultural Studies and Digital Imaging. Recent and forthcoming publications include chapters in edited collections on the spectacle of the real, computer games and twenty-first century Gothic, and journal articles on 'torture porn' and Korean horror.

Paul Long: Senior Lecturer in Media and Cultural Theory in the Birmingham School of Media, Birmingham City University. His published work has concerned topics as varied as Charles Parker, DJ John Peel and popular music radio, local history and the cultural politics and redevelopment of his hometown of Birmingham. His book *Only in the Common People: The Aesthetics of Class in Post-War Britain* was recently published by Cambridge Scholars Publishing. He is the editor of the 'Friends of Philip Donnellan' website: http://www.philipdonnellan.co.uk

Angus McDonald: Senior Lecturer in Law, Law School, Staffordshire University, active in research in critical legal theory, law and cultural studies, including papers and publications on law and film, fiction and painting.

Martin Myers: Freelance researcher and writer whose recent work has concentrated on Gypsy families and their experiences of education. He is currently finishing an ESRC funded PhD entitled 'Narrative, Identity and the Crossing of Local Boundaries', which examines relationships between Gypsies in the UK and their neighbours. He is the joint author (with Kalwant Bhopal) of *Insiders, Outsiders* *and Others: Gypsies and Identity* (University of Hertfordshire Press, 2008). He has been listening to The Fall for over 30 years.

Richard Osborne: Fellow of the London Consortium. He was recently awarded a doctorate for his research into the history of vinyl records. His writing on music has appeared in the journals *Critical Quarterly*, *Réseaux* and *Popular Music History*. He currently lectures on the music industry at the University of Surrey and researches films for the project 'Colonial Film: Moving Images of the British Empire'.

Robin Purves: Lecturer in English Literature at the University of Central Lancashire. His principal research interest is in British and American poetry since the Second World War. He has also written on nineteenth-century French poetics and art criticism, with a particular focus on the poetry and prose of Charles Baudelaire and Arthur Rimbaud, and published essays analysing the work of Isidore Ducasse, J.H. Prynne, Denise Riley, Andrea Brady and W.S. Graham, among others. He is currently writing a book on Jacques Lacan and poetry.

Robert Walker: Sound designer, mixer and musician with credits across independent feature films, TV, short films, animation and documentary. He studied Film and Media at the University of Stirling and as a postgraduate studied Film Production (Sound) at UCLA. He teaches Film Sound at Edinburgh Napier University, based at Screen Academy Scotland.

Paul Wilson: Researcher and lecturer at the University of Leeds. His main research interest centres on the relationships between typography, writing and elements of everyday life, most notably sound and place. Recent work has investigated the transformative capacity of new technologies: where images, artefacts and typefaces have been reprocessed into sound. In 2006 he produced a commissioned 'sound-text' for *The Wire*, where twelve months of the magazine's front cover images were remade into a 12-minute audio montage. His contribution to the 'Paintwork: The Fall' exhibition in Berlin in May 2006 was two audiovisual installations derived from the cover artwork to *The Twenty Seven Points* (1995).

Richard Witts: Music lecturer at the University of Edinburgh. His most recent book, *The Velvet Underground* (Indiana University Press), came out in 2006, and he has contributed a chapter on post-punk recordings for the forthcoming *Cambridge Companion to Recorded Music* (Cambridge University Press). He lived in Manchester between 1968 and 1985, co-founded the Manchester Musicians' Collective, was active in Rock Against Racism, played in a local band (The Passage), was founding music editor of *The New Manchester Review* and *City Life*, was – with Margi Clark – Tony Wilson's replacement on Granada TV's *What's On*, was hypothetically The Fall's first manager and introduced Michael Clark to Mark E. Smith.

Andy Wood: was awarded a PHD in 2008 for his thesis '"Come What May, We Are Here To Stay": Popular Cultures and the Formation of Asian and Black British Identities'. He first saw The Fall at Manchester Ritz circa 1987 and owns more Fall records (and other records) than is sensible. He has published fanzines, written for publications including *Is This Music?* and contributed essays to a number of books and publications including *The Routledge Companion to Black British Culture* (Routledge, 2002), *Wasafari* and *A Black British Canon?* (Macmillan, 2007).

General Editor's Preface

The upheaval that occurred in musicology during the last two decades of the twentieth century has created a new urgency for the study of popular music alongside the development of new critical and theoretical models. A relativistic outlook has replaced the universal perspective of modernism (the international ambitions of the 12-note style); the grand narrative of the evolution and dissolution of tonality has been challenged, and emphasis has shifted to cultural context, reception and subject position. Together, these have conspired to eat away at the status of canonical composers and categories of high and low in music. A need has arisen, also, to recognize and address the emergence of crossovers, mixed and new genres, to engage in debates concerning the vexed problem of what constitutes authenticity in music and to offer a critique of musical practice as the product of free, individual expression.

Popular musicology is now a vital and exciting area of scholarship, and the *Ashgate Popular and Folk Music Series* presents some of the best research in the field. Authors are concerned with locating musical practices, values and meanings in cultural context, and may draw upon methodologies and theories developed in cultural studies, semiotics, poststructuralism, psychology and sociology. The series focuses on popular musics of the twentieth and twenty-first centuries. It is designed to embrace the world's popular musics from Acid Jazz to Zydeco, whether high tech or low tech, commercial or non-commercial, contemporary or traditional.

Derek B. Scott,
Professor of Critical Musicology,
University of Leeds, UK

Acknowledgements

The editors would like to acknowledge a number of individuals and organizations who made this publication possible. Thanks go to the Communication, Culture and Media (CCM) Research Centre at the University of Salford, which supported the event 'Messing up the Paintwork', out of which this publication emerged. Special thanks are due to George McKay, Director of the Adelphi Research Institute and of CCM, who supported the project from the outset and both Debbie Hughes and Deborah Woodman who provided essential administrative support. We would also like to acknowledge for their participation in the event Alan Wise, Grant Showbiz and Mick Middles; while they have not contributed chapters to this volume, their presence at the event certainly contributed invaluably towards its realization. David Sanjek, C.P. Lee and Amy McNulty also made valuable contributions to the day as did the art/performance group Globo. Special mention should be made of Irene and Carolyn Smith whose 'visitation' rendered the day even more memorable. We would also like to thank the staff of the Kings Arms, not only for their support of our event but for continuing to provide a unique Salfordian cultural environment. Thanks are due to the Manchester District Music Archive and specifically Matthew Norman and Alison Surtees for documenting the event. Thanks to Simon Reynolds whose pioneering work in the field and encouraging words were very inspiring. Special thanks are also due to Mark Fisher, whose work on The Fall was an inspiration for both the symposium and this publication, and to Richard Witts, who made invaluable contributions to both projects. We would also like to thank all our other authors. Thanks are particularly due to Derek Scott, the *Ashgate Popular and Folk Music Series* General Editor for enthusiastic support of the project and to Heidi Bishop and the team at Ashgate.

Finally we would like to thank Mark E. Smith for casting the runes in the first place.

Image Acknowledgements

The authors gratefully acknowledge the following people and organizations for their assistance in locating and providing images, and granting permissions for their use. Front cover image: Dan Maier (Mark E. Smith, at the Galtymore in Cricklewood, 30 November 2007). Introduction images: Benjamin Halligan. Chapter 1: Figures 1.1, 1.2, North West Film Archive at Manchester Metropolitan University, with thanks to ILS at the University of Salford for granting permission for use; Figure 2.3, Benjamin Halligan; Figures 1.4, 1.5, John Davis and the Visual Resources Centre, Manchester Metropolitan University. Chapter 3:

Figure 3.1, Brendan Jackson (www.brendanjackson.co.uk); Figure 3.2, Nick Blinko, courtesy of Henry Boxer Gallery. Chapter 14: reproduced by kind permission of Rob Waite.

Lyrics Acknowledgements

Lyrics from the following works are reproduced by the kind permission of Kassner Associated Publishers, Ltd:

'New Puritan': Words and music by Mark E. Smith/Marc Riley/Steve Hanley/ Craig Scanlon. © 2006 Cherry Red Songs for The World. Administered by Kassner Associated Publishers Ltd. Used by permission. All rights reserved.

'City Hobgoblins': Words and music by Mark E. Smith/Marc Riley/Steve Hanley/ Craig Scanlon. © 2006 Cherry Red Songs for The World. Administered by Kassner Associated Publishers Ltd. Used by permission. All rights reserved.

Introduction
'Messing up the Paintwork'

Michael Goddard and Benjamin Halligan

One Day in May

On the 9 May 2008, around thirty people gathered for a symposium, which as several participants noted was far from being a typical academic conference. This symposium, 'Messing up the Paintwork', set out to engage with the art and politics of Mark E. Smith and The Fall and from the beginning encountered antagonism and questions of territory, even before the day of the conference itself. From the time it was first proposed, there was a lively discussion thread about the conference on the unofficial Fall website, The Fall Online, most of it sceptical. The contributors questioned everything from the price of admission to the value of highbrow academic discussion led by 'chin stroking grey haired professors' on The Fall or indeed on rock music in general. This antagonism far from being a discouragement was taken as a positive sign, in that the event was engaging directly and conflictually with a unique fan culture who in some cases exhibited highly sophisticated responses to the event even while disparaging it. An example of this interaction was one contributor to the discussion, 'Granny on Bongos', who offered up a series of 'pre-cog' conclusions to the conference topics such as the following:

> * Mark E. Smith and (Northern) working class culture: Likes a pint, doesn't keep pigeons, may or may not like leek soup. Can't keep whippets due to touring. (The Fall Online, 2007)

Ranging from the flippantly sarcastic to the incisive, these ideas about The Fall would have been perfectly at home at the conference itself, even if their intention was to save Fall fans £30 and the waste of a day with a bunch of academics.

The conference itself, while nominally following an academic structure during the day, was composed of a mixture of academics, fans (often combined in the same person) and some associates of The Fall such as producer Grant Showbiz, promoter Alan Wise and music journalist Mick Middles. While the anticipated 'grey-haired professors' were largely absent, there was nevertheless a high level of intellectual analysis during the day but an analysis that responded to the 'territories' of The Fall whether they be defined in geographical, fan cultural, political or aesthetic terms. This ranged in methodologies from close analysis of particular recordings to the interrogation of specific techniques to the more general investigation of the place of Mark E. Smith in relation to media and culture and the North, a diversity of approaches that is fully attested to by this volume of essays.

Towards the end of the afternoon the relatively normal tone of the conference began to shift, a shift marked by Alan Wise's Edgar Allen Poe-like description of Mark E. Smith's Prestwich abode and the latter's psychic powers, which he claimed were fully operational both in his ritualistic live performances and in daily life. Wise kept reminding the audience that there were limits to what he was 'authorized' to say and at one point broke off his discourse to refer to the fact that spies sent by Smith were present in the audience to keep an eye on things. Wise noted that he himself was under psychic observation and at one point during his talk suddenly jolted, which he explained by saying that he feared he may just have gone too far. These unlikely assertions seemed to be validated when, after the conference had moved to the Kings Arms pub, relatives of Smith materialized, demanding to know who had authorized the event and who was getting the royalties (a negative sum as it turned out). This irruption of local (sur)reality, which came in the middle of Mick Middles' talk and screening of his unreleased film on The Fall, completely disrupting it, became incorporated into the event itself, although this was only made possible by skilful diplomacy on the part of Grant Showbiz and others. In the middle of Grant's own talk, a telephone call was received from Mark E. Smith himself, which the former took on stage, telling Mark that it had been a great day and he really should have been there. That some of the event's critics seemed to have come around to the idea was evidenced by comments after the event such as the following:

> I have to say this was the most bizarre conference I've ever attended. Truly a one-off. The Kings Arms evening was unforgettable, with Mark's ethereal interjections, via family and mobile phone, lending weight to Alan Wise's amazing and brilliant talk about MES and his superpowers. (The Fall Online, 2008)

What these shifting relations between this academic event and The Fall Online attest to is a form of 'general intellect' operating between the academy and popular culture, comprised of intellectual rigour, what is generally relegated to trivial 'fan knowledge' and constitutive weirdness within which this collection of essays can also be usefully situated. However, as a collection of writings on The Fall rather than a live event, it necessarily has another immediate context, namely that of existing writing on The Fall, which will be examined in the next section.

Writing on The Fall

A decade ago, it might have been more accurate to entitle this section *not* writing on The Fall and even today in the context of the considerable retroactive interest in punk and post-punk music, The Fall are certainly yet to be accorded the degree of attention of their Mancunian contemporaries Joy Division and their Factory label.[1] Paul Morley, a key figure in the construction of the Manchester Factory myth, has lucidly described his reasons for not writing about The Fall relative to his beloved Warsaw/Joy Division:

> Mark E. Smith … was exactly what he was always going to be as soon as the first Fall played their first show, as if he had already picked out in his buggered brilliant head the songs and albums and jackets and rhythms and melodies and gigs and drinks and arguments and shoes and musicians and marriages and blackouts and birthdays he would live through … Mark E. Smith's coruscating confidence in his own terrible, fully-formed genius verged on the indecent … and did not point me toward intellectual and emotional salvation. (Morley 2008, 32)

The Fall offered none of the transcendence of the Mancunian environment that Joy Division would briefly provide but they instead turned it inside out, uncovering layers of weirdness lurking within the everyday; more importantly, rather than the vague inchoate myth of Joy Division that needed writers like Morley to articulate it in another register, The Fall and especially Smith had no need of such myth-making and in fact positively repelled any such attempts, making them from the beginning daunting figures for prospective interviewers. Some like Ian Penman or Mark Sinker took the risk but little more substantial than short interviews emerged on The Fall until quite recently, with the exception of small circulation books like Brian Edge's *Paintwork* (1989) or the bilingual book of Fall lyrics apparently produced at the request of a German fan of the band (Smith 1985).

In the early 2000s, however, corresponding to the reviving fortunes of the group itself, two books appeared that approached The Fall in radically different ways, emphasizing some of the challenges and difficulties of writing about The Fall.[2] Mick Middles, in his book simply entitled *The Fall* (2003) and for which Mark E. Smith was given a co-authorship credit, clearly felt that something other than a standard rock biography was needed. At any rate, it seems that Smith himself was reluctant to engage in any straight linear account of the group. As Middles quotes Smith in the dialogue that opens the book, 'I don't want there to be any of that retro crap … Don't want it to be another linear rock biography … on The Fall … that would be so dull' (Middles and Smith 2003, ix). Middles' idea was based on having experienced the brilliance of Smith not only on stage but in conversation, which he hoped to recapture 'live' by taking Smith off to the Lake District, plying him with sufficient beers and allowing the brilliant weirdness of Smith's mind sufficient space to express itself. By Middles' own account this was a difficult

---

[1]   On the Factory 'cartel', see Witts in Chapter 1 of this volume.

[2]   In the same year Dave Thompson's excellent annotated discography of The Fall also appeared. See Thompson (2003).

experience and one that resulted in a sprawling and uneven book and yet one that does indeed contain flashes of brilliance.

The opposite approach was taken by the art historian Simon Ford. While Ford was clearly drawn to writing on The Fall out of intellectual curiosity, his book *Hip Priest* (2003) reads surprisingly like a conventional rock biography, with little space devoted to any intellectual analysis. Ford's more academic and linear approach, along with his academic credentials, certainly did not endear him to Smith who declined to participate in the project, and so Ford's book is constructed through a combination of accounts by former band members and a rereading of already existing writings on The Fall. For all its meticulous research into this history, Ford's book is intellectually thin and there are probably more musings as to the significance of The Fall from Middles. It is telling that in ending his book Ford cites a comment from Smith that seems to preclude precisely any intellectual approach: 'The Fall, [Smith] hoped, would always escape analysis: "I don't think established high-art theories apply to The Fall. I'd much rather be seen as a failed pop singer, to be honest"' (Ford 2003, 280). It is as if Ford was at pains to disguise his academic credentials and to adhere to Smith's anti-academic stance and all the more so due to the latter's non-participation in the project.

After a relative lapse in publishing, 2008 was a veritable bumper year for Fall writing, with not only the re-release of the books by Dave Thompson and Middles but new books by Smith himself, the long awaited *Renegade* and Dave Simpson's fascinating book, *The Fallen*. Coming in the wake of renewed interested in The Fall occasioned by the many tributes to John Peel following his untimely death in 2004, and the BBC4 documentary *The Fall: The Wonderful and Frightening World of Mark E. Smith* (2005), in which the ubiquitous Morley participated, and bolstered by the relatively high profile release of *Imperial Wax Solvent* in 2008, The Fall were now occupying a more prominent place in the media landscape than they had for many years.

Renegade itself was something of a disappointment, for the most part lacking the occasional bursts of brilliance evident in the book with Middles or the quality of writing evident in Ford's book. Essentially a series of rants on a variety of topics from musicians to football to marriage, Smith seems to play up to his media persona of a cantankerous, Northern 'fifty year old man' without revealing very much. Part of the problem is the writing style which is neither true to Smith's speech rhythms nor transposed into any writerly style but is instead expressed in a stilted and muted idiom; direct transcripts from Smith's dictaphone would have been preferable. Nevertheless occasional caustic remarks do shine through the text as do the typewritten passages entitled 'Voices' in which Smith cuts up fragments of speech and memories in a disjointed but poetic manner resonant with some of his best lyrics: 'Constant experimentation ... Many a time he's exploded ... They reek of self-pity and confusion ... I'll meet you at the Red at 3.00 ... I hope to become an afternoon amnesiac' (Smith 2008a, 47). These passages rather than talking about Smith and his creative processes actually embody them and are in many ways more revealing than the rest of the book.

Finally, Simpson's *The Fallen* takes the reader on a strange journey in which the writer embarks on the fully admitted obsessional task of tracking down as many Fall members as possible to try to understand the phenomenon of The Fall from the series of intimate perspectives provided by former band members. Surprisingly, this project which would seem to be anathema to Smith given his disparaging views on musicians, ex-members of The Fall and nostalgia, actually includes his participation in an opening interview. Simpson's claim in the book that once touched by The Fall, musicians are never quite the same again is equally applicable to fans and indeed one of the things the book most intimately recounts is the toll of Simpson's own obsession with The Fall on his personal life, particularly on the relationship that falls apart during the writing of the book. Simpson's drive to understand the madness of The Fall clearly borders on a barely controlled obsessional voyeurism on Simpson's part that fully reflects the book's subject.

What this existing literature on The Fall demonstrates is the irreducibly enigmatic nature of The Fall and the impossibility of an exhaustive account. It also shows limits and constraints in getting access to The Fall and Smith's private world, whether in the case of authorized or unauthorized accounts, linear histories or more fluid and non-linear explorations. As a response to this enigma and the self-censorship it seems to have imposed, this volume will break at least one of the unwritten rules of writing on The Fall, namely by being unapologetically intellectual and applying a variety of intellectual methodologies to thinking and writing about The Fall. This is not done in the vain attempt to provide a superior understanding of The Fall relative to previous accounts but in order to provide a different layer of engagement with The Fall, precisely through the kind of intellectual analysis that has so far been avoided. Nevertheless we would maintain that The Fall, as a uniquely intelligent music group, deserves an equally intelligent response and so the variety of essays presented here should be seen as an attempt to come up with ideas adequate to thinking *with* The Fall, a display of intelligent response which is in no way reserved to an academic context. As such this volume aims to complement and extend the already existing writing on The Fall and is no less kaleidoscopic and multi-perspectival than this existing work or indeed the work of the band that inspired it.

From Punk to Post-Punk

In his study of glam rock, Auslander (2006) posits a moment of its inception: the sudden and unwelcome appearance of an unapologetic theatricality rather than authenticity, and showmanship rather than a spontaneous living-in-the-moment, denoting a return to a 1950s conformism rather than a progression of 1960s radicalism, in the midst of the counter-culture. Specifically, this was Phil Ochs performing – to a booing audience – in a gold lamé suit in New York's Carnegie Hall in 1970 (Auslander 2006, 10ff.). Counter-cultural rock music, for Auslander, is marked and structured by its authenticity, as evidenced in the often poor singing voices, interspaced with the lengthy guitar solos that are both qualitative, in respect of musical virtuosity and art, and quantitative, in respect of the need to break out of the commercial confines of pop music. Glam, with a postmodern brio, jettisoned the authentic and embraced the inauthentic – a belated and appropriately perverse Futurist impulse to celebrate the dehumanized, dehumanizing new. Caught between these two poles, as the story goes, the fledgling punks ransacked and then wished a plague on both these houses. The pop-as-event of glam was synthesized with the vaunted authenticity of feeling of psychedelia for an assault on the ossified and moribund music scene, which was emblematic of the wider 'scene' of English life in the mid-1970s.

But what of the rejection that gave rise to post-punk? Here the narrative becomes hazy. Reynolds (2009, x) attributes this, in part, to a lack of research and analysis but anticipates the kind of attention previously afforded to earlier eras. Even at the end of his second volume on post-punk, Reynolds skirts around a firm definition of the subject at hand and, after eventually offering a number of commercial framings for the phenomenon, identifies post-punk as '*a space of possibility*' for new genres of music and a creative response to punk's destructive response to boredom, '*the* problem facing youth in the affluent West' (Reynolds 2009, 408, 415; his italics). In terms of personnel, specifically the trajectory of the Buzzcocks, Joy Division and the links between the Sex Pistols and Public Image Ltd. post-punk represented a second shot at punk. This punk after punk was more thoroughgoing, had overcome opposition-for-the-sake-of-opposition and offered a content recalibrated to form – the 1918 Leninist moment, when the means of production have been seized and the question arises: what now is to be done? Punk and post-punk maintain the relationship of negative correlation, therefore; a mutual antagonism, certainly, but within a shared set of coordinates and concerns. The implication of Mark E. Smith's provocative reading of punk is that post-punk, in the project of The Fall, sought to respond to questions that had remained suspended in the years immediately prior:

> Punk was a safety net for a lot of people, a refuge of sorts from the reality that was 70s Britain. On one side, it was something that the kids could fall into, and out of when it all got a bit too complicated and harsh; and for the older generation, instead of concentrating their minds on the undeniable mess of the State, it provided them with an almost manageable problem. (Smith 2008a, 41)

The answer came in a hanging up of the leather jackets and a binning of the safety pins: music as lifestyle option replaced by music as a critical, philosophical engagement with the world around. But was something lost in this maturing? Punk was vainglorious but – as Savage (1991) and Derek Jarman (in his 1977 film *Jubilee*) recognized – romantic in its radicalism; the world could still be changed. The new manager of the 'almost manageable problem', Margaret Thatcher, who came to office in the same year (*pace* Reynolds) of post-punk's beginning, now precluded the idea of such a possibility. Her quoting of St Francis of Assisi as she arrived at 10 Downing Street could well have been a riposte to the problem of punk – 'where there is discord, may we bring harmony'. What more could be done with dampened utopian impulses but to take stock, regroup and go underground? It is not entirely appropriate to conflate The Fall and post-punk, which is their usual categorization. However, the movement between punk and post-punk is a tendency from and within which the elusive cultural context of The Fall can be considered.

The Fall in Context

A number of essays in this volume note The Fall's uneasy position in the history of contemporary Manchester music; if this history is considered as something of a party and, indeed, it has seemed mostly given over to celebrations and anniversaries, the unwise renewal of acquaintances with old flames and matters of civic pride, then it is a party to which Mark E. Smith has not been invited. This observation holds for a wider consideration of British pop music too: Mark E. Smith rejects The Fall's claim to the pantheon of punk as a matter of course; while acknowledged as an undeniable influence on Britpop by John Harris (2004), The Fall receive only occasional mentions in passing in his history of 1990s music and even The Fall's usual categorization as a post-punk band suggests – in the negative correlation of this term – that they are only to be grasped in respect to that which they are not. The Fall are a lacuna in these ways – an interloper caught between these histories, between locations (are they Mancunian or Salfordian?), between the singular and plural (Smith, or Smith and/or group), between past and present (the sound of the old, post-industrial North? And yet surely the critique of the new?) and between a number of generations. A quick glance around at the baffling demographics of the uncategorizable crowds at Fall gigs will confirm this latter point.[3] The Fall do not pander to nostalgia and so their back catalogue and their critical standing are not historical burdens, or self-declared standards to which they can be then held to account. In this volume, both Long and McDonald suggest that such a turn of events occurs with the perception of The Fall and an appreciation of The Fall as marks of authenticity – unsubsumable within that most homogenizing and conservative of all sectors of the entertainment industry: pop. The rapid turnover of group members works to forever remake The Fall –

---

[3]   Smith describes this 'Fall army' as 'Rigsby pilled up' – seemingly an allusion to Leonard Rossiter's character in the 1970s British sitcom *Rising Damp* (Smith 2008a, 72). Perhaps sartorially and in terms of temperament but certainly in the way in which this older generation is now forced to rub shoulders with the young (Rigsby is a landlord to ne'er-do-well students in his dilapidated Victorian house in Yorkshire), Smith is quite correct in his observation of Fall crowds.

a constant, obsessive-compulsive shedding of skins which gives rise to a protean, shape-shifting, self-renewing entity.

But if such a turnover is understood as the symptom rather than the cause, a reading that Smith himself advances when defending the firings in his autobiography, then what can account for this seemingly bottomless pit of creative energy? It is here that a more useful critical context emerges for The Fall: the long-distance running of the Northern outsider. The immediate precedent could be said to be the Northern stand-up comic, whose milieu (the working men's club) was initially shared with The Fall and whose unending, inexhaustible monologues seemed possessed of inner perpetual motion. Such a 'Northernness' effects an oblique take on the world, neither essentially condemnatory nor celebratory, neither entirely humorous nor doleful. This characteristic is often lazily reduced to 'cynicism' or a Northern 'straight talking' and with an unpolished and scruffy demeanour mistaken for paucity or slovenliness. And yet, as the Vorticists claimed for their manifesto, it is a characteristic that represents a particular vantage point and role for the Northern commentator-creator: 'Tragic humour is the birthright of the North/Any great Northern Art will partake of this insidious and volcanic chaos' (Lewis 2009, 38). Chaos presupposes flux, and flux requires a change that outmanoeuvres that tendency – academic, historical, curatorial or journalistic – to freeze a creative project, round up its associates and belongings and jail the lot in the museum of art. The Fall remain in a state of 'becoming', to borrow Deleuze and Guattari's term, evading capture, shunning identification and confounding analysis.

The Fall in Concert

The lacuna status is a fundamental necessity for The Fall as we encounter them, rather than an historical blind spot. John Peel's often quoted description of The Fall – 'always different, always the same' (quoted in Garner 2007, 282) – seems disarmingly accurate in this light. This lacuna status is in operation in the live experience of The Fall – indeed, it goes some way to explaining the bizarreness of their live appearances. The performances are contingent – seemingly coloured by mishaps, the urgent need for Smith to fiddle with amps or reposition musicians and other obscure concerns that override the temptations to deliver 'the songs', or indeed songs at all. This operating within a field of contingency seems to occur even to the point of abandonment of the stage, the gigs or even the tour, often through or leading to mass sackings (surely the real sense in which The Fall is a post-industrial band). Nothing can be assumed, nothing should be expected – from the earliest days: from a review of a 1979 London Lyceum gig, 'Mark E. Smith was met on stage by a skinhead who poured a pint of lager over his head and landed two punches on his jaw. Smith continued to perform' (quoted in Time Out editors 2008, 198); to the most recent – Smith performed an April 2009 Camden gig in a wheelchair and physically exited three songs before the end, his voice, however, remaining via radio mike from his dressing room. The poet Simon Armitage, in his *Gig*, recalls another such occasion of 'just the standard oddness' arising from Smith's absenting or semi-absenting himself: 'At one stage, Smith walks into the wings and makes a life-mask of his face by covering his head with the curtain, and sings into the microphone through the heavy cloth' (Armitage 2008, 80). In this condition of the unexpected, the project of The Fall – when at their best – remains live, unsettled and in a state of happening. The songs become the sum of their parts; remixed live (via Smith's amp rebalancing work), experimentally and deconstructively, a disassemblage rather than a showcasing as the end in itself. This could be compared with the treatment of the Rolling Stones and 'Sympathy for the Devil' at the hands of Jean-Luc Godard in *One Plus One* (1968), the abstractions of Cubism or the poetry of Francis Ponge. In the context of most groups who have remained active across three decades, such happenstance-liveness reinvents and so redeems the music: it de-karaokizes the songs and de-deifies their singer.

Figures 0.1–0.6   The Fall live in Manchester Academy One, 18 July 2009

Whereas most groups will vamp their imminent arrival, building the expectations that they will, must or can meet with a dazzling beginning, in recent years The Fall defy this frisson of anticipation. Looped film and video clips of singers and performers (from orchestra conductors to heavy metal singers mid-scream to a Boy George *Top of the Pops* entrance) are projected onto the back of the stage; the clips are only a second's worth of real time, but are sometimes stretched or extracted *in medias res*, so that the sound – at some volume – distorts and unnerves and the gestures are rendered as the involuntary, spasmodic jerkings of those in physical or mental distress. The effect is one of a caustic cleansing of the aural palette and deflection of the gaze away from the central point of the venue. Thus when The Fall do take to the stage, once the barrage stops, it cannot but be to a collective relief – the fast broken, the conditioning complete – the corollary of which is a willingness to now generously take any sound or vision on its own terms. This process seems to relate to the importance of 'de-cluttering', which Smith discusses in relation to creative and domestic concerns – from the preparation of lyrics to the number of chairs appropriate to a household (Smith 2008a, 136). Thereafter, then, the songs can be and are explored – often to the ends of being de-articulated rather than re-articulated, and de-familiarized, short-circuiting the unity that comes from that concert audience cry of recognition. This is not so much a process of negation but of a dialogue with the songs as the interlocutor continues to shape and interpret them. The stage becomes a laboratory to this end, although Smith can pace it as if a factory floor manager. Is it any wonder that there are so few bands exemplifying the musical influence of The Fall, and yet a legion who would ape this attitude? For this reason too, the authors of this volume have shunned nostalgia; this is not a history of The Fall, but a contemporary consideration – and therefore the very opposite of Simpson's investigations (2008) into the origins and back-stories of the group.

The Fall and the North

In Part I, three directions are offered as a means of situating The Fall: as in dialogue with geographical, sociological, historical and even architectural framings of the North and its cultures (from Richard Witts), as uniquely a part of the cultural scene of a specific time and particular place (from Katie Hannon) and via the mesh of approaches that give rise to a 'psychogeographical' discourse for Mark Goodall. For Witts, The Fall offers the potential for a splintering of the received histories, social and cultural, of Manchester and Salford. The ideological bias of these narratives, as identified by Witts, underwrites the self-mythologizing embedded in the new tales of the two cities, not least via media representations which Witts dissects forensically and so serves the various creators of and coteries in the industries of Northern cultural heritage. In this respect, the story of Manchester and Salford, accessed through The Fall, is seen to have been subject to that which Raymond Williams (1973) identified as the 'selective tradition'. This 'official' history, limited and circumscribed within tight parameters and given meanings, and often associated with individuals and heroic individuality (rather than collectives and communal achievements), serves only the conception of the past most useful to the dominant forces of the present. Conversely, spinning the story of The Fall through considerations of Manchester and Salford – which is the dramatic arc and narrative relation usually employed by critical commentators and historians of pop music (the checklist here includes dull dole days, pub basement rehearsal rooms, the brother of a girlfriend who plays bass and so on) – is surely part of this problem. For Witts, The Fall delimits: thinking and writing about The Fall effects and necessitates a methodological shift which we hold to be the essential first step for this volume.

Hannon's essay melds an instinctive understanding of this need for an unshackling of The Fall with an insider's perspective. That is, she generously lends her thoughts as an example of the one group with an honourable, irrevocable claim to The Fall: fans, concert-goers, album listeners, compilers of clippings, those whose histories place The Fall down as a marker, mapping life's high and low points onto various Fall gigs. In Hannon's discussion of The Fall, a 'Fall Scene' leads to a series of more local reconsiderations of The Fall's status, origins, meanings and the commentaries to which they give rise. Goodall in contrast calls on a psychogeographical discourse to pin down the mercurial nature of Smith and the history of The Fall – psychically, historically and geographically mapping the lineaments of a rhizomatic, subterranean network of influences and connections, allusions and borrowings. In this respect, at the hands of the psychogeographer-exorcist The Fall seems to be an ectoplasmic materialization – and indeed is often rudely puked out into polite society (one thinks of Smith's occasional and striking television appearances; on the BBC's *Newsnight* in 2004 in relation to the passing of John Peel is the most celebrated) – to be teased out from the spiritual(ist) stirrings in the ether.

The Techniques and Tactics of The Fall

In Part II, the essays hone in on the specific techniques employed by The Fall, in order to invent new forms of music irreducible to pre-existing categories and genres by experimenting with a range of different techniques. While this emphasis on originality, invention and experimentation was a feature shared with many post-punk groups, The Fall explicitly distanced themselves from their contemporaries, ranging from the early punk scene, through the post-punk period dominated in Manchester by Factory records and on up to 'Madchester' and new 'indie' groups like Oasis. Andy Wood's essay focuses on these acts of distinction on the part of The Fall as essential to the music and philosophy of the group over this entire period.

The next two essays in this section focus more directly on specific techniques employed by The Fall, namely their approach to the vinyl record and the distinctive means Smith uses to record his voice, which Robert Walker refers to as 'dictaphonics'. Both essays show the way that the recording techniques employed by The Fall challenge ideas of sonic professionalism whether by mixing 'proper' rock techniques with cheap and homemade instruments or by splicing professional recordings with home recordings, in some cases accidental ones. Whereas

Richard Osborne situates these techniques in relation to the vinyl record, Walker focuses more on production itself, specifically on Smith's use of microphones, dictaphones and other voice recording devices. Drawing on Chion's work on film sound, Walker refers to these practices of voice recording as 'dictaphonics', which he sees as a coherent and consistent strategy used throughout the career of The Fall to generate a different, more active engagement on the part of the listener than that afforded by standard sound recording techniques. In this way the focus on techniques in all three of these essays leads directly to the questions of aesthetics that will be dealt with in Part III. Finally, Owen Hatherley's essay takes on a completely different arena of tactics, namely Smith's notorious approach to band management, contrasting it usefully with Taylor's account of the disciplined worker. In this light the contrast between The Fall and the bands grouped under the Factory umbrella takes on both an aesthetic and a political dimension, as radically divergent modes of production.

The Aesthetics of The Fall

The use of the term aesthetics is probably one that will result in an impression of an inappropriate mixing of high and popular cultures and yet, as the essays in Part III demonstrate, this impure mixture is precisely what is going on in the work of The Fall itself. Mark Fisher's '"Memorex for the Krakens": The Fall's Pulp Modernism', focuses on the relations between The Fall and what Fisher refers to as 'pulp modernism', specifically the works of writers that are associated with 'weird fiction' such as H.P. Lovecraft and M.R. James. References to these authors abound, especially in the period of The Fall from *Dragnet* (1979) to *Hex Enduction Hour* (1982), which is the focus of Fisher's essay. If weird fiction already points to an ambiguous domain between modernist invention and pulp consumption, this is heightened in tracks like 'Spectre vs. Rector', which is a sonically and lyrically complex tale making explicit reference to the abovementioned authors. Fisher sees Smith's inhabitation of this domain as a way of dealing with the contradictions between his proletarian origins and desire to produce intelligent, difficult work, while at the same time avoiding being assimilated into middle-class aesthetics and values. According to Fisher, Smith's engagement with the Weird also accounts for the transformations of media culture in The Fall as well as their transformations of literary modernism by opening up an ambiguous space between the two. Paul Wilson approaches the aesthetics of The Fall in a completely different way, namely through a focus on The Fall's album covers in relation to modern typography. As with the sonic techniques explored earlier, The Fall's album covers bear witness to a consistent deformation of the norms of presentation of recordings, especially through the incorporation of Smith's cryptically scrawled handwriting and the other techniques analysed by Wilson. While it may seem counter-intuitive to analyse The Fall in visual terms, Wilson makes a strong case that Fall album covers are as original a deformation of modernist norms of typography as their music is of the norms of popular music.

The next essay in this section is largely devoted to the close analysis of a single song by The Fall, 'Iceland' (1982), although this is not done through attention to the lyrics at the expense of the music. Rather Robin Purves situates this song in relation to the problematic field of improvisation, claiming that in distinction to the ideologies of free improvisation, this track combines elements of both spontaneity and structure. Purves' analysis shows how the situation in which the musicians were hearing the lyrics for the first time, while the singer was unaware what music would be produced, created a unique situation of mutual, 'idiomatic' improvisation in a much more unstable and tense situation than the ideals of improvisational community. Finally in the last chapter in this section, Martin Myers explores the otherness of The Fall, making reference to Simmel's concept of the stranger. For Myers, however, The Fall are not so much foreign to their cultural environment as the stranger within, at once familiar and strange, and have a transformative effect on the local culture they inhabit and render strange through their otherness to cultural norms. This essay therefore opens up the questions of Mark E. Smith and The Fall's place in contemporary media culture and cultural politics which are addressed in the final section of the book.

The Fall, the Media and Cultural Politics

Part IV opens with Angus McDonald's consideration of The Fall's implicit countering and outmanoeuvring of the media machine and the resultant, diminishing mediation visited upon the band, a media which includes, as McDonald points out, the discipline of Cultural Studies. The Fall, for McDonald, substantially operate in a space outside the industrial imperatives of products to sell and wares to flaunt, a space from which a certain relationship between the followers of The Fall and Smith becomes possible – and one that mirrors and justifies the *praxis* of Smith. Such a consideration allows the notion of authenticity to emerge – an authenticity of both artistic expression and of the give-and-take of the typically personal relationship established between the Fall follower and the band. Friendship, as a relationship necessitating truth, is an appropriate and illuminating term to use in this context, and McDonald returns to the roots of the idea of friendship to this end.

The existence of the authentic has long been held to be an anathema in the postmodern critiques of the workings of the mediasphere and the emotional weightlessness of its 24/7 discourse. It is in this context that Paul Long posits the late disc jockey John Peel as a self-defining media persona in and through his championing of The Fall, and The Fall as authenticated by Peel in turn. The one becomes the talisman to the other: a protection, and a warding off of the evil spirits who would steal the souls of the pure. This relationship confirms Peel's status – *the*

DJ, in British terms, and no more so than in the post-punk era – as essentially an exception in that most postmodern of cultural phenomenon: DJ culture.

Chris Atton offers us an archaeology of The Fall. In the 'fan discourse' of the fanzine, a proto or Ur-pop media of the type that finds its virtual recreation and sometime institutionalization via MySpace and the like, is visible. The dynamism and sophistication of this pre-digital community in articulating and illustrating its own interests, formed and found and founded its own constituency. Such questions of authenticity and consumption, which are explicitly addressed in this section of the volume, and might be termed a 'political economy' of The Fall sound, are mitigated, as Atton, MacDonald and Long indicate, by the way in which commercial considerations never seem to quite capture the essence of The Fall. Their elusive element, seemingly resistant to the effects of commercial exploitation, is founded on the longevity and very continuum of the project of The Fall, and so collapses the several generations of technological advance since The Fall's inception, from photocopier to World Wide Web, into one. To paraphrase Peel: the world may be different, but The Fall remain there all the same. The 'Fall army' – as if directed by Che Guevara (perhaps the only revolutionary Communist leader to whom Smith is not likened by the authors in this volume) – engages on its own grounds and its own terms.

Clearly the relationship between The Fall and the fans is complex and multifarious, and so has prompted our contributors to reach, at times, for a number of 'difficult' philosophical concepts and theorists. Likewise, for the final chapter, Janice Kearns and Dean Lockwood, in setting out to hunt down the nature of Smith's persona in the media, draw on Deleuze and Guattari's theory of a 'minoritarian culture'. Smith's gadfly cameos, and the licences granted to him for as much, and the wider haunting of today's media by the spirit (or spirits) of post-punk, suggest that various issues of an ideological and cultural bent, issues that can be situated at the inception of the post-punk period, do not remain at rest. Kearns and Lockwood, however, buck Brecht's maxim of urging us to forget the good old days in favour of the bad news ones by galvanizing the remarkable legacy of The Fall in relation to what, they anticipate, is still to come.

PART I
The Fall and 'The North'

Chapter One

Building up a Band: Music for a Second City

Richard Witts

There are many good reasons for writing about The Fall, but I will take the worst. The story of The Fall helps us to understand the post-war history of Manchester where the story of Factory falls short of it. Yet in the five years between 2002 and 2007 there has been a concerted attempt to fix a stiff narrative frame around this city's musical life. It has been applied by a cartel associated with Factory and keen to raise their 'heritage' status in the city's cultural profile.

They have done so in order to delimit general sequences of events around the specificities of Factory Records, its founder the television journalist Tony Wilson (1950–2007), its original club night The Factory (1978–80), which was succeeded by its nightclub The Haçienda (1982–97), and the bands associated with the enterprise, chiefly New Order.[1] By constructing and advancing a received post-punk narrative they have swept bands like The Fall out of that history. Yet the stories provided by practitioners and resources such as The Fall, John Cooper Clarke, New Hormones Records,[2] Rabid Records, Band On The Wall[3] or the Manchester Musicians' Collective[4] provide much richer accounts of impacts, scenes, activities, realizations and conflicts than the monochrome frame tightly set around Factory.

This retortive campaign grew from the dismay of Factory associates to a general media critique and marginalization of their venture in the 1990s. Such a reappraisal appeared to precipitate Factory Records' bankruptcy in 1992 and the decline around that time of the fortunes of the Haçienda club, leading to its closure in 1997 and demolition in 2002. The singer of rival group The Smiths mocked Factory's parochial character, while the most successful Manchester band of the 1990s, Oasis, had nothing to do with Factory. Sarah Champion's modish book *And God Created Manchester* (1990) was a flippant survey of the scene that belittled Factory. She wrote of Joy Division's impact, '[y]et even at their peak ... hyped to death by writers like Paul Morley, it was nothing compared to the 90s Manc boom'

---

[1]   A band known as Warsaw (1976–77), then Joy Division (1977–80) that changed its name to New Order (1981–) following the suicide of singer Ian Curtis (1956–80).

[2]   For Justin Toland's history of that label, see http://newhormonesinfo.com

[3]   See http://www.bandonthewall.org/news3.html

[4]   For its history see http://manchestermusicianscollective.org. Also see Messthetics CD No.106: The Manchester Musicians' Collective 1977–82 (Westminster, Mass., November 2008).

(Champion 1990, 11). In contrast, Champion hailed Mark E. Smith as 'the Robin Hood of alternative pop' (Champion 1990, 30).

Nevertheless four recent films have stamped the Factory story onto that of Manchester. Michael Winterbottom's fictional *24 Hour Party People* (2002) was succeeded by three films which circulated in the same year following Wilson's cancer-related death: Chris Rodley's documentary *Manchester from Joy Division to Happy Mondays* (BBC 2007), Anton Corbijn's *Control* (2007) and Grant Gee's documentary *Joy Division* (2007). Associated with these are no less than five books, chiefly Deborah Curtis's *Touching From A Distance: Ian Curtis and Joy Division* (2001), Tony Wilson's *24 Hour Party People: What the Sleeve Notes Never Tell You* (2002) and Mick Middles and Lindsay Reade's *Torn Apart: The Life of Ian Curtis* (2007).[5] It is significant that the Factory story that is being told most loudly is not its near-comical decline (rendered in Winterbottom's film) but that of the project's abrupt rise, an ascent associated with the punctuation mark of Curtis's death. It is Wilson's death, however, that has provided the setting for the former to be iconically portrayed.[6]

In each of the four films the Manchester conurbation of the 1970s is revealed as dilapidated, derelict and deprived. Row upon row of rain-spattered terrace houses are juxtaposed with shots of demolition hammers smashing them down while mucky kids mooch in the rubble. These highly edited images offer a bewildering message; were the people of Manchester and Salford living in caravans parked out of the film crew's sight? The commentaries add to this depressing vista. In Rodley's film journalist Paul Morley, in an image he must have taken years to hone, talks of how 'the street lights somehow made things darker, not lighter'. Both Rodley and Gee, fine directors, told me of the limited range of post-war footage available of the conurbation. Most of what is accessible is held in the North West Film Archive. Both directors used a promotional film from its library shot in 1967 for Salford Council, titled *The Changing Face of Salford*. It is a 'before' and 'after' portrayal of improvements to the Ordsall area, and the rubble sequences come from the former section. I have made a table of Rodley's opening shots (Table 1.1) which lists the sequences. The year of the filming of each segment is shown in the final column, and the whole reveals that Rodley used material shot over two decades to exemplify an impressionistic image of the central 1970s.

---

[5]   The others are Colin Sharp's *Who Killed Martin Hannett? The Story of Factory Records' Musical Magician* (2007), Paul Morley's *Joy Division: Piece by Piece* (2008) and David Nolan's *Bernard Sumner: Confusion: Joy Division, Electronic and New Order versus the World* (2007).

[6]   I suspect that the spate of films in 2007 followed the urgent need to interview and consult with Wilson once his cancer was known about in 2006.

Table 1.1   Opening shots: *Factory: Manchester from Joy Division to Happy Mondays* (Chris Rodley, BBC4, first transmission 21.09.2007)

Shot	Description	Chroma	Time	Duration (secs)	Year
01	Aerial profile church, terraced streets, Ordsall	Clr	00:00	02	1967
02	Smoking chimneys	Clr	00:02	03	1967
03–07	Factory Records sequence	Clr	00:05	23	–
08	Title: Factory – Manchester …	Clr	00:28	11	–
09	Title: The Early Shift	Clr	00:39	03	–
10	Aerial shot of city centre	B&W	00:42	09	1946
11	Piccadilly Square	B&W	00:51	02	1946
12	Ordsall housing estate	B&W	00:53	06	1946
13	Demolition of walls	Clr	00:59	04	1967
14	'Bloody Slums' on wall	Clr	01:03	05	1967
15	Paul Morley	Clr	01:08	04	–
16	Rain on pavements, woman with umbrella, headscarf	Clr	01:12	04	1967
17	Canal, Refuge Building	Clr	01:16	04	1967
18	Canal, gas holder reflection	Clr	01:20	02	1967
19	Rain, puddle, pavement	Clr	01:22	02	1967
20	Car, street	Clr	01:24	02	1967
21	Passage, man walking	Clr	01:26	03	1967
22	Smoking chimneys, terrace houses	B&W	01:29	04	1955
23	Dock gates (a) Barney Sumner v/o	B&W	01:33	04	1955
24	Dock gates (b)	B&W	01:37	02	1946
25	Dock gates end of day (c)	B&W	01:39	06	1955
26	Barney Sumner	Clr	01:45	04	–
27	Street, man, bike	Clr	01:49	03	1967
28	Street, woman, dog	Clr	01:52	03	1967
29	Tony Wilson	Clr	01:55	06	–
30	Demolition ball	Clr	02:01	03	1967
31	Man, sack, rubble	Clr	02:04	06	1967

Meanwhile Tony Wilson in his book version of *24 Hour Party People* set out the premise of the legend that continues to drive the Factory narrative, of how Factory provoked urban renewal:

This was the home of the Industrial Revolution, changing the habits of homo sapiens the way the agrarian revolution had done ten thousand years earlier. And what did that heritage mean? It meant slums. It meant shite ... The remnants, derelict working-class housing zones, empty redbrick mills and warehouses, and a sense of self that included loss and pride in equal if confused measures. (Wilson 2002, 14)

In his demotic way he echoes Disraeli who wrote in 1844 that, 'What Art was to the ancient world, Science is to the modern ... Rightly understood, Manchester is as great a human exploit as Athens' (Disraeli 1948). Having fashioned his trajectory – of how energetic Victorian emprise degenerated into post-industrial inertia – Wilson meshed his big picture with the small when, in Gee's documentary on Joy Division, he led off, 'I don't see this as the story of a rock group. I see it as the story of a city', adding, 'The revolution that Joy Division started has resulted in this modern city ... The vibrancy of the city and all the things like that are the legacy of Joy Division', referring finally to 'The story of the rebuilding of a city that began with them.' This eschatology is endorsed by Gee's 'scriptwriter' – though there is no script – Jon Savage, who wrote an essay to support the documentary in the Spring 2008 edition of *Critical Quarterly*, where his rather rambling discourse is there to back the inclusion of bleak grey photographs he took of Manchester buildings in 1977 (Savage 2008). It seems the sun never shone when Savage was around.

Conversely, let us shine a light on the facts. In the Manchester-Salford complex a period of avid metropolitan modernist planning took place in the 1950s and 1960s, with the objective, first laid out in the 1945 City of Manchester Plan, to eradicate a Victorian heritage of unplanned urban sprawl, one turned to further disarray by momentous wartime damage, and due to which Manchester lacked a vivid civic identity. Instead, the corporation planned a circle of satellite towns in the 'garden city' style of 1930s Wythenshawe, the hub for which would be an entirely regenerated city centre of impressive modern offices and prominent civic amenities, a flagship city to compete with other second cities like Chicago, Manchester's model (HMSO 1995, 11–20).

Meanwhile the post-war pressure for council housing, and the lack of cash and resources, had led not to garden cities, but to a huge inner-city demolition programme. It began in 1954, and in connection with it came the hurried construction of overspill estates such as Hattersley and Langley (HMSO 1995, 24). Yet the re-housing schemes moved too slowly to meet both national and local objectives. Pressure to find cursory solutions was applied by both Conservative (1951–64) and Labour regimes (1964–70). The Corporation produced a second-phase Development Plan to erect new flats in the demolished spaces. Out of this sprouted those inner-city modernist monsters Fort Ardwick, Fort Beswick and the Hulme Crescents, all completed by 1972 and so hastily built that within two years many of the units were uninhabitable (Shapely 2006, 73).

Nevertheless, from the start of the modernist development of Manchester in the mid-1950s until the postmodern shift in the mid-1970s, the vigorous scale of post-war neo-modernist commercial and institutional building resulted in 25 major modernist concrete, glass and steel buildings planned and built for the city complex. Table 1.2 lists these, starting with the surreal 'Toast Rack' domestic science college of 1958 (designed by a local civic architect), progressing through the Towers – such as the iconic Co-op of 1962, Owen's Park 1964, Moberley 1965 and the Maths Tower of 1968 – to the Royal Exchange's spectacular 'space pod' of 1976. This list is not inclusive and excludes, for example, the Arndale Centre, a massive but protracted and piecemeal retail development of the 1970s that was completed only in 1980.

Table 1.2   Manchester's post-war modernist buildings

No.	Name of new building	Year completed
01	Hollings Campus (The Toast Rack)	1958
02	Albert Bridge House	1959
03	Peter House	1959
04	Television House	1959
05	Elizabeth House	1960
06	Oxford Road Station	1960
07	Granada Studios	1962
08	CIS [Co-op] Tower	1962
09	St. John's College	1962
10	Owen's Park Tower	1964
11	St. James's House	1964
12	Piccadilly Plaza complex	1965
13	Moberley Tower	1965
14	Maths Tower	1968
15	Renold Building, UMIST	1968
16	NatWest Building	1969
17	Pall Mall Court	1969
18	Piccadilly Station Approach	1969
19	Portland Tower	1970
20	Bank of England Northern HQ	1971
21	Magistrates' Court	1971
22	Precinct Centre	1972
23	Eagle Star House	1973
24	Royal Northern College of Music	1973
25	Royal Exchange Theatre	1976

Figures 1.1 and 1.2   The 1976 'space pod' in the Royal Exchange Theatre,
                       Manchester. Images from the 1981 documentary *Exchange*

Figure 1.3   The Exchange Theatre today

However, many of the new concrete, steel and glass commercial and institutional buildings were neither varied nor coordinated enough to withstand public disapproval, a notorious example being the complex around the Maths Tower, the Precinct Centre and the Royal Northern College, where the 'streets in the sky' walkways were designed at different heights and so couldn't be connected up. Thus, contrary to the view promoted in the Factory story, the image that Manchester presented to the world was not of a derelict city but of a comprehensively modern one – that had got it wrong. In fact, those were the words that Councillor Allan Roberts, chair of Manchester Council's Housing Committee, expressed in 1977, adding, 'Manchester's not been doing its job.' He admitted this after being cornered by burgeoning sets of tenants' action groups whose campaigns, and the Council's reactions, are well documented in Peter Shapely's essay for the journal *Social History* (Shapely 2006).

The newly formed metropolitan county, the Greater Manchester Council of 1974, identified a clear solution, which materialized as the default postmodern architectural reaction of the period translated to the housing, amenities and image needs of the conurbation: that is, conversion of existing buildings rather than their demolition, identifying conservation areas such as Castlefields, marketing notions of legacy, pedestrianizing the city centre and making the initial attempts within the city to cage modernism within a bricked heritage, firstly and most sensationally at the Royal Exchange Theatre in 1976 and, in that sense following on, the Haçienda of 1982 and, nearby it, both the Cornerhouse visual arts centre and the Greenroom Theatre of 1983. In other words, Factory's nightclub represented a commercial contribution to a public postmodern design project.

In terms of cityscapes and epochs, then, it appears to be in this postmodern context that we must place the birth of The Fall. Yet if we do so we slip into the same trap in which the Factory story has found itself caught. It is a coarse and quixotic determinism that conjures up the grids and correspondences needed to bond building sites and bands, civic plans and popular songs in the way that the Factory faction has done. The Fall certainly emerged – as did Joy Divison – from a set of circumstances tied to urban environment and class, but not wreckage and squalor. And in strictly musical terms we find in the births of these bands continuities from beyond the punk scene, such as Ian Curtis's 'German' look and Smith's Beat style (the bass of The Fall's founder, Tony Friel, was called Jaco, after the jazz bassist Pastorius). Nevertheless, if we are to test whether Factory's modernist claims suit the times, we must check how far a modernist aesthetic was already present in the city's music scene.[7] We can indeed identify bands spawned in the area at the time of the late 1960s that were progressive, utopian and internationalist in tendency: Barclay James Harvest, Van der Graaf Generator,

---

[7]   Sociologist Nick Prior argues interestingly that punk marks the start of popular music's modernist phase (personal communication). I don't agree, but we do agree anyway that these grand epochal categories only seem to work by imposing an aesthetic homomorphism on diverse scenes and forms.

10cc. The short mid-1970s punk scene was definitely a cartoon-like negation of groups like them. But in reaction to that, the effervescent post-punk scene was in general more integrative, tending to mesh convention – such as song form – with experimentation, and to link punk's gestural Luddism with a progressive curiosity for technology and sound production (on stage and in the studio). In the end it might be claimed that Van der Graaf Generator's appearance at the University of Manchester Institute of Science and Technology on 8 May 1976 was more influential to local post-punk aesthetics than the Sex Pistols' two gigs at the Lesser Free Trade Hall on 4 June and 20 July of that year (see Nolan 2006).

Figures 1.4 and 1.5   The 1958 'toast rack' – the Hollings Building,
                        Fallowfield, Manchester, late 1970s

Existent co-ordinates in the mid-1970s air informed this post-punk integrative disposition. One such co-ordinate was the resurgent folk music scene of that time, through which singer-comedians such as Mike Harding and Bob Williamson propelled the Lancashire accent. Yet the conscious assertion of a local lingo, in line with the emergent promotion of a heritage culture, turned to deep embarrassment among progressive minds with the national success in April 1978 of Brian and Michael's glutinous homage to local painter L.S. Lowry, 'Matchstalk Men and Matchstalk Cats and Dogs', and, while Ian Curtis of Joy Division maintained his affected American brogue in order to summon ghosts, others, like Mark E. Smith, gradually adopted ironized or embroidered accents, not in order to 'represent', but to stress the exceptional act of performance. Nevertheless, in 1978, Paul Morley would excitedly review in the *New Musical Express* (NME) a Manchester Musicians' Collective gig under the headline, 'These are the *Mancunian* Mancunians' (see Morley 1978).

And when the conurbation started to re-assess its matchstalk inheritance it found, inside its dilapidated warehouses, post-punk musicians already there, practising. In 'renting the heritage', they were doing little for their health in those dank, freezing echo chambers, but they were working there together to prepare for gigs in old buildings such as The Squat (a derelict music college) or dishevelled clubs with dog-eared music licences such as the Cyprus Tavern and the Russell Club. Rehearsal rooms, 4-track studios such as Graveyard and Revolution, the 'gentle giant' tour manager Chas Banks, Oz PA Hire, promoter Alan Wise and Rabid Records were all part of the micro music industry that sprang up in a state of alternative enterprise, in which Factory acted out the role of Icarus. It was New Hormones, run by the non-Mancunian Richard Boon, that did succeed and that gave The Fall its start in a recording studio. Factory was not the brightest thread in the skein of yarns spun about those times.

Much of the city music scene, even Factory through its proclivity for Situationism, was driven by political critique, and in the experience of many the most class-conscious of all of the bands was The Fall. It always passed a common litmus test for the worth of a band at the time: would it play for free for Rock Against Racism? It would, but Mark E. Smith and Una Baines often stressed that what they believed in formed the content of their work and was not to be confined to a slogan on a banner, for The Fall was critical of both the state we were then leaving and the state that was arriving, and it has remained an agent of broad (as well as picky) critique, the general target of which is, as Smith put it as recently as 26 April 2008 to the *Daily Telegraph*, 'the threat of some kind of standardised horrible society run by a bunch of fucking wankers' (Blincoe 2008).

The vigour and width of this critique surely explains the richness of the material produced in the music and also in the lyrics, and accounts for its range between simplicity ('Repetition') and density ('Spectre vs. Rector'), which informs the entire wayward output of the last 30 years. I emphasize music here because composer Trevor Wishart and I in the Manchester Musicians' Collective (MMC) loved the music of the band, especially the dissonance achieved through three means – tuning, bitonality and looseness of co-ordination.[8] The understandable tendency for reviewers to focus on Mark's lyrics unduly subordinates the sound world in which they're set, and discounts the musicians who contribute so much to the fabric of the experience. After all, The Fall is a band that plays songs. What fascinated Trevor and I was the way that those songs were not so much constructed as discovered, realized by the members working out through time random ideas that were connected only by the presence of the people in the room at that moment.

It is for this reason that I persist in calling The Fall a band, meaning that a band is a team of musicians singled out by a corporate name. The individual identities of the musicians contribute to the integrity of the overall sound, but those identities are of less interest than the aural result. A band is closer to, say, Manchester's Hallé Orchestra, which will take in deputies and visiting players, while the audience, so long as expectations are satisfied, will consider it has heard the Hallé at 100 per cent, not 90 per cent. Conversely, I consider a group to be an assembly of named personalities, who work together but may individually harbour creative ventures. When a group loses a member, it often has difficulty in finding a replacement who will satisfy an audience of the group's fresh integrity. Perhaps the Rolling Stones was the first British rock band to become a group, prompted by the maverick behaviour of Brian Jones, while The Fall is a band that has stayed a band. A tension arises between a band mediated as an entity and the needs of the media to attend to it within the conventional expressions of personality. The person in a position to assume identity on behalf of the band is not necessarily the one in control but the one who can most directly presume authority.

Control is achieved because the band is an entity (as one thing) and it can therefore be framed conceptually (as one thing), and it is through this framing that power is claimed and asserted. In a band it is commonly the person physically closest to the public, the one who takes and needs the least internal co-ordination, the fewest cues.

Smith has alleged in his 2008 autobiography, that 'They [the band] didn't want to be in The Fall. The whole concept of The Fall back then was mine. They didn't get it. The audience did, but not them' (Smith 2008a, 46). In fact its bass player, Tony Friel, started The Fall in 1976. Friel resigned on a matter of principle around Christmas 1977 when Mark introduced his new girlfriend, Kay Carroll, as the band's manager. The result was that the singer took control, turning a once collective venture into a business enterprise under his leadership.

It is this sense of entrepreneurism that most chimes with Manchester's recent history, one which might be crudely termed the Thatcherization of the city. Manchester's Labour-led administration was a target of the (1979–90) Thatcher government's plan *Streamlining the Cities* (1983) which resulted in the 1986 abolition of the Greater Manchester Council and in its place a directive to elevate economic dynamism through the privatization of resources which in turn would generate competition in services, a formulation known as 'entrepreneurial urbanism'

---

[8]   For the relation of The Fall to the MMC, see Ford (2002).

(Ward 2003, 116; Williams 2003, 53–6). This was a move from government to governance, an ideology that New Labour (1997–) persisted with as eagerly as had the Conservatives (1979–97).[9] But it was also designed to impel an assertive urban consumption economy, one which measured prosperity by possessions and which emerged forcefully through the flowering of two related reactionary phenomena in the late 1980s and 1990s – 'Madchester', 'laddism'[10] – focused around the leisure market, mainly in football, alcohol and drugs, and epitomized in the local music scene firstly by Factory's band The Happy Mondays and then supremely by Oasis. Tickell and Peck point out how the privatizing shift of power from elected local authorities to business-led bodies led to the naturalization of male power 'as the legitimate conduit for effective local governance' (1996, 595), signifying how far the story of the Manchester conurbation's apparent resurgence may be read as a reversionary one. There are no happy women in the Factory story.

Indeed, a return to aggressive neo-modernism that so strongly symbolized rejuvenation and success for the Manchester conurbation may explain the surge of high-rise concrete and glass buildings around the city complex, a style derided by Smith as 'glorified fridge boxes' (Smith 2008a, 98).[11] Most noticeable are the 47-storey Beetham Tower (2006) and the Great Northern Tower (2007) among a quasi-modernist resurgence of civic and business showpieces that followed in the wake of the IRA bombing of the Arndale Centre in 1996. The picture is somewhat complicated by, firstly, the introduction of urban grant-aid from the European Union (Bridgewater Hall, 1996) and the advent in 1993 of the National Lottery, which, as a result of campaigns by the architecture profession, offered millions of pounds for new building in sport, heritage and the arts, benefiting major projects in East Manchester and Salford Quays such as the Lowry Centre (2000) and the Imperial War Museum North (2002) (see also Hetherington 2007). Overall, then, Manchester has returned to its modernist mission after a postmodern digression in which Factory played a part. Whether this time the conurbation has got it right rather than wrong is too early to say.

If my remark about Thatcherization and entrepreneurism suggests that Smith is a free market kind of guy, then it needs correcting. He criticized the selfishness of her era, arguing, 'Thatcher's an antagonist … but people voted her in for their

---

[9]   The term New Labour was taken from a 1996 manifesto titled 'New Labour, New Life for Britain'. It differs chiefly from the traditional or 'old' Labour Party (1906–) in its re-writing of the constitution's Clause Four, omitting the term 'common ownership' or nationalization. It is sometimes said that New Labour is socially left-wing and economically right-wing, while Old Labour is socially right-wing and economically left-wing.

[10]   Smith satirizes 'Madchester' in his song 'Idiot Joy Showland' (1991) while the conurbation's feeling of resurgence is dealt with in 'City Dweller' (1994).

[11]   The full quote widens the issue: 'Nowadays the ultimate aim is to get the working class out, that's what gentrification's all about. They think that by building glorified fridge boxes and passing them off as "modern" and "progressive", everybody who walks by them will in time transform into the likes of them!' (Smith 2008a, 98–9).

own greed, all looking at rewards' (Ford 2003, 97). Yet he supported that side of
Thatcher's project that promoted an ethic for gainful work as a personal obligation,
as opposed to a unionized one (an undeniable irony in Thatcher's case, as her
policies were the cause of dramatically high unemployment). In his autobiography
he declares: 'The more you make of your life, then the more you fucking do …
Thomas Carlyle, the Scottish writer, said, "Produce, produce – it's the only thing
you're there for." This is what I'm talking about' (Smith 2008a, 32).[12] Smith adds
that he has a 'very desk-job attitude' to The Fall (2008a, 32). Here the ideological
link is rooted more to principles of 'old' Labour, which through its very title
promotes the centrality of the concept of productive endeavour.

Above all Smith embodies the 'Old' working-class disposition of the
autodidact, who, as Bourdieu states, 'has not acquired his culture in the legitimate
order established by the educational system' and is 'fundamentally defined by a
reverence for culture which was induced by abrupt and early exclusion' (1984, 328).
And in his splendid account of British working-class intellectual life, Jonathan
Rose adds that in order 'to become individual agents in framing an understanding
of the world' autodidacts 'resisted ideologies imposed from above' (2001, 12).
They did so, as did Smith, by reading and arguing, and out of the reading came
the writing. Smith's interest in esoterica reflects autodidacticism, and his late-teen
discovery of another performing/writing Smith, Patti – together with the general
rehabilitation at that time of her Beat forebears, such as William Burroughs whose
cut-up technique inspired the Lancashire Smith – came about just as a resurgence
of radical individual anarchism superseded communal leftist campaigning such
as Rock Against Racism.[13] He is not quite the Manchester one-off he is portrayed
as: the wonderful cartoonist Ray Lowry and cyber-novelist Jeff Noon spring to
mind, in those days good drinkers like Smith. Yet his achievement in gathering
information, gaining knowledge and placing it imaginatively back into public
space is undeniable, while his lyrics that comment on and describe issues around
mental health, linked to the patients he knew at Prestwich Hospital, are unique
and significant. Smith's approach is doubtless informed by the way post-war
Beat ideology dismissed modernist utopianism and replaced it with a voyeuristic
interest in the 'real life' routines of the outlawed and the disenfranchised. The Beat
aesthetic further accounts for The Fall's confluence of experimentation (a very Beat
'living the moment') with its default garage band style, one clearly influenced by

---

[12]   In 'The Philosophy of Clothes', Carlyle writes: 'work it out therefrom; and
working, believe, live, be free! Produce! produce! Work while it is called to-day' (Carlyle
[1832] 2000, 145).

[13]   Shapely (2006) points out how the Manchester tenants' action groups were
undermined by their consumerist priorities, an issue that might also be raised about Rock
Against Racism. Yet the Miners' Strike of 1984–85 and the Poll Tax actions of 1990 showed
that communal acts could be renewed on occasion.

The Velvet Underground, another Beat-influenced band that chopped and changed its members.[14]

Mention of the Velvets connects The Fall with Joy Division, which the Factory story does not permit, although Ian Curtis was almost as much the autodidact as Smith. The Factory story so flattens Manchester that only the Factory and its tenants are left standing. Yet, as Wilson's beloved Situationists declared, 'Beneath the pavements – the beach!' It is through the rubble of what is left, once the Factory story has been foisted on us as the received narrative, that The Fall and the others will provide, as an alternative, the richest, most potent, most kinetic history of that city. As I said, this is the worst possible reason for writing about The Fall, and so I am sorry for wasting your time.

---

[14]   However, Smith would have to leave his own band to go as far as the Velvets did.

Chapter Two
The Fall: A Manchester Band?

Katie Hannon

Is The Fall a 'Manchester band'? The short answer is no; the long answer is no, with a few caveats. In a 2008 article in the *Manchester Evening News*, conveniently titled 'Mark E. Smith: We're not a Manchester band', Smith declared: 'I just don't think we're a Manchester group. We just didn't fit in. We couldn't even get a gig anywhere in Manchester for years' (Clegg 2008). Though it is tempting to use this as conclusive evidence, Smith's disassociation deserves further investigation. While The Fall, and Smith in particular, may be strongly associated with a Northern ethos, the implications of being a musical group from Manchester are entirely different from those of just being Northern. The association with certain movements – like new wave or post-punk in the 1970s and Madchester of the late 1980s – is so strong that 'Manchester' is almost a genre unto itself. However, the same could be said of The Fall, a band that has fused countless influences from across different genres of music, literature and art. It is this fusion that helps them escape being defined by something as simplistic as their city of origin.

In music journalism, the term 'Manchester band' serves as a shortcut for a certain sound or persona that has, thanks to a handful of groups, become associated with the city. The mythology of Manchester's music scene is well-trodden territory: from the Sex Pistols at the Lesser Free Trade Hall in 1976, a gig whose likely musical worth has long been surpassed by its cultural legend, to Stephen Morrissey's awkward beginnings as a bandless lyricist, to Inspiral Carpets roadie Noel Gallagher's life-changing revelation upon hearing The Stone Roses, it's all rather incestuous. Surely bands within a geographical area interact, and may even influence each other to a degree, and certainly there's pride to be had in seeing someone with one's own style and accent receive national acclaim. But media perpetuations about a cohesive Manchester scene or sound over the years border on the fetishistic. Journalists are quick to mention The Fall in passing when discussing Manchester bands, but usually fail to pursue the subject as more than a curiosity. Joy Division and New Order's association with Factory means that, musically and aesthetically, they are the embodiment of Manchester for some. Morrissey has never been shy about his Hulme upbringing, incorporating notable Manchester locales like Salford Lads' Club and the Rusholme neighbourhood into The Smiths' imagery. However, without associating themselves with any particular Manchester hotspot, The Fall is perhaps the band that best represents late twentieth-century Manchester: inscrutable, tense and ever changing.

What sets The Fall apart from other Northern music progenitors is a commitment to complexity and high-mindedness, when this is not a trait often ascribed to Northern cultural products by the mainstream music press, nor to rock 'n' roll as a genre. Mark E. Smith's oblique lyrics do not inspire the same kind of escapism as those about having a good time in the summer sunshine, nor do they fit with the gloom and doom of Ian Curtis or the lovelorn missives perpetuated by Pete Shelley of the Buzzcocks. Because mainstream journalists lack such a shortcut to describe the band, they are often excluded from discussion of the Manchester aesthetic, which is dominated by about half a dozen bands and figures. The moodiness of Joy Division, the pathos of The Smiths, the misplaced self-confidence of The Stone Roses, Happy Mondays' voracious appetite for drugs and the brashness of Oasis are all traits that have come to define the Manchester aesthetic over the last 30 years, and the work of men like Martin Hannett, Peter Saville and Tony Wilson gets highlighted to the detriment of many others who toiled offstage.

Whether or not these personae were affectations is moot; theirs are the images that came across to millions of fans and are ones that have reinforced ideas of Northern music clustering at either end of the overly miserable/overly simplistic continuum. And while The Fall and Mark E. Smith are no strangers to drugs, moodiness or bombastic statements, none of these traits is the dominant characteristic of the group. Nor can we point to The Fall's individualistic sound as the sole reason for their exclusion from perennial celebrations of Manchester's musical culture; there is room in the Manchester aesthetic for a variety of sounds. Consider the music of Joy Division against the music of Oasis, or the Buzzcocks compared to Happy Mondays. Because this collection is something of a mixed bag, musically, we can say that a musical style does not necessarily define what makes a Manchester band, but rather a broad appeal based on music, image, lifestyle or some combination of the three; origins in Manchester; and a clear association with a notable popular culture movement in which Manchester had a predominant role. The Fall, then, adheres to only one of these requirements – origins in the city – yet still dismisses the importance of such a fact. And any casual observer can see that there has never been much consumer desire to replicate The Fall's image or lifestyle. This lack of accoutrements beyond the music is key to understanding The Fall's otherness in regard to Manchester's heavy hitters. The absence of marketability from the group's outset meant that they would be exiled from the mainstream as long as their image remained under Smith's tight control. Luckily, for Mark E. Smith, and for his dedicated fan base, this was of little consequence in The Fall's artistic progression over the years.

Despite their dissociation with Manchester music on the whole, there is a part of The Fall's success that is very much indebted to Manchester. Manchester's distance from London has allowed Smith to forego major record label politics, under which The Fall would not have been able to survive. Geoff Travis of Rough Trade Records, erstwhile home of the group, asserts that Smith 'will always consider himself the spokesman of the Northern roots culture, a culture centered in Manchester' (Kent 1985). Indeed, many of their songs are Northern science fiction homages – 'Lie Dream of a Casino Soul', 'City Hobgoblins', 'The N.W.R.A.' – and the entirety of sophomore album *Dragnet* plays like a paranoid fantasy of the grey north, teeming with spirits and shadowy figures. 'Even when I did romanticize in my music', says Smith, 'it was always about Manchester. That's what I knew best' (2008a, 87). And for all the praise heaped upon other cultures, Smith also finds that travelling has a deleterious effect:

> If someone told me I couldn't leave this country again it wouldn't bother me …
> the more you travel, the more you get away from yourself. You sometimes meet
> these people who have been everywhere and you sort of know they can't get
> themselves together. They don't know what they're about. (Rom 1986)

In the same interview, Smith offers the city a backhanded compliment: he decided to stay in Manchester because he's 'always liked it … I'm not madly in love with the place, it just would be really depressing being in London all the time' (Rom 1986). Frustrating as these conflicting statements may be, they illustrate that Smith is making the best with what he has in Manchester, but not glorifying the city's influence any more than he thinks is reasonable. Being identified with Manchester by a Londoner like Geoff Travis comes off as slightly derogatory, a way to ghettoize The Fall's aesthetic as something niche, and unable to be understood outside its birthplace, relegating Smith to life as a Northern eccentric. Smith may be a Manchester character, but to write him off in such a manner is insulting both to him and to Northern art as a whole, just as to assert that The Fall has no ties to Manchester would be irresponsible. However, as concerns the notion of a continuous scene or adherence to mainstream ideas of what deems a band worthy of the Manchester label, The Fall is detached from its geographical peers in several ways.

There are two overarching ways to explain how The Fall has evaded a regionalized definition. Firstly, the notion of a music scene, especially local and regional scenes, is temporally restrictive, and implies qualities about a band's personnel and music that align it with other bands from that time and place. Secondly, Mark E. Smith both passively and purposefully rejects a simplistic compartmentalization of his music. The proof of The Fall as something bigger than a city, a genre or even its frontman is in the product. With a catalogue containing what is conservatively estimated at 28 studio albums, two spoken word albums, a play, a ballet and a handful of books over four decades, and the number of members and contributors nearing triple digits, daring to use the shortcut of 'Manchester band' would be foolhardy indeed. While the same argument could be made for, perhaps, The Smiths, whose mythos has much to do with their singer, we must also consider that one facet of The Smiths held dear by their fans was the escape fantasy, the hope of transcending where you come from. For Morrissey, Manchester was a large part of that, and hence the specific baggage of Manchester was integral to the group's appeal. The cultural appeal of The Fall, however, is scattered across more categories, with the Manchester or even the Northern identity playing a smaller role in the light of the band's many engaging qualities.

Mark E. Smith has been clear about his desire, personally and for his band, to remain free of misleading labels. The notion of a regional scene is often as much a media fabrication as it is an actual representation, and Smith's statements about Manchester's so-called scenes, in the late 1980s and early 1990s in particular, reveal the hypocrisy and posturing contained therein. Interviewed by Gaz Top on *APB* in 1988, Smith describes any preceding Manchester scene as 'a myth. But it's coming true now. That's what I like to think, anyway' (*APB* 1988). Rejecting the notion of a cohesive local scene necessarily means that The Fall could not and did not want to be included in such a scene. Smith flirted with a Madchester-like sound in songs like 'Telephone Thing' (1990), 'High Tension Line' (1990) and even 'Hit the North' which, with its 1987 release, may have been influential to some of the bands that emerged shortly thereafter. However, he simultaneously rejected the mere notion of a Manchester sound, asserting that one may incorporate certain stylistic and genre elements without being defined by them, elements that in this case were associated with both a sound and a city. Madchester could be considered Manchester's most hyped and least enduring musical movement of the last 30 years, and Smith is right to distance himself from it. Not only did most bands tarred with the Madchester brush fall by the wayside rather quickly after their early-1990s peak, but the genre was almost completely irrelevant to The Fall's music; rarely have The Fall been described as funky or danceable. And despite sharing some influences, like psychedelia and perhaps Smith's beloved Italian house music, the way these influences manifested themselves in and through the work of Happy Mondays, The Stone Roses et al. revealed a much less dynamic interpretation than Mark E. Smith's.

Moving backward from this era, we encounter a Manchester scene that would not be so blatantly mismatched with The Fall's music. Post-punk is one of the more accurate shortcuts used to describe The Fall, but that term itself serves as a catch-all for bands that emerged during the hangover of punk in the very late 1970s and early 1980s. And while The Fall emerged at the same time as Joy Division and the Buzzcocks – and Smith did attend the aforementioned Sex Pistols show in 1976 – he conceived of The Fall as something different from the start. In a 1989 interview, Smith explained:

> I do dislike it a lot when people nowadays go, "You're one of the survivors of the punk movement." But we weren't even a part of that. We used to play with The Buzzcocks and all that but we always were different. I think the Sex Pistols made it into a fashion thing … people were throwing bottles and it wasn't because we were shit, but because we weren't punk. That was really annoying because I considered us as apart of the start of it. That made us quite cynical of punk from the start. (Segal 1989)

In the same interview, Smith pre-emptively knocks down the notion that The Fall may have been had any kinship with the Manchester punk scene at the time, noting that they came from North Manchester, and 'all those other bands were from the south part' (Segal 1989). This is the dominant tactic that Smith uses in interviews to delineate the differences between The Fall and other Manchester bands. South Manchester was looked askance at by Smith, and its cultural and socioeconomic differences from North Manchester gave The Fall's musical uniqueness an ideological underpinning. Indeed, calling someone 'South Manchester' is derogatory in Smith's book, indicative of a dearth of character. Smith has referred to Morrissey as 'a South Manchester Paddy' (Brown and O'Hagan 1989), accused Happy Mondays, who are from Smith's North Manchester hometown of Salford, of practising 'their North Manchester accents', and noted that Tony Wilson, also originally from Salford, 'comes up to me and asks where I buy my clothes' (Peart 1990). In one of The Fall's notable northern-themed songs, 'The N.W.R.A.' from *A Part of America Therein* (1982), Smith delivers a musical condemnation of one 'Tony', described as a 'business friend' of RT XVII, also known as Smith's alter-ego R. Totale. Though there is no forthcoming evidence of Wilson ever having attempted to sign The Fall to Factory, the passage imagines that he may have, as well as Smith's possible reaction.[1] From this, along with Smith's verbal barbs delivered via the media, we can understand that what he resents is the performance of, or false association with, a North Manchester identity for profit or the illusion of authenticity for which so many bands strive. While Wilson and Shaun Ryder may have, like Smith, originated in Salford, Factory Records and the Manchester movement very much benefited from both South and Central Manchester and nationwide patronage and media attention, and bands like The Stone Roses and The Charlatans originated in South Manchester and its environs. Interpreting Happy Mondays as something of a North Manchester minstrel show is illustrative of the disingenuousness of the Factory/Madchester movement as perceived by Smith, and plays another important part in his rejection of the Manchester scene idea.

The second form of The Fall's intentional disaffiliation with Manchester can be found in Smith's rejection of Northern stereotypes, die-hard regional allegiance and the transient culture that comes with music scenes as defined by the media. Smith's relationship with the music press over the years has not been so free and easy. Though he can at times be open, lucid and playful, he just as often comes across as short or cryptic in his answers. Early interviews are heavy on the former incarnation of Smith, but as The Fall grew in both reputation and body of work, so did the perhaps unfounded image of Smith as an unapologetic curmudgeon. His defensiveness about perceived Northern musical and cultural qualities is apparent in a 1981 interview, where he posits that there is an expectation of failure towards Northern, working people both from Southerners and from Northerners themselves:

---

[1]   For these and other lyrics cited, please see 'Lyrics Parade' at The Fall Online: http://fall.byethost13.com/lyrics.html

'I'm Northern; we're all Northern as well, and I don't like the way Northern people degrade themselves; 'cos it's not even a poverty factor … Northern people are so media-hurt that they think something's got to come from somewhere else to be good' (Gill 1981).

There is an interesting dualism in Smith's assessment. Certainly he has always maintained a confident and intelligent persona, and his opinion of how Northerners perceive themselves would then imply that he is not a typical Northerner. And while he seems to take pride in his upbringing, continuing to live in Prestwich, North Manchester, he often stresses the fact that his Northernness – and his Manchester – is one that is entirely different from the one perceived by outsiders. Many Fall songs delineate, bluntly or indirectly, the separation between the band's aesthetic and that of others in the various Manchester scenes. 'Room to Live', from the 1982 album of the same name, contains more anti-Factory sentiment, mocking the clientele of The Haçienda, Factory's nightclub that had opened earlier that year (see Haslam 2003). Released during the dying days of Madchester, in 1991, *Shift-Work*'s 'Idiot Joy Showland' is a clear send-up of trendy Manchester groups, sparing no vitriol for their sartorial choices. 'Choc-Stock', from 1979's *Dragnet*, shuts undesirables out of the Fall's in-jokes while 'City Dweller' from 1995's *Middle Class Revolt*, delivers a sharp command to those who might claim Manchester as their own: 'Get out of my city/You mediocre pseuds.' As national media focus on Manchester dwindled along with Factory Records during the late 1990s and beyond, so did Smith's tendency to address this issue in his lyrics; there are fewer examples of his distaste for the 'scene' to be found post-1995, likely due to his well-known aversion to revisiting the past. However, during Manchester's 15 or so years in the media spotlight, opportunists, posers and hangers-on were perennial favourites for Smith to skewer both in interviews and in his writing.

In another 1981 interview with an American journalist, he twice notes that he is ideologically and geographically removed from the perceived locus of action, '[Joy Division] was a romantic, sentimental, maudlin scene. See, I don't talk or hang around with those people at all, I live at the opposite end of town from Factory Records', and says that he can drink in Prestwich pubs unmolested, whereas if he goes 'to the south side of town, where the student population is, and where Factory Records is … I always get recognized and all that shit' (Marvin 1981). The implication here is that even though Smith is from Manchester, it is *his* Manchester – not the idealized copy broadcasted to outsiders. Smith also uses his association with non-English nationals as a caveat for his regional affiliations. His autobiography stresses repeatedly that he was surrounded by Irish families in his youth, he speaks highly of Americans and American culture, particularly their openness to The Fall, and he briefly exiled himself to Edinburgh in the late 1980s. By pressing these points, Smith damns regional pride as a form of closed-mindedness.

One of The Fall's most salient features is its oft-changing personnel. Regardless of what this may say about Smith as a leader, these changes have played a key role in revitalizing the band's music at critical points, and its sound has evolved over the years because of these changes. And because of this, there is no Fall Mark I or II. Fall fans may each have a favourite line-up, but there is really no consensus as to a watershed album or personnel change that divides the band's legacy in two. This has allowed the group to exist outside any temporal limits that an association with a Manchester scene or an all-Manchester line-up would impose. Aligning oneself with a musical genre is stunting in that these genres tend to remain static in a period of time. Smith calls punk a 'quick statement', acknowledging that its relevance would fade over time (Smith 2008a, 44). And while Manchester has weathered several 'scenes' in the last 30 years, none is sufficient to contain The Fall's music. Moreover, the line-ups often included musicians who did not come from Manchester, bringing with them a different and often refreshing musical sensibility.

The Fall has achieved something remarkable with its body of work: art that makes a statement unencumbered by pretension and irony. Certainly a Northern sensibility – one that can be best described as highly discretionary when it comes to phoniness – has helped in this respect. After eliminating, apparently systematically, unwanted student and 'indie idiot' followings with the *Slates* EP and the 'Hit the North' single, respectively, Smith claimed in 1990 that their fan base was now 'The Manc-est … Survival of the Mancs!' (Collins 1990). He has always sung the virtues of his Northern followers, from the Yorkshire Fall Army to miners from Wakefield. It is sensed that these fans can appreciate Smith as one of their peers, and he enjoys being thought of as such, as it keeps him grounded outside of the music business that he so loathes. So while The Fall is definitely not a Manchester band in the way that may be used as a media shortcut – an approach that is defined by an opportunistic, outsider's point of view – it is every bit a Manchester band in its defiance of this superficial label and in its embracing of an 'other' Manchester. Perhaps it can be best understood by accepting that Mark E. Smith's version of the city is the ideological and geographical opposite of the one tenuously grasped by those unfamiliar with The Fall. As Smith has actively kept The Fall separate from the historically accepted Manchester scenes, he has simultaneously created his own permanent scene just out of town – the only one to which The Fall can ever belong.

Chapter Three

Salford Drift: A Psychogeography of The Fall

Mark Goodall

Music … if it were pursued one-sidedly and without connexion with other field of form, thought, and culture, seemed … a stunting specialization, humanly speaking. (Mann 1968, 73)

The occult is not in Egypt, but in the pubs of the East End – on your doorstep basically. (Smith 2008a, 80)

Why use psychogeography to talk about pop music? The landscape formed by the works of a group such as Mark E. Smith and The Fall offers a diversity of scenes: local, international, cosmic. Thus, how does a person, given that the output of this group is so unique, varied and extensive, 'explain' this terrain? The journey one takes (which in this essay will be 'psychogeographical') is the point of the exercise and the explanation. The search for some sort of 'conclusion' may be fruitless but the diversity of a journey through some aspects of The Fall's output will revive the possibility of something 'authentic'; that which Guy Debord describes as 'journeys within an authentic life that is itself understood as a journey containing its whole meaning within itself' (2003, 70). This drift will incorporate the work of The Fall, Mark E. Smith and the writers and artists that inspired the group and its leader.

Here I wish to suggest that such an experimental approach obfuscating any clear borders while celebrating an eclecticism (the use of parallel processes etc.) can be fruitful. The Lettrist theory of hypergraphy, metagraphics or post-writing where text is combined with other media (photos etc.), for example, can be related to The Fall – especially their record covers.[1] Indeed, the psychogeographical practice of using writing to visualize a location, to render a place in text, is in effect a metagraphic expression. This approach is being applied in another aspect of my work in the study of films.[2]

---

[1] Hypergraphy is an 'ensemble of signs capable of transmitting the reality served by the consciousness more exactly than all the former fragmentary and partial practices (phonetic alphabets, algebra, geometry, painting, music, and so forth)' (Ford 2003, 20). Sound examples of this, where the link between Smith's vocal technique and that of other avant-garde performance is tangible, can be found on the LP recording *Poèmes Letteristes 1944–1999* by Isidore Isou (1999, Alga Marghen).

[2] 'The Wild Eye: Experimental film studies' is a project designed to invigorate, after Robert B. Ray, the discipline of film studies, by encouraging vanguard interactions between

In this essay I will begin with a psychogeographical account of the personality of Mark E. Smith before moving on to the more interesting analysis of the words and music of his group. The quotations placed above demonstrate that it is not sufficient to talk about music simply as sound, and that it is not necessary to have a degree in English Literature or Philosophy to understand the magic beyond the boredom of the everyday. Any 'analysis' of a subject should take the reader off into other areas of discovery, like a dog sniffing a trail. Theory 'for the sake of theory' comes unstuck with a subject as sprawling and rarefied as The Fall. The insect-like network of Fall obsessives will not approve of such arch practices, but as they generally sneer and criticize from the safety of the fanzine/internet it doesn't really matter. The point of the project is to look at The Fall afresh. That is all.

The Drunken King

Looking at the picture of Mark E. Smith in Figure 3.1 takes me back to when the LP *Dragnet* from which it was taken first came out and I bought it. Smith peers inside a derelict (now renovated) greyhound track in Manchester. Viewing the image retrospectively, Smith is situated in the grim landscape of the past – 'the horror of the normal' (Smith 2008a, 79) – a past defined by the urban geographical surrounding of the area he stood in and expressed later through the songs of his group The Fall. To better understand The Fall – psychogeographically – we can begin with the personality of the leader of the group, Mark E. Smith. This is the least fruitful area of exploration because, unless you know a person intimately, it is surely all second-hand supposition. The first thing people want to know about an individual is a portrait, a psychoanalysis of their being (their psyche).

It's true that there are certainly aspects of the personality, habits and organizational strategies of Smith that are echoed in key practitioners of psychogeography, most notably Guy Debord the leader of one of the groups that 'utilized' psychogeography (although *not* the leader of the group that first proclaimed its use),[3] and this is covered in detail elsewhere in the volume.[4] Debord's superb aphorisms neatly apply to the habits of Smith. My favourite is Debord's appropriation of Baltasar Gracian: 'There are those who have got drunk only once, but it has lasted a lifetime' (2004, 30). Debord's admission, after Li Po, that 'For thirty years I have hidden my fame in taverns' (2004, 30) seems also to apply to Smith (see 'In My Area' for a good selection of Smith's aphorisms). Both writers devote chapters of their autobiographies to drinking. Yet this is not the most interesting aspect of linking those radical avant-garde groups with the work

a disparate range of disciplines, techniques and individuals.

[3]   That was Isidore Isou, chief theorist of Lettrism.

[4]   Debord and Smith are characterized by sharing: a megalomaniacal desire to control their collaborators; a fondness for cultivating the company of 'amateurs'; defining their work as a 'game of war'; a delight in violent expulsions; a fondness for alcohol abuse.

Figure 3.1   Mark E. Smith at Belle Vue Greyhound Stadium, Gorton, Southeast Manchester, 1978

of Mark E. Smith and The Fall. Generally the use of Situationist International (SI) texts in discussing The Fall tends to focus on 'negation', of which the early Debord was a master theoretician, and which Smith also arguably celebrates; his work often does not reflect the literary 'visionary tradition' of psychogeography but rather appears to oppose liberal politics and romanticism using sour existential critique. But this tells only part of the story.

The 'classic' French psychogeographers of the 1950s, of course, carried out their experiments in and around the area of the French capital. Paris was by then long renowned as a city of revolution, poetry and art. The ordering principles of the Haussmann re-design of Paris, incorporating the *Grand Boulevards* were seen by psychogeographers as the enemy of play, experimentation, freedom and instinct. Psychogeography is thus often associated with metropolitan excursions and practices (British psychogeography is advocated by a London-centric gaggle made up of the likes of writers Iain Sinclair and Will Self, and filmmakers such as Chris Petit and Patrick Keiller). *In my view, though, psychogeography can be practised anywhere, certainly in a Salford that is real or imaginary.* Many Fall songs reflect on Northern landscape and geography ('In My Area', 'New Puritan', 'M5', etc.). Therefore, in examining the work of The Fall, we must mentally, as well as physically, 'leave the capital'.

A New Urbanism

What, then, would a psychogeography of The Fall look like? Psychogeography, according to the SI, is 'the study of the specific effects of the geographical environment (whether consciously organized or not) on the emotions and behaviour of individuals' (Andreotti and Costa 1996, 69). 'Dreams spring from reality and are realized in it', observed Ivan Chtcheglov in his psychogeographical masterpiece 'Formulary for a New Urbanism' (1996, 15). Psychogeography has a 'pleasing vagueness' (Debord 1996, 18) and the bizarre array of uses of the term and its practices make it challenging and exciting to define, while elusive. Chtcheglov's text incorporates the phrase 'The Haçienda must be built'. This of course links the work of the SI, Manchester's famous nightclub and The Fall. This experiment with The Fall will incorporate real objects such as songs ('Arms Control Poseur', 'Spectre vs. Rector', 'City Hobgoblins'), photographs, record sleeves and lyrics. From these I will project and create readings and interpretations that may become dream-like. The 'drifts' of songs, poetry and art can be magical and elusive, but are always inspired by concrete expression and real environments. Smith, like Chtcheglov, is well read. The books and ideas that inspired the psychogeographers are also those that inspired a shipping clerk from Salford.

The above psychogeographical approach, 'the study of the specific effects', allows for the free interpretation of elements within works and the journeying ('dériving') from particular texts to other sometimes extreme regions of expression. With a complex body of work like that of The Fall it is possible to draw out intriguing aspects that are historical, cultural, poetic, occult and experimental. I will certainly wish to raise some of the literary influences on the words of Mark E. Smith, especially writers Arthur Machen (incidentally also a pioneer of psychogeography) and Malcolm Lowry. Both are regularly acknowledged by Smith to be of major significance and yet are rarely discussed in analyses of The Fall's songs.[5] Also significant is the way in which psychogeography can foreground a personal (psychic and spatial) response to works of art. Psychogeographical approaches allow their user to utilize a particular location as a point of departure for analysis, in this case the North Manchester area of Salford or a song by The Fall and to 'drift' towards ever more eccentric locations and places, both real and imagined. It is an approach encouraging a comparatist/interdisciplinary/alchemical/poetic method, and one which eschews conventional borders and encourages eclecticism and the possibility of bringing 'parallel processes' into the study of cultural phenomena.[6]

The most exciting psychogeographical projects are concerned with Chtcheglov's idea that 'dreams spring from reality and are realized in it' (1996, 15). I believe that the work of The Fall is ideal for this mode of inquiry. The dark humour of The Fall is often absent from any critique and this also can be brought to bear with psychogeographical methodologies. So rather than Debord, it is the work of other figures in the pre-SI psychogeographical movement that will be of primary interest, especially the writings of Chtcheglov,[7] together with other key literary influences on the world of Mark E. Smith that I will now outline.

'Lunar Caustic'

An important influence on the expressions of Mark E. Smith is the British writer Malcolm Lowry. Lowry is a neglected figure, but one who will no doubt rise again upon the centenary of his birth.[8] Smith has noted this lack of esteem and once acclaimed Lowry as 'one of the *best* bloody writers, he wrote the *best* books' (Herrington 1996, 29). Lowry's work has to be read several times in order to gain

---

[5]   Both Machen and Lowry were influenced by Edgar Allen Poe, another favourite of Mark E. Smith, and both were also interested in occult phenomena such as the cabbala. There are precedents for the dérive such as Baudelaire's *Spleen de Paris* and Aragon's *Paris Peasant*. The dérive is best defined as 'a mode of experimental behaviour linked to the conditions of urban society: a technique of transient passage through varied ambiences' (Andreotti and Costa, 1996, 69).

[6]   See also the author's 'Wild Eye' project run in conjunction with De Montfort University.

[7]   In particular Chtcheglov's 1953 text 'Formulary for a New Urbanism'. See Andreotti and Costa (1996, 14–17).

[8]   A Malcolm Lowry tribute was held in Liverpool in the autumn of 2009. This complemented a conference in Vancouver, Canada, the acknowledged centre for the study of Lowry's writing.

the full power of its expression; the text is bursting with rich language, poetic diversions, streams of consciousness, symbolism, experimental modes. Lowry's work rewards re-reading. In the same way the songs of The Fall have to be listened to several times over in order to obtain the fullest experience of the way the words and sounds correspond or clash. The obtuse manner of the phrasing and wording is not always 'obvious'. This partly explains, I think, the negative reviews, particularly of the early Fall singles (see Ford 2003, 55). Lowry was a keen exponent of the occult and was fascinated, like Smith, by the writings of P.D. Ouspensky. Ouspensky was a Russian-born mystical philosopher who devised a 'system' of higher logic. He devised four forms of the manifestations of consciousness. The fourth form could be achieved by 'men of cosmic consciousness', capable of obtaining 'conscious automatism' (Ouspensky 1981, 284). I believe that most of the writers that Smith enjoys – including Lowry – were obsessed with this anaesthetic state. Ouspensky also quotes from Dostoevsky, one of Lowry's key influences. Intriguingly, Ouspensky, who was as uninterested in material wealth as both Lowry and Smith, died in the same year as Arthur Machen (1947), the year in which both *Under the Volcano* and *Doctor Faustus* were published (the work of Thomas Mann is also acknowledged by Smith).

The Fall makes reference to Lowry in a number of ways. One of Lowry's best stories is a short one, 'Lunar Caustic' (1963). This tale of an alcoholic's spell in a mental institution is harrowing, bleak and ominous. This theme, of course, echoes Lowry's greatest work, *Under the Volcano*. The title of the Fall LP *Cerebral Caustic* is surely a nod to Lowry. Lowry's own theories about what makes the best writing echoes The Fall: 'a satisfactory work of art … is full of affects and dissonances … the best kind of novel was something that is bald and winnowed like Sibelius and that makes an odd and splendid din, like Beiderbecke' (1985a, 28). Lowry's obsession with booze can be related to one of Smith's key pastimes. Like many of his heroes (see Debord, Poe, etc.) drinking is important to Lowry. The main character in *Under the Volcano*, Geoffrey Firmin, known as the Consul, treats drinking like a religion where each drink is an act of devoted worship: 'as if I were taking an eternal sacrament he claims' (Markson 1978, 24). The Consul has alcoholic psychosis causing horrific insect visions. We find this echoed in the fiends of 'City Hobgoblins' where the infestation means that 'we cannot walk the floor at night in peace'.

Like Smith, Lowry was obsessed by chance, coincidence, the occult (see for example his letter to Jonathan Cape listing coincidental links between his life and the novel; Lowry 1985b). Lowry once admitted that *Under the Volcano* was, like mescal, 'difficult to get down'. Yet his texts reward re-reading and, like Smith, Lowry was criticized for 'eccentric word-spinning and too much stream-of-consciousness stuff' (Lowry, 1985b, 60). Lowry's obsession with fate is evidenced by his love of the Faust myth and Kretschmar's idea that 'relationship is everything' (Mann, 1968, 49) and manifests itself in a belief in the symbolism of the Jewish cabbala. *Under the Volcano* is made up of twelve chapters, structured in accordance with the 'universal unit' of the number twelve (Lowry 1985b, 65).

Lowry and Smith are influenced by the Faust legend, the idea that one sells one's soul to the devil in order to endure genius. The gothic visions of Goethe's version of the myth would have influenced Smith. Marlowe's use of 'blank verse' for his reading of the legend is echoed in Smith's often deliberately monotonous play with words and poetics. In 'C.R.E.E.P', for example, Smith goes 'beyond the pop lyric with strange lyrics that mean nothing' (Neal 1987, 97). The title of the song is chanted and pronounced and the song is introduced with spoken words in a female voice. The extended scripts of 'Prole Art Threat' (from *Slates, etc.* – see also the text reproduced on the back sleeve that resembles a screenplay) and 'C'n'C-S Mithering' (from *Grotesque*) are built from large sections of the non-rhyming rhythms of the blank verse form. In the song 'Arms Control Poseur', from the LP *Extricate*, the spirit of Malcolm Lowry is evoked when Smith speaks some words from Lowry's diaries ('Death of a sense of humour/'N death of sense /How do you recover from this?'). The way in which blank verse synthesizes into rant/rap in many of The Fall's songs is poetry akin to the work of another Smith – R.T. Smith – whose words form lists of seemingly disjointed thoughts and observations.[9]

Holy Terrors

Another writer important to Mark E. Smith, and one rarely investigated, is the Welsh author and journalist Arthur Machen. It is interesting and probably significant to note that Machen was a pioneer of psychogeography and especially interested in the interconnection between landscape and the mind. Through his strange wanderings he was also interested in what lies beneath the surface: 'the eternal beauty hidden beneath the crust of common and yet commonplace things' (Machen quoted in Coverley 2006, 48). Machen's 1929 story 'The Cosy Room' (Machen 1946a) mines this field of the commonplace occult. The story centres on strange occurrences in a quiet London street as the principal character, having committed a murder, flees to a 'thoroughly pleasant room' in order to escape detection. His guilt and paranoia gradually close in, exposing him to suspicion. In the end his 'cosy room' becomes a 'condemned cell' (Machen 1946a, 104). Machen was acutely aware of the terror lurking in the capital and the irony that in a metropolis one can feel both free to move around unknown while at the same time pursued by fear, much as Smith, 'When I'm in London I feel how a madman would feel. Like there's people whispering behind me back all the time' (quoted in Ford 2003, 93).

An encounter with Machen's earlier story 'The Happy Children' (Machen 1946b) also yields interesting psychogeographical phenomena. The story concerns the visit of a journalist to a town during the First World War and the supernatural phenomena he witnesses one night there, experiences that link the sinking of the *Lusitania* with the Abbey perched high on the cliffs. The story is based on Machen's

---

[9]   See, for example, Smith's collection *The Hollow Log Lounge* (2003).

trip to the town to cover a story relating to the war. Initially I had no idea that the story was about Whitby. But as I read it I realized that the 'North-Eastern district' was indeed that location. I then located another copy of the story in a booklet entitled *Town of a Magic Dream: Arthur Machen in Whitby* (Valentine 1987). This was unearthed in the dusty and parochial surroundings of Whitby Museum. Whitby is of course famous as the setting for part of Bram Stoker's novel *Dracula* and the town is a twice yearly host to a 'Goth Weekend'. The first thing that is noticeable about the booklet is the startling cover illustration by Nick Blinko who also happens to be the singer and guitarist in Rudimentary Peni (Figure 3.2).

While Mark E. Smith's interest in the gothic is well known, The Fall are clearly not a goth band. There seems little to link The Fall with the seaside town (we know how much Smith hates rural spaces). However, as a former paid-up member of the Friends of Arthur Machen (FOAM), Mark E. Smith once attended an Arthur Machen AGM meeting in Whitby, staying at the dark, atmospheric hotel the White Horse & Griffin and drinking in the Angel Hotel, where Machen had stayed. One of the FOAM organizers told me:

> The main thing I remember is an impromptu folk-guitar jam session by society members in the bar of the White Horse and Griffin in which Mark E. Smith was 'treated' to renditions of Velvet Underground classics and *Old Shep is Dead*. He didn't himself join in but looked suitably sardonic. Alas I cannot recall any commentary on Machen as such. (M. Valentine, personal communication, 7/5/2008)

Machen also wrote 'The Novel of the White Powder', a story that clearly influenced another Smith favourite, H.P. Lovecraft. Machen's style of writing horror and the supernatural into everyday occurrences, especially urban metropolitan settings, is echoed in The Fall's urban gothic. The horror is located under the surface of things, an observation Ford makes about Smith's writing (Ford 2003, 13). The Fall's concerns with what Thomas Mann expresses as the 'weirdnesses of nature' (1968, 25) are laid bare for all to see and hear. Even Smith's invention of the alter ego Roman Totale XVII, a figure who 'fled from Lancashire and settled in the Welsh mountains' (Ford 2003, 40), owes its character to Machen (the 'Welsh hills' also occur in the text on the back of the single 'Fiery Jack' which Ford also describes as 'Lovecraft-influenced' (2003, 77). The supernatural can be located across the LP *Dragnet* where psychic phenomena are expressed and conjured. Numerous Fall songs relating the experience of drugs are drawn not just from the personal habits of the group but from the supernatural obsession with the transference offered by substance abuse, particularly Machen's 'The Novel of the White Powder', which Smith described as 'a great drug story' (2008a, 79).

Figure 3.2   Cover illustration by Nick Blinko for *Town of a Magic Dream: Arthur Machen in Whitby* (Valentine 1987)

'City Hobgoblins': Channeling Chtcheglov and Others

> We'll stick punk rock up your fucking arse. Right, here's a good one – it's a bit
> of fucking culture for you. Right, Hobgoblins! Davies! Hit the fucking cowbell
> quick! (Spoken intro to 'City Hobgoblins', Friday 13 June 1980, Eindhoven, the
> Netherlands)[10]

In 1980 The Fall released a single called 'How I Wrote "Elastic Man"'. The B-side
of this single, 'City Hobgoblins', expresses beautifully the range of influences on
The Fall. The song celebrates the absurd, drawing on favourite writers such as
Camus, Sartre and especially Alfred Jarry, whose *Ubu Roi* was a key Fall/Smith
text. The music is a clattering fast-paced romp structured around a rising riff
that slides up the scale. These aspects, of course, can be 'psychogeographically'
explained. In linking Chtcheglov's text with Smith's we can better understand
how art and poetry of the occult can express ongoing truths about the world. A
psychogeography of a song like 'City Hobgoblins' can possibly act as a blueprint
for future investigations into what is often termed the 'wonderful and frightening
world of The Fall'.

Various literary references are associated with the group: 'Bend Sinister' is
also the name of a 1947 Nabokov novel; the group is named after Albert Camus's
The Fall (1956) (the group was originally going to be called The Outsiders). Smith
has expressed approval of Luke Rheinhart's infamous novel *The Dice Man* and
Thomas Pynchon (his essay 'Is it OK to be a Luddite?' will strike a chord with
fans of The Fall). Moreover, for all his love of pop/pulp writings it is clear that a
substantial range of European modernist literary texts have been devoured or at
least scoured for inspiration by Smith. Literary tropes such as collage, cut-ups,
wordplay and temporal experiments are clear in the lyrics. As Charles Neal notes:

> Smith's lyrics often bear no rational symmetry to the actual music, and at
> times he becomes a storyteller addressing things obliquely rather than directly.
> These allegories are often best consumed through album covers and sleeves.
> (1987, 94)

It's interesting that in Smith's live introduction, quoted above, he links the song
with a statement against the derivative, stupid nature of what punk rock had
become. It defines 'City Hobgoblins' and the songs of The Fall, The Fall 'project',
as operating outside and against any generic codes. For me the song acts as a good
example of The Fall as a form of (unconscious?) avant-garde.

Another thing to notice is that in 'City Hobgoblins' we find a parallel interest with
Lettrist/SI writings in the weirdness of locations, especially those of the urban sphere.
'Formulary for a New Urbanism' contains a list of strange locations identified via

---

[10]   Quoted at http://www.culturewars.org.uk/index.php/site/article/dead_hands/

Parisian street locations. Chtcheglov undertakes a series of wordplays to emphasize the strangeness of the Parisian habit of naming shops after the street name:

> Showerbath of the Patriarchs
> Meat Cutting Machines
> Notre Dame Zoo
> Sports Pharmacy
> Martyrs Provisions
> Translucent Concrete
> Golden Touch Sawmill
> Center for Functional Recuperation
> Saint Anne Ambulance
> Café Fifth Avenue
> Prolonged Volunteers Street
> Family Boarding House in the Garden
> Hotel of Strangers
> Wild Street (Chtcheglov 1996, 14)

Looking at this text it strikes me that lists like this appear in Fall songs (sometimes as chants, for example, 'Ludd Gang'). Smith, like Lowry and Chtcheglov, is clearly curious as to how the mundane can be altered, using drink, drugs or other altered states, and is searching for something 'beyond'. The modernist landscape is a veneer, masking both decay and surprise, 'a past merely overlaid with presentness' (Mann 1968, 39). This can often manifest itself, as it did for Chtcheglov, in terms of the mystical or the occult. Both Chtcheglov and Smith write celebrations of run-down areas. Both wrote of psychiatric hospitals: Chtcheglov on Saint Anne (Chtcheglov 1996, 14) a famous Parisian asylum, while Smith 'sang about mental hospitals and paranoia' (Middles 2002, 52). This is evident both in the 1977 song 'Repetition' – 'Oh mental hospitals/They put electrodes in your brain' – and in proclaiming 'the madness in my area' ('In my Area'); Ivan Chtcheglov ended his days incarcerated in a mental institution.

The locations that lie at the heart of the group's formation echo the kinds of spectral sites that Chtcheglov wanted to transform in Paris (for example Mick Middles describes Oozits Club in Shude Hill as 'lost deep in a maze of intimidating streets, flanked with long thin evil shadows and grimly beckoning pubs' with a 'down-at-heel ambience, or beauty' ; 2002, 52). Chtcheglov speaks of a 'fragmentary vision … that must be sought in the magical locales of fairy tales and surrealist writings … forgotten bars … casino mirrors' (1996, 15). His notion of the 'Sinister Quarter' (Chtcheglov 1996, 17) existing as a space ideal for evil happenings is reflected in many Fall songs; the cover of the LP *Dragnet* is scrawled with text from Smith and one of these phrases, 'the streets are full of mercenary eyes', appears to express the horror of the everyday. Smith claimed that 'writing about Prestwich is just as valid as Dante writing about his inferno' (2008a, 86). This 'everyday horror' echoes another of Smith's favourite writers,

H.P. Lovecraft. In particular Lovecraft's short story 'Cool Air' (1928) opens with a statement expressing this mode of ordinary madness: 'It is a mistake to fancy that horror is associated inextricably with darkness, silence and solitude. I found it in the glare of mid-afternoon' (Lovecraft 1964, 59). There is nightmarish unearthly sensation in 'Repetition', an expression of a person trapped in a zone of fear and so the song is a good example of what the SI, in defining the psychogeographical dérive as a 'science-fiction of urbanism',[11] imagined as an account of the brutalizing effect of the modern world.

So much for words. Chtcheglov's unforgettable line was that 'dreams spring from reality and are realized in it'. His work was an experiment in the avant-garde; his technique echoes the improvisation that is evident in the working methods of The Fall (see, for example, 'Spectre vs. Rector'). The art Chtcheglov imagined here was both textual (Poe) and visual (the paintings of Claude Lorrain). His text has a wonderful lyrical quality to it; I suggest that this is what made most critics suspicious of this text and more favourable to the more 'political' writings of the groups that superseded Lettrism.

Clearly, though, songs by The Fall have an audio-musical aspect that cannot be dismissed. Smith, like Isou with his metagraphic expressions (grunts, shouts, wordplay), uses the spoken word to great effect. The sound of 'City Hobgoblins', beginning with the 'pagan' clang of the cowbell, recalls the sound of the group's key musical influences, in particular the 'garage' sound of groups such as The Monks, two of whose songs The Fall covered for *Extricate*, and the avant-rock of German group Can, where again the notion of the 'made-up words' of their singer Damo Suzuki comes into play. Although The Fall were always keen to distance themselves from any movement and in particular the punk movement, there can be discerned elements drawn from a group such as Rudimentary Peni, notably that group's emphasis on noise, use of drones and choice of subject matter. See, for example, 'Macabre Heritage' on *Cacophony*, a tribute album to H.P. Lovecraft, which repeats the names of decadent writers such as Poe, Huysmans, Machen and M.R. James. In other works by The Fall, of course, musical/sound elements are subject to experimentation. 'Live at the Witch Trials' is a brief fragment with spoken words and eerie descending single guitar notes. In 'Muzorewi's Daughter' a tribal sound is used; in 'Spectre vs. Rector' a frightening drone expresses the group's attempt at 'writing *out* of the song' (Smith 2008a, 84). As Smith noted recently: 'If you are going to play it out of tune, then play it out of tune properly' (2008a, 84).

---

[11]   'Psychogeography, the study of the laws and precise effects of a consciously or unconsciously elaborated geographical environment acting directly on affective behaviour, subsumes itself as the science fiction of urbanism' (Khatib 1996, 72).

Futures and Pasts ...

This essay has briefly drifted through varied biographical, lyrical and musical ambiences of the work of Mark E. Smith and The Fall. Along the way, associated fragments have emerged and been examined before being put back. The drift can be useful in negotiating a body of work that transcends the normal criteria associated with its origin (in this case 'rock' music). It helps the writer and the reader towards a different perspective on a collection of artistic expressions. The drift invents a 'passage through a brief moment in time' and presents a poetical, as opposed to an ideological, understanding of interesting combinations of words, music and sound. I would like to see further experiments with writing about music using the methods of the dérive – and not all of them within the academic sphere. It is clear that artists often try to obscure their influences and lineage. A form of analysis that encourages a free-form, associative trip is able to perform a kind of 'theory jam' that can with skill replicate the best musical jam sessions and through experimental processes peel back some of these masked intriguing layers of relevance.[12] The best of this work will enliven the art under discussion and send the reader back to the recordings with renewed vigour. The drift can discover, reveal or amplify the 'occult territory' of the pop song.[13] I suppose that the only real rule is that if you want to go on a kind of dérive, make sure that you take the best artists and writers with you. In searching for a statement that encapsulates the philosophy of Mark E. Smith and The Fall, I have been unable to find a better summation of the radical work of this group and especially its leader than the following. Significantly, it is by one of Smith's favourite authors:

> He ... sought for something more than respectability ... He journeyed on a strange adventure; he sought for a nobler chalice than the cup in which non-alcoholic beverages are contained. (Machen 1918, 62)

---

[12]   I'm clearly here not talking about tedious and self-indulgent manifestations of the jam but rather an example such as The Fall track 'Iceland'.

[13]   The term 'occult territory' was coined by Arthur Machen. It relates to many of his literary works, most notably his 1907 story *The Hill of Dreams*.

PART II
The Techniques and Tactics of The Fall

Chapter Four

'Rebellious Jukebox': The Fall and the War against Conformity

Andy Wood

Mark E. Smith and The Fall have always occupied an ambiguous and contentious place within popular culture and the music industry. Continually playing against expectations and refusing to play by the unwritten rules of the culture industries, The Fall have largely disdained scenes, trends and fashions and, by continually reinventing themselves, looking forward and avoiding looking back or playing up to past glories, have continued to produce vital new work. This has made them one of, if not *the* most important group to evolve out of the British punk scene. It could also be argued that this refusal of, or war against, conformity has damaged the band's commercial and critical appeal. Equally, it could be argued that it is precisely this combination of obtuseness and a principled stand that has allowed Mark E. Smith and The Fall to continue to create and innovate consistently over a period of three decades, when many other artists have fallen by the wayside, found themselves and their music compromised or have simply become another cabaret act on the punk revival circuit.

In this essay, I will explore the position of The Fall within the different music scenes of the last 30 years, not only as participants and actors but also as ongoing cultural commentators. The Fall have operated to combine experimentalism within the structure of the pop song. Early songs such as 'Music Scene' and 'It's the New Thing' are caustically observed analyses of the record industry and its obsession with fashion, packaging, marketing and profit as opposed to music. Later songs such as 'Idiot Joy Showland' excoriate the Manchester scene of the late 1980s and early 1990s as a second generation of working-class bands both conformed to and played up to metropolitan music critics' preconceptions of 'thick Northerners' in exchange for acclaim and recording contracts.

Record companies and bands are not the only targets of Smith and The Fall's scathing wit and insight. Journalists and critics are often the recipients of criticism, both in song and interviews. This has contributed to Smith's continual portrayal, not entirely undeserved, as an awkward individual. In their heyday, from the mid-1970s to the mid-1990s, the music weeklies could make and break band careers, yet The Fall managed to navigate their way through this potentially dangerous terrain, often enjoying commercial and critical acclaim without making concessions or toning down their critiques of either the music scene or journalists and magazine editors. I will examine this trajectory, as well as the fact that The Fall have appeared to maintain an outsider position, while being signed to a number of major independent labels as well as a major record company, Phonogram. Despite their longevity as 'the best underground band in the country ... because the overground won't accept us' (Lowenstein 1978, 43), Mark E. Smith and The Fall have often occupied a position close to the centre rather than the periphery of the British music scene, an interesting paradox that deserves investigation.

The Fall versus the New Punk Orthodoxy

In terms of critical discourse, The Fall has been a band that has consistently eluded being fixed or firmly positioned within a specific genre, scene or even a physical location. A punk or post-punk band whose leader denies ever being a punk or having liked much of the music, particularly as many of the main players disintegrated or lapsed into producing simplistic, slogan laden statements and adopted retrograde 'rockist' posturing as punks' initial blitzkrieg impact was absorbed into the mainstream and the form itself rapidly became reduced to a series of clichés and dogmas. Histories of British punk often ignore The Fall or pay scant attention to them. Even Jon Savage, in *England's Dreaming*, barely finds space to mention the band despite noting that, along with groups such as The Slits and Subway Sect, The Fall 'offered a sense of possibility that had been squeezed out elsewhere' (1991, 419–20).

Smith, like Subway Sect's maverick leader Vic Godard, had quickly identified the limitations of punk's vanguard along with the potential contradictions and limitations inherent in the likes of the Sex Pistols and the Clash and their legion of imitators. Despite media proclamations that punk represented a pop cultural year zero and the end of rock 'n' roll, it was swiftly becoming another form of rock 'n' roll as a mixture of new bands and old hands donned the emperor's new clothes to position themselves as punks. Acts such as former Glam rockers Slaughter and the Dogs along with the likes of Sham 69 and The Vibrators were among some of those who adopted or bought into the trappings of punk as imagined by tabloid newspaper editors and record labels as punk became stratified between the poles of the new wave (loud, fast guitars, pop references played up) and Oi! (loud, fast guitars, lumpen thuggishness played up). Punk seemed to be rapidly co-opted, commercialized and remarketed as a series of new orthodoxies, its potential for radical action swiftly neutered for chart appeal. Mark E. Smith described the scene with a scathing insider outsider's eye in 'C'n'C-S Mithering' on 1980's *Grotesque*. As with many Fall songs, 'C'n'C-S Mithering' makes very specific references to individuals, events and periods, leaving a sense of the lyrics, if not the music, being historically fixed in a time and place. The words reference the influence, not only of a set of very polarized ideas and concepts that had developed out of punk's originary moment but also the marketable variants of new wave (thin ties), the first inklings of the new pop/romanticism (miserable songs) and the orthodox racket of the next generation of 'punk' bands, big on slogans, short on ideas (circles with

A in the middle). The latter proved to be promoting a doctrinaire and dogmatic view of what punk should look and sound like, which seemed to operate to close down the more complex point of view held by a number of post-punk acts.

Garry Bushell had arrived at *Sounds* in 1978 as the champion and promoter of this heavily orthodox vision of punk as espoused by bands such as Sham 69 and UK Subs. Bushell championed Oi! It was described by one member of an Oi! band in 1980 as a genre that stood 'for punk as bootboy music. Oi! is working class, and if you're not working class you'll get a kick in the bollocks.'[1] As well as writing about and promoting the music, Bushell set up a record label, also called Oi!, which would be heavily featured in the pages of *Sounds*. Smith describes this clique-ish insiderism and the obvious conflict of interests involved in Bushell's work in a way that is both humorous and scathing as he sums up the scenario with the bittersweet observation that the actors involved represent 'A circle of low IQs.' TV Smith of punk band The Adverts noted that both *Sounds* and punk's new direction under the considerable influence of Bushell had seen both punk and the weekly paper threatening to 'descend into [all] that fake working-class agenda, which had nothing to do with … [punk]. It was like Garry Bushell introduces the Right To Be Thick' (Heylin 2007, 463).

Well before 1980, punk had become a rather diffuse and nebulous term as the scene rapidly fragmented into different factions. On the one hand, there were the groups and individuals who had used it as a starting point to develop their own sound and world view. On the other, there were those who perceived it as a chance to reinvent themselves and chose to jump on a bandwagon in one last attempt to relaunch their careers. On both sides, a number of bands, often beginning with limited musical skills and options, would re-imagine themselves into often startling and innovative forms while others, hindered by a lack of vision, retreated into punk as a form of back-to-basics music, relying upon increasingly staid and limited musical licks and lyrical messages purporting to be a form of authentic social realism.

Stepping Out: Scenes and Subcultures

For The Fall and a number of their peers, punk was an inspiration and a stepping stone for taking pre-existing ideas and influences and bringing them to some sort of fruition in front of potential audiences. Many of the influences supposedly introduced by punk were already loosely in place well before the Sex Pistols supposedly acted as the catalysts for the birth of a Manchester music scene by appearing twice at the Lesser Free Trade Hall in 1976. For the members of The Fall who had been using Una Baines and Mark E. Smith's flat as a base, listening to music, swapping records and books and experimenting with music, words and drugs, it was not the Pistols' music as such that fired them up. Discussing

---

[1]   Stinky Turner, quoted at http://www.garry-bushell.co.uk/oi/index.asp

the impact of the Pistols' first two visits to Manchester, events much mythologized in accounts of the city's punk scene, not least in Michael Winterbottom's film *24 Hour Party People* (2002), Smith recalled that:

> It was crap … and anyone who says differently is lying. But what it did do was to break things down. That was perhaps the point. Actually, I'm not that convinced that it was, but that is what has happened. We came away certain that we could do a lot better. I mean, I loved the Pistols, really. I loved Johnny Rotten's vocals. I certainly connected with that. The way he used his non voice. That was absolutely fantastic even though, in many respects, the Pistols were a pretty bad heavy metal band. (Middles and Smith 2003, 70)

What the Pistols initial forays into Manchester had provided for some, including The Fall, was a catalyst for their formative ventures into public performance, a move that many of the individuals who would go on to play a role in both the punk and post-punk periods had previously believed was not a realistic option unless you played covers or were a glam or metal band, with both those genres enjoying a degree of popularity in the city or, as Smith suggested, you had 'a million pounds'.[2] Live performances were, for bands looking to perform sets largely made up of their own compositions, not an option for unknown bands. The members of The Fall, who had mainly been a band only in name and from within the confines of Baines and Smith's flat, now felt galvanized by both the potentialities and the musical limitations of punk in the form of the Sex Pistols to begin stepping out in public.

Of course The Fall were not alone in this as other bands began to stumble from out of bedrooms, bedsits and dingy rehearsal rooms, some in a more musically advanced state than others, for example the Buzzcocks who had debuted as a support at the second Sex Pistols show at the Lesser Free Trade Hall in July 1976, while others, including Warsaw and The Fall, were still developing their sound and lyrical world view in front of audiences. Although beginning from fairly base materials and embracing an untutored, intuitive approach to making music, they were now in the public eye.

Although a sense of common purpose, influences and a similarity in approaches existed, giving the sense of a new scene, there also existed a great deal of competitiveness and a sense of rivalry between the new bands despite these linkages. As with any nascent subcultural scene where access to limited resources – spaces for performance, publicity, a record deal – combined with a fiery sense of self-belief, this initial rivalry intensified between bands as they scrambled to stand out from one another. At the same time, writers were attempting via fanzines, the local press and the weekly music papers to portray a close-knit Manchester scene, one that was developing in a distinctive fashion away from the metropolitan punk

---

2   Quoted in the BBC 4 documentary *The Fall: The Wonderful and Frightening World of Mark E. Smith* (2005).

capital. The initial promotion of Manchester as a distinct regional scene would prove fortuitous to The Fall in the form of press coverage and also in the support and patronage of the Buzzcocks and Richard Boon who provided the band with valuable gigs and recording time. It would also provide Smith with an opportunity for some mischief and myth-making of his own, something he would continue to do in a highly personal and idiosyncratic way over the next 30 plus years. Richard Boon and Pete Shelley financed the recording of the band's first record via New Hormones. Over the decades Smith has continually maintained the view that Boon only did so because 'he was pissed off with the Buzzcocks because they were going really poppy ... and so he might have recorded us to piss them off a bit' (Heylin, 2007, 321), thus developing the view of The Fall as a continual fly in the ointment of the Manchester scene; a band capable of antagonizing and irritating those who had 'sold out' or gone soft. Myth-making apart, as I have suggested earlier, The Fall and Smith sought to distance themselves from both the local and the national punk scene, which they had rapidly began to perceive as less of a revolutionary movement than one with its own potentially restrictive set of hierarchies, rules and doctrinaire approaches to lyrics, music and performance. Speaking for the band, Martin Bramah stated that:

> We hated most of the other bands, 'cause we felt that they were just crude punk rockers. We felt we'd left punk behind after just a few months. We didn't really think we were punks, even six months after seeing the Pistols, because it immediately became clear that it had become a fashion movement. It was all about safety pins and bondage trousers. We'd never dress like that. The Sex Pistols didn't dress like that when we first saw them. It was this Oxfam chic. (Heylin 2007, 320)

The Fall, having started off as The Outsiders, both names being references to Albert Camus novels, were actively positioning themselves as outsiders, with other bands being something to define themselves against.[3] However, this was less a nihilistic punk move than a position and mode of operation that Smith would continue to develop and modify over the years. In songs such as 'It's the New Thing', 'Music Scene' and 'In My Area', The Fall would criticize other bands and scenes while proclaiming their outsider credentials. In 'It's the New Thing' Smith tells anyone listening, 'We have never sold out/Spent hours on a clever act' while 'In My Area' berates other nameless bands and scenesters: 'Your highs are contrived/The bands are getting too contrived, recent/Your audience is not even decent.'

Subcultures also have their own rules. They may be unwritten or informal but they are nonetheless rules. Although they are often operating in defiance of or with complete disregard to the mainstream, these rules, which may initially provide a

---

[3]   Colin Wilson's book, *The Outsider*, first published in 1956, was also influential on Smith's thinking and work.

sense of autonomous space in which to develop a distinct sense of identity, can also become restricting. Punk and post-punk bands contested the perceived or real structures of hegemony of the mainstream cultural industries, encompassing the recording, media and fashion industries. Nevertheless, they were still engaged with aspects of those industries, from the debates over the signing of a number of the major and many minor players to major record companies, to the terms of engagement with the media and audiences. The irony of The Clash proclaiming themselves to be a 'garage band' with 'Complete Control' while locked in a series of bureaucratic battles with CBS Records was not lost on a number of bands and commentators in this period. Other issues, such as authenticity, representation and image would perplex and perturb a number of bands and individuals, whether they signed contracts with independent or major labels.

Issues of scenes and the myths built up around those involved either centrally or peripherally with them are also a site of intense contestation. The Fall and Mark E. Smith have continually resisted being co-opted into scenes, showing a keen awareness of both the limitations and the limited time spans of such constructs and therefore the potential problems facing those involved. The Fall, however, were actively inventing their own myths and rules in their actions, music and lyrics and within the pages of the music press. Smith has on numerous occasions debated the limitations of a conventional education, whether that be school, further education or musical education, and has consistently argued that motivated individuals can learn more outside of 'the curriculum', by refusing to accept narrow concepts and perceived canonical wisdom whether offered by formal education, music journalists or cultural commentators (Middles and Smith 2003, 9). He has learnt lasting lessons from the punk scene, particularly from the mistakes of a number of that scene's protagonists, thus allowing The Fall to develop in their own unique way over a long period of time, rarely staying the same or standing still long enough to be wholly pinned down or categorized.

Such actions though are not without their consequences. Rightly or wrongly, Smith and The Fall were increasingly portrayed as being difficult, both musically and personally. Even in the punk era when difficult, even outright obnoxious behaviour seemed to be expected if not actively encouraged, The Fall struggled to find an acceptable record label to release their music and struggled to play live regularly. By the time the 'Bingo-Master's Break-Out' EP arrived in August 1978 on Step Forward, the line-up had drastically changed. It could be argued that the time lapse between the band's debut gig and first record had allowed them the space and freedom to explore and expand upon the dynamics of their sound and songs. Earlier songs such as 'Dresden Dolls' and 'Race Hatred' had been dropped along with any overt traces of a punk sound or perceived sloganeering, which had been rapidly expunged from the set at an early stage when The Fall had been categorized as just another Manchester punk band. The release of the band's debut album *Live at the Witch Trials* in March 1979 cleared the deck for new material and *Dragnet* followed only seven months later as The Fall showed new musical and lyrical directions leading to a period of intense creativity for the band. Equally, it could be argued that this delay in releasing material heightened and highlighted tensions within the band and bred a sense of resentment, distrust and bitterness as The Fall remained unsigned while a number of remarkably inferior bands and their peers found themselves being signed up. Smith has often expressed a sense of bitterness at the ways in which he felt that The Fall were relatively ignored or dismissed in Manchester.

In 1990, at the peak of the hype surrounding the Manchester scene, Smith declared to the *NME* that 'with this Manchester thing going on – as from January 1 we're from Salford! We're not from Manchester anymore' (Collins 1990, 25). Smith appeared keen to distance himself from Manchester and its current status as the fashionable centre of the universe, as embodied in a popular, slightly jingoistic slogan, emblazoned on T-shirts, 'God created Manchester'. A degree of bittersweet irony was revealed in the same interview:

> It's all nonsense. The Fall have always been apart from that anyway. There was a Manchester scene in '78, a Manchester scene in 1981, and it doesn't concern us ... I'm glad we're sort of overlooked in that way. (Collins 1990, 25)

Ironically, The Fall had been enjoying an extended creatively and commercially successful period and had been embracing aspects of contemporary dance music as an influence, working with Coldcut on the single 'Telephone Thing' and as co-producers on their first major label album *Extricate*. The Fall's involvement with contemporary electronic and dance musics was far more radical than the supposed adoption of such musical influences by the 'Madchester' bands and, at the same time, less contrived sounding. Perhaps this was due to the way that the rhythm section had always played an integral element in The Fall's sound, particularly through Stephen Hanley's distinctive bass sound and style. The Fall were not content either to simply follow the rules of the new technology but adapted it to their own idiosyncratic style of recording.

The Fall versus the Media

The Fall had enjoyed a constant media presence and critical acclaim despite the often abrasive nature of the meetings with various representatives of the weekly papers, with The Fall, especially Smith, providing good copy. Although portrayed as archetypal Northerners with a chip on each shoulder, The Fall graced a number of front covers and were given increasing column inches in the 1980s and 1990s. In this arena, Smith could be witty, biting, erudite, perplexing and opaque but was always entertaining and memorable. Mark and Brix even appeared in *Smash Hits*, the teen pop bible, in October 1986 in which William Shaw summed them up as a band who would carry on regardless while 'still never making it within a mile of *Top of the Pops*' (1986, 49). The pair also appeared famously in *NME* as Lord Nelson and Lady Hamilton. This media friendly approach was tempered with classic interviews where Smith would often play devil's advocate, winding up journalists and readers alike.

Although The Fall have often been described as being wilfully uncommercial Smith has never claimed this position, in fact quite the opposite. As far back as 1978 he stated that, as far as he was concerned, the music industry was another job, albeit one with less job security:

> We're not into being uncommercial. That's silly. That's middle-class … When you leave work to concentrate on rock and roll you're really swapping one trap for another, only at least at work you get a wage. You have unions and that. When you sell your soul to a factory you at least get bread for it. The music industry is the most medieval system there is. (McCullough 1978, 15)

What The Fall had done and continue to do was to make the records they wanted in the manner they wished to work. Cries of 'sell-out' were muttered in some corners of the media when the band charted with covers of 'There's a Ghost in my House' and 'Victoria' and later when the band signed to Phonogram. Accusations of 'sell-out' were common in the independent scene in the 1980s but, in my opinion, there was no dilution or compromise in The Fall's work. Smith had suggested that he left Beggars Banquet because the label was unwilling or unable to finance his vision for *Extricate*. In contrast, Phonogram was able to offer The Fall a degree of financial security without compromise. This was not something a number of The Fall's previous independent labels had been able to do.

The Myths of Madchester

Prior to *Extricate* Smith had relocated to Edinburgh where he resided for a period of around 18 months. In part, the move was undertaken to maintain a sense of distance from the Manchester scene, a scene that he felt he was being 'held slightly responsible for' (Lester 1990, 42). If *Extricate* was the sound of someone reasonably at ease with their position, 1991's *Shift-Work* was an album full of vitriol for the current music scene, particularly the madness at large in Smith's own area. 'Idiot Joy Showland' was a brilliant, twisted attack, ostensibly on the Manchester scene, although no names were mentioned. In the first verse Smith lambasts 'idiot groups' with 'no shape or form'.[4] The song takes the attack further though with its humorous but scathing critique of the music business. In the third verse Smith takes direct aim at the groups involved but seems also to be targeting the cultural commentators, specifically middle-class journalists, excitedly reporting the antics of working-class bands acting out stereotypical roles as they played up

---

[4]   For these lyrics, please see 'Lyrics Parade' at The Fall Online: http://fall.byethost13.com/lyrics.html

to the media circus. In the lyrics the bands are both the perpetrators and the victims of the war against intelligence.

Smith's disgust here is double-edged. The 'working-class has been shafted' but some of the victims are in fact, fifth columnists. In 'Idiot Joy Showland' the supposedly working-class culture of Madchester is no more authentic than Disneyland or Blackpool's Funland, it is an artificial construct where class and cultural tourists can come like 'locusts' for cheap, voyeuristic thrills. In the penultimate verse, Smith dissects the way working-class cultures operate from an ambiguous and precarious position. Referring to the footballer Paul Gascoigne's tears at the 1990 World Cup semi-finals in the line, 'Your sportsmen's tears are laudanum', he makes the subtle correlation between sport and music as predominant forms of identity formation as well as social narcotics that can be both applauded and condemned. In times of need such as war, the battle to drive up export figures, defining a sense of national identity against an 'other', the working class are lauded, championed and welcomed into the national body. At other points, they are portrayed as a society within, an expendable, ignorant underclass. For Smith and The Fall, these are traps to be avoided. Starring in a debased version of a culture such as that portrayed in 'Idiot Joy Showland' is a dead-end, reductive position. In contrast, Smith's description of The Fall in September 1990 was just as apt for 1978 or 2008:

> If you wanna talk about The Fall, we always try and stimulate the brain, we always have … Our intention now is pretty much what it always has been: to produce intelligent lyrics over shit-hot music that's fuckin' raw and fuckin' basic. And it's got a fuckin' rhythm, you know, which is the 'in' thing to say but a lot of people don't have it. (Lester 1990, 42)

The Fall and Mark E. Smith continue to be an irritant, a thorn in the side, yet continue to thrive despite seemingly bleak patches and often self-inflicted attempts by Smith to sabotage a conventional career path. In *24 Hour Party People*, he has a brief cameo, the contemporary Mark E. Smith looking on at younger participants of a now heavily mythologized Manchester, a view particularly mediated and promoted by the late Tony Wilson. It is as though Smith is appearing as a warning that although we may believe this version there is another version still to be told. Although the film hints at this through Coogan/Wilson's status as an unreliable narrator, Smith here is the ghost in the machine but one that is still flesh and blood, still railing and kicking against conformists and orthodoxies long after his peers are repackaging and revising their past as a golden age of music and creativity.

Despite periods of turmoil including numerous changes in band personnel and labels, along with periods where Smith and The Fall have fallen out of favour with the media, in 2008 they appeared to be undergoing a renaissance period, though for a band that have often been written off only to subvert expectations, perhaps this was not a wholly unusual situation. Mark E. Smith and The Fall never do comebacks for they never truly go away. The release of the album

Imperial Wax Solvent (2008) along with Smith's autobiography *Renegade* (2008) saw both receiving enthusiastic reviews and critical acclaim, while the album went on to become the best-selling Fall album for over a decade. The journalist Dave Simpson also published his book *The Fallen* in 2008, a story of his journey to find out what happened to the 40 plus former members of the band but also to discover what Mark E. Smith and The Fall were truly about. Simpson sought to find the true essence of a band and front man among the contradictions, myths and evasions. In the end the author had to admit defeat with both the man and the group being described as 'uncategorizable' and driven by a 'guarded doctrine of creative tension' (Simpson 2008, 11, 13), remaining an unknowable enigma. Describing Smith and the way he operates, Kay Carroll, the band's former manager, suggested that Smith 'basically rewrites events to fit the Mark E. character, just like an author in a novel. Mark is the writer' (Ford 2003, 281). In this way The Fall remain a difficult band to define and are always moving on, always changing, yet somehow giving the sense that they are always the same as they refuse to play by the rules of the game.

Chapter Five

'I curse your preoccupation with your record collection': The Fall on Vinyl 1978–83

Richard Osborne

The New Puritan

The moment occurs towards the end of 'New Puritan', one of the tracks off the *Totale's Turns* LP that was recorded in 'other places'; this time 'at home during which said home was attacked by a drunk, which accounts for the tension on that track' (Smith 1980). The narrative is all over the place. Mark E. Smith first hails the new puritan, and then he becomes him: 'All hard-core fiends/Will die by me', he declares, 'And all decadent sins/Will reap discipline.' The lyrics then go on to describe LA, where the 'window opener switch/Is like a dinosaur cackle'; they next turn to Britain, finding 'the scream of electric pumps in a renovated pub'. Then we are back with first person declarations. Smith cries out, 'Don't call me Peter I can't go/Salem's just up the road/I've got work to do.' Finally, after we have been asked to hail the new puritan a few more times, we get this:

> I curse your preoccupation
> With your record collection
> New puritan has no time
> It's only music, John
> (The Fall, 'New Puritan')

It is preoccupations, record collections and curses that I wish to discuss here; primarily, the collection of records that The Fall released between 1978 and 1983, the first six years of their recorded existence. In the following I will outline the ways in which this output exposed and undermined previous record collecting practice. I also discuss one of the perverse ways in which this ambition was achieved: The Fall's early releases display a lyrical preoccupation with recordings. The objects that will be under discussion are vinyl records. It is important to note that prior to 1983 The Fall's music was released solely in this format.[1] In the following I wish to outline just how central the vinyl record was as both subject and context of the band's original work.

---

[1]   The first official Fall release to come out in more than one format was 1983's *Perverted By Language*, which was issued on both LP and cassette.

The Preoccupation

It is the grooved analogue disc that has preoccupied record collectors. As early as 1970 the jazz critic Derek Langridge was commenting that 'Collectors find an attraction in discs that they do not find in tapes' (1970, 10). More recently, Ian Shirley, editor of the *Rare Record Price Guide*, has conceded that CDs are 'just not as sexy as vinyl. They lack that allure' (quoted in Jones 2006). This has been reflected in financial terms. In 2004 the *Record Collector* magazine celebrated its twenty-fifth anniversary by compiling a top 100 of the UK's most collectable records. Out of this top 100, ninety-seven were released on either vinyl or shellac discs ('100 Rarest Records' 2004). Mark E. Smith is among those who favour vinyl. In *Renegade* he writes that the format is 'very underrated', adding 'I still think in terms of vinyl – sides one and two' (Smith 2008a, 197, 151).

To uncover the roots of vinyl's allure, we must turn back to the music industry's first format war. In the first decade of the twentieth century the phonograph cylinder invented by Thomas Edison in 1877 yielded its position as the leading recording format to the gramophone disc, patented by Emile Berliner a decade later. This victory was by no means a foregone conclusion. It is generally agreed that the cylinder afforded the superior method of sound reproduction. It also, unlike the disc, provided a home-recording function for the amateur enthusiast. The disc, meanwhile, was only able to offer pre-recorded material. Initially, its principal selling points were that it was easier to duplicate than the cylinder, that it was louder, that it was more robust and that it could be stored more conveniently.

Nevertheless, the factor that proved to be truly decisive was repertoire. And what is curious here is that what could be perceived as the disc's weakness – that there was no home-recording ability – turned out to be an advantage. First, it meant that gramophone companies, from the beginning, focused on professional recordings. This assumed importance when it was discovered that the public had little appetite for listening to recordings of themselves: because it had never been 'tainted by amateur offerings' (Barfe 2004, 26) the disc could promote itself as a luxury good. To this end, gramophone companies pursued a policy of signing the world's most renowned artists to exclusive contracts. At first they targeted the operatic stars of Europe, with the signing of Enrico Caruso in 1902 representing the significant breakthrough; later, when the recording of orchestras improved, they also signed conductors and soloists. Parallel to this process, the gramophone, which had originally been viewed as a technical machine, was now being marketed as a domestically acceptable piece of furniture, as indicated by the names given to new models: 'Sheraton', 'Chippendale', 'Queen Anne'. These policies established the gramophone as a must-have commodity.

The exclusivity of analogue discs has been essential in establishing their special status. Uniquely among sound recording media there has never been a successful method by which you can record your own shellac or vinyl discs at home. Two further quirks of the disc-manufacturing process also helped to bring forth the record collector. The first of these is the 'record label', the paper insert in the middle of the disc, which acquired such importance that it soon became synonymous with record companies themselves. This was another development that only arose as a result of the restrictive nature of analogue disc manufacture. As a disc's groove winds ever tighter towards its centre, sound quality decreases (unlike the groove of a cylinder, which maintains uniform sound quality throughout). Eventually, it reaches a point beyond which it cannot acceptably reproduce audio information. This leaves a void at the centre of the disc. A use was immediately found for it: information relating to the recording could be detailed here. At first these details were etched directly into the record's surface. Then, in the early years of the twentieth century, the paper label was introduced. This innovation not only dignified the factory-produced disc, it also allowed records to be colour-coded by genre, with the most revered label being the 'red seal' of classical recordings. Soon records were being collected for their status as objects, as well as for the music that they contained. The recording historian Louis Barfe has pointed out that 'Later collectors noted the preponderance of mint single-sided Red Seals and were led to conclude that they were rarely if ever played' (2004, 66).

The other quirk that helped to bring forth the record collector is the fact that, although analogue records are mass produced, each disc can be differentiated. On the one hand, records degrade in accordance with usage: the groove captures dust if it is exposed, and it wears in relation to the number of times that it is played. On the other hand, records are produced in separate and distinguishable batches. Combined, these factors have led to the fetishization of the mint, first pressing of the disc. The vinyl long-playing record, introduced by Columbia in 1948, elevated the disc to even greater heights. Although vinyl was more robust than the shellac that it replaced, the LP's delicate microgroove attracted dust more easily. In addition, its finer recording quality meant than any glitches in reproduction were more easily noted. It was also an expensive product. The first British LPs were introduced in 1952, with prices ranging from 22s. to 39s. At this time the average weekly wage for men over 21 was £8.30 per week (see Marwick 1982, 114). Elaborate rituals evolved for taking care of these precious discs: specific ways of holding, cleaning and storing them. Packaging played a part in establishing the LP's exalted status: these records were the first to regularly receive picture sleeves, inner sleeves and sleeve notes. There was also the matter of repertoire. The LP was developed principally for classical music, the genre that made up the bulk of early releases. It was established as a grown-up and sophisticated product. It was aided in this process by virtue of the fact that it soon had an opposite: in 1949 RCA Victor launched the 45rpm, 7″ vinyl record, which was quickly cast as the vehicle for more commercial forms of popular music.

Mark E. Smith is surely not alone in his troubled experience of trying to play 45s on his family's hi-fi system:

> We never really had records in our home when I was young. We had a record player but, if we did play a record, my dad would say 'You are breakin' the fuckin' record player. Take that off!' It would just be some rock 'n' roll record …

Elvis Presley or something, but my dad would never have it. 'You think you are being funny, playin' that, don't you? Take it off. Take it off, now. It's breaking all the equipment.' (Middles and Smith 2003, 35)

The reverence for elite, professional, and expensive vinyl records evidently niggled Mark E. Smith. There is an early live version of the song 'Music Scene' in which he breaks off from the usual lyrics, informing the crowd:

When you go to the record shop you don't get in for free. In fact, you get about five pound; you put five pound on the counter: you get about half an hour. Ha-ha! Half an hour for five pound! Seven-inch, 80 pence. Eighty pence for about five minutes. But the sleeves are very nice, yes, the sleeves are very nice. (quoted in Edge 1989, 13)

The John Peel session version of 'New Puritan' takes matters further. Here, Mark E. Smith asks: 'Why don't you ask your local record dealer how many bribes he took today?' This rendition has the amended lyrics:

I curse the self-copulation
Of your lousy record collection
New puritan says 'Coffee table LPs never breathe.'
(The Fall, 'New Puritan' *John Peel Sessions*)

The Fall thereby put a hex on the antiseptic elitism of the recorded music scene and they did this by making records that sound as though they might 'break all the equipment'.

The Curse

During the late 1960s, popular music split into two camps: 'rock' which was supposedly serious, artistic and anti-establishment and 'pop' which was derided by rock aficionados as being commercial, disposable and crass. One of the ways in which this fracture occurred was along format lines. Rock music colonized the LP, absorbing the format's classicism, its high-quality musicianship and hi-fidelity recording techniques, as well as the artistry of its sleeves. Pop, meanwhile, continued to be associated with the 45rpm single and its generic-label bags.

By 1978, when The Fall commenced their recorded music career, the LP was the established receptacle for portentous statements by rock's leading players. Groups such as Led Zeppelin and Pink Floyd refused to release 7″ singles; the idea being that each album release should remain sacrosanct. These long playing statements were to be anticipated, pored over and revered. It was amid this rarefied world that The Fall's curse was most effective: they did not make coffee table LPs. The Fall's albums of their first six years effectively undermined notions of what an LP should be. They are records that consistently mock recording perfectionism and musical professionalism.

The first LP, *Live at the Witch Trials*, was proudly recorded in just one day. One of the songs, 'Mother-Sister!', opens with the profound question: 'Er, what's this song about?', receiving the reply, 'Er, nothing.' 'Music Scene', the lengthy track that concludes the LP, is conscious of the fact that it is heading towards progressive territory. Consequently, it is broken with cries of 'OK, studio, that's plenty', as well as featuring time-checks detailing how far the recording has moved on. It is also interrupted with lo-fi home tape recordings. Mark E. Smith readily endorsed the tape cassette, which rose to prominence during this era. This format represented a return to the days of the phonograph cylinder: once again amateurs could record themselves. The cassette recording provided the perfect means with which The Fall could puncture vinyl's professionalism; it has gate-crashed numerous tracks during the band's lengthy career.

Dragnet, The Fall's second album, was completed in three days, with the then novice Grant Showbiz at the controls. Smith has stated: 'It panned out okay, though, and looking back it wasn't such a bad thing using an inexperienced producer.' He adds:

> Most of it is purposefully out of tune. But later we found out that Cargo Studios in Rochdale [where the album was recorded] didn't want to let it out. It was a heavy metal studio and they were nervous about releasing it because of its sound. They thought it'd reflect badly on them. (Smith 2008a, 80)

More than any other Fall album, *Dragnet* is obsessed with the group's presence within and difference from the established world of professional recording. Many of the lyrics almost sound like catchy hooks but then they back away. For instance there is 'Choc-Stock', with its hilarious 'breakdown' section. Some of the songs too are almost sophisticated. But then the production breaks through. Just as we're enjoying the atmosphere of 'A Figure Walks', a ridiculously loud crashing cymbal breaks it.[2] The playful 'Choc-Stock' is followed by the astonishing and agonizing 'Spectre vs. Rector'. The majority of this latter piece was recorded on a cheap cassette player. Smith delivered the results to Grant Showbiz, informing him, 'that's the track'.[3]

Totale's Turns, the next album, is of even lower sound quality, being made up of various abandoned cassette tape recordings: 'They were lying around in a studio somewhere' (Smith 2008a, 85). It was released by Rough Trade, who regarded it

---

[2]   Speaking at the 'Messing up the Paintwork' conference, Grant Showbiz revealed the reasons for the volume levels on this track. The cymbal player was Mark E. Smith and the reason why the instrument could not be mixed any lower is because he was playing it at the same time as he recorded his vocal; the volume of the cymbal is the volume at which it bled into the vocal microphone.

[3]   Recalled by Grant Showbiz at the 'Messing up the Paintwork' conference.

as 'one of the worst quality recordings ever committed to vinyl' (Thompson 2003, 45). According to Smith: 'In the band's eyes it was commercial suicide releasing this dirge; they couldn't see the soul that lay behind it. That's musicians for you' (Smith 2008a, 85).

This LP was followed by *Grotesque*, which apparently cost only £300 to produce, this sum including the band's first full-colour sleeve. The album contains the unique lo-fi excursion, 'W.M.C.-Blob 59', about which the group claimed: 'This is a very funny track. It's a pity you can't hear what's going on' (press release for *Grotesque*, quoted in Ford 2003, 87). An established jazz sleeve-note convention had been to list the quality equipment used in the making of an LP. This was parodied by The Fall. A press release detailed the components of this track:

1 x Shure microphone (B-roke);

1 x 'Schitti' 15w amp;

1 x 1964 Red 'New Beat' plastic guitar;

1 x model no. 90000 AC Lewis's tape recorder with special 'Hopeless' black-grey mike. (quoted in Ford 2003, 87)

These weren't the only Fall instruments to break with convention. The first album is characterized by Una Baines' 'Snoopy' keyboard (played by Yvonne Pawlett), the cheapest device on the market and reviewed by *Melody Maker* as the worst you could buy. From *Dragnet* onwards the band made frequent use of the kazoo; a working-class riposte to the horn sections then in vogue.

The Fall were also fond of choosing unusual locations for their recordings: a damp warehouse for 'Spectre vs. Rector', the home recording of 'New Puritan', Iceland and a cinema in Hitchin for *Hex Enduction Hour*. Their statements about their LPs were equally unconventional. Whereas the rock elite promoted their albums as the latest instalment of their developing art, The Fall's records, sleeve notes and press releases are littered with self-abuse: 'I don't sing, I just shout' (from 'Your Heart Out'), 'the mistakes are glorious' (from the press release for 'In My Area'), 'white crap let loose in a studio but still in control' (from the notes for *Dragnet*), 'Call yourselves bloody professionals?' (from the sleeve notes for *Totale's Turns*).

And then there are the sleeves. It was in the retail environment that The Fall displayed their difference most brilliantly. Not for this group the elaborate Hipgnosis packaging that surrounded Pink Floyd and Led Zeppelin LPs; nor did they lean towards the sophisticated graphic design that their contemporaries on Factory and Fast Records were displaying. Instead, The Fall's early records are housed in sleeves that feature scrappy cartoons, blurred and badly cropped photographs of the group, or grainy pictures of Prestwich. In addition, most of the sleeves feature the unique Smith scrawl. This ranges from the simple declarations of the Northern towns in which the band performed the *Totale's Turns* live recordings, of which

Mark E. Smith has claimed: 'Nobody wanted to release it, because nobody played the sort of venues that you hear on it – places like Doncaster and Preston. It wasn't the done thing to promote ourselves like that' (Smith 2008a, 84), to the graffiti splurge of *Hex Enduction Hour*, which so horrified the HMV retail chain that they informed staff to display the sleeve backwards (see Edge 1989, 49).

The Record Collection

The Fall's wilful abuse of their recorded status went some way towards making the curse of 'New Puritan' effective. The record collector's preoccupation with the material object and with the technical specifics of recording, rather than with music itself, was exposed and undermined. What interests me here, however, is the identity of 'John', the everyman record collector who is being cursed in the song. Is he the rock record buyer? Is he the purchaser of the *Totale's Turns* LP? Or could he, perhaps, be Mark E. Smith himself? Most intriguing is the latter idea. The shifting narrative of 'New Puritan' means that it is never clear whether it is the new puritan/Smith who delivers the curse, or whether it is the new puritan/Smith who receives it. Moreover, it is a curse from which the speaker cannot escape; as it is made he reveals his preoccupation with the preoccupation with records.

There is ample evidence that Mark E. Smith has been obsessed with recordings. His appetite is revealed in the live version of 'C'n'C-S Mithering', during which he announces, 'I'll feast on 45s.' On the occasion of The Fall's twenty-fifth anniversary he stated:

> I regard the twenty-fifth year as 25 years after our first record, not 25 years since we got together in some bedroom, somewhere. Who cares about that? (Middles and Smith 2003, 141)

Mark E. Smith has always used his records to talk about his records. In The Fall's early output cross-references abound: 'Container Drivers' name-checks 'Fiery Jack'; the protagonist of 'I'm into C.B.' says 'I should have listened to "New Face in Hell"'; the *Totale's Turns* version of 'Spectre vs. Rector' recalls the earlier version on *Dragnet*, informing the listener that 'This is the second half of spectre versus rector/The rector lived in Hampshire/You probably know this if you've got the record.' Elsewhere, Mark E. Smith uses the Peel session versions of songs to tell listeners about the recorded versions. During 'No Xmas for John Quays' he states 'Make sure this album is in your Christmas stocking'; as part of 'New Face in Hell' we are informed, 'This is off the new LP.'

This record referencing isn't limited to the releases by his own band: we also discover the other artists that Mark E. Smith has been checking out. The lyrics of The Fall's early records find room for Bjorn and Benny, the Worst, Frankie Lymon, Jake Burns, Joe Strummer, Faust, Johnny Rotten, Bill Haley, the Beat, Wah! Heat, Captain Beefheart, the Ramones, Elton John, Megas Jonsson, D. Bowie, the Moody Blues, Kevin Ayers, Link Wray, the B.E.F., Louis Armstrong, Shakin' Stevens and King Crimson. By virtue of the fact that their music had appeared on vinyl, The Fall had been promoted to this league of recorded sound. The fact that the group's releases would be racked alongside Abba and Shakin' Stevens evidently both thrilled and appalled Mark E. Smith. These new professional peers are commented upon and absorbed. Early Fall records betray some surprising influences: 'Rowche Rumble' owes an admitted debt to Racey's 'Some Girls'; Trio's 'Da Da Da' can be glimpsed in the intro to 'Fortress'; the imprint of 'Ring of Fire' is all over 'Fiery Jack'; 'Hassle Schmuck' is inspired by Coast to Coast's 'Do the Hucklebuck'.

Meanwhile, in the group's lyrics, Mark E. Smith examines his place at the music industry table. His talk is full of the likes of 'Big A&M Herb' (in 'C'n'C - S Mithering) and 'fucking Jimmy Saville' (in 'Fortress'). At the beginning of 'The N.W.R.A.' he imagines the situation whereby:

> 'Junior Choice' played one morning. The song was 'English Scheme.' Mine. They'd changed it with a grand piano and turned it into a love song. How they did it I don't know.

In the BBC Fall documentary, Paul Morley argues that The Fall's music 'fitted into the John Peel show because it was, in a way, made out of the John Peel show' (*The Fall: The Wonderful and Frightening World of Mark E. Smith*, 2005). Smith's ambitions were, nevertheless, greater than that. In *Renegade* he states mournfully:

> The idea was that you did John Peel, then progressed on to the 7 till 9 slot and so on. We never went that far from Peel, and ultimately that was a limitation for us. You become known as a 'Peel group'. (Smith 2008a, 102)

'Junior Choice' may have been stretching things a little far but it is clear that Mark E. Smith always contextualized his records among more mainstream releases. It is telling that he can still recall each LP's contemporaries: Aztec Camera, Scritti Politti and Duran Duran for *Slates*; Spandau Ballet and Elvis Costello for *Hex Enduction Hour*; Echo and the Bunnymen for *Perverted By Language*. The fact that he derides these bands' audiences reveals the ambiguity of his position. Futurists are berated on *Hex Enduction Hour*; new romantics on *Room to Live*; 'the 77 shit pile' during 'In My Area' on *Totale's Turns*.

Call Yourselves Bloody Professionals?

One of the factors that makes The Fall's early output continually fascinating is Mark E. Smith's mixture of arrogance and insecurity. The dual perspective of 'New Puritan' exposing his own obsession with record collections at the same time that he criticizes that of others is one example of this tendency. The same holds true for The Fall's attack upon 'coffee table LPs'. The Fall's scrappy records undermined the seriousness that had been accorded to contemporary rock albums but in doing so they ran the danger of undermining their own status as vinyl records. Nevertheless this is not what happened. What makes the curse in 'New Puritan' resonate is the fact that it is contained on a record, one that will be ranked alongside and collated amid the owner's previous collection. From the beginning The Fall attracted a particularly obsessive following. Mark E. Smith was surely aware that one of the ways that this obsession would manifest itself would be in the practice of collecting the band's releases. The curse comes across as a knowing acknowledgement of this fact.

However, what he presumably could not have predicted was just how collectable the band's output would be. The Fall's early singles and LPs formed part of the late 1970s boom in cheaply packaged and produced independent records. The great irony of these releases is that, far from being regarded as inferior to their more polished peers, they were often more highly valued. The romantic 'handmade' nature of the records accounts for some of their appeal. This was as effective in distinguishing these discs from the mass-produced herd as the 'red seal' record label had been three-quarters of a century earlier. The fact that many of these releases were manufactured in low numbers also helped to make them collectors' items. This was one of the eras in which record collecting took a great leap forward. In 1977 the *New Musical Express* commented, 'some customers are buying everything from the independent labels … They realise the investment might pay off' (Bell 1977, 26). In relation to The Fall, it has been the independent records of their early years that have proven to be the most collectable: these are the recordings that are most highly valued in the *Rare Record Price Guide*.[4]

And would Mark E. Smith still curse his fans for collecting the records of these first six years? I don't think so. Several years later, appearing in another of his guises, this time as the 'Big New Prinz', he would turn another song's narrative towards himself.[5] This song has the self-referential complaint, 'he is not appreciated'. For evidence, Mark E. Smith urges the listener to go out and 'check the track record. Check the guy's track record.'

---

[4]   In the 2008 edition (Shirley 2006) original vinyl copies of the early albums are valued as follows: *Live at the Witch Trials*, £12; *Dragnet*, £15; *Totale's Turns*, £15; *Grotesque*, £14; *Slates*, £10; *Hex Enduction Hour*, £12; and *Perverted By Language*, £15.

[5]   Here we have a character-driven Fall song that refers to and quotes from another character-driven Fall song, 'Hip Priest'. 'Big New Prinz' is written in the third-person and it extols the virtues of the 'Hip Priest'. As for the identity of the 'Hip Priest', this is another song in which the narrative fluctuates: Smith sings of the Hip Priest, and he sings as the Hip Priest. As so often with his song's characters doubt remains as to the degree of self-portrayal. Nevertheless, in live performances of recent years the main refrain of 'Big New Prinz' has taken on a more concrete meaning. The audience knows that Smith is the Hip Priest and, although adored by his loyal following, this latent national institution accepts the call-and-response refrain that it is 'he' who 'is not appreciated'.

Chapter Six

'Dictaphonics': Acoustics and Primitive Recording in the Music of The Fall

Robert Walker

In the many words written about The Fall and Mark E. Smith, there is little which considers why his voice has undergone so many transformations. Aside from the lyrical content of The Fall's work, there has been a restless variation in the tonal quality of the treatments applied to Mark E. Smith's voice. Whether singing through a guitar amp, a megaphone or jamming a microphone inside a bass drum, the voice has rarely been allowed to rest in the default sound of the vocal booth favoured by most recording artists.

The use of amateur recording devices such as dictaphones[1] and domestic tape recorders has been a regular feature of The Fall's studio output and live shows throughout their career. As a tonal device these might at first be considered just some of the many manipulations applied by Smith and his collaborators to every aspect of their music for the sake of experimentation. However, the technique that I have termed 'dictaphonics' goes much deeper than this, challenging how we listen to recorded music; the other presence taking on the various roles of ghost backing band, recorder of blemished reality and angry intervener. It can blur the line between writing and recording, a direct injection of the nascent idea into the artifice of the rock record.

Dictaphonics poses a number of key questions: Can we define it in relation to other established definitions of audio aesthetics and practice? How does The Fall's use of it fit into a wider context of tape use in music? Can we identify what effects it creates in the mind of the listener? I will address these questions while mapping out the sonic territory created by The Fall's use of dictaphonics. I will show how Smith has never settled on any one use of the technique throughout the group's career, instead employing it in a variety of contexts in relation to the song (both structurally and acoustically) with differing consequences.

---

[1]   Dictaphone is a registered trademark of Nuance Communications, Inc. (Healthcare Division) and its affiliates in the United States and/or other countries. It is used here as a generic term for a dictation audio recorder and not in reference to any specific product.

What is Dictaphonics?

We are all familiar with the distinct sound of a dictaphone. It comprises distortion, interference, artificially compressed dynamic range, hiss, wow and flutter over arrhythmic clicks and punctuating squeals as it drags a tape back and forth. We also get the scratchy clunks of handling noise from the user adjusting their grip and a further loss in clarity as the recorder picks up excessive reverberation. The cheap electronics of the built-in microphone, the pre amplifier, the tape itself, the alignment of the heads, the amplification and the speaker all conspire to colour the sound. Like a photocopy of a photograph of a familiar face it can be a fascinating facsimile. The associations we attach to this sonic character include non-professional, unprepared recording and the sound of an audio sketch unconcerned with fidelity and only with content. The cheaper the recorder, the more coloured the sound and the more DIY the aesthetic effect. I will therefore be considering any sounds which obviously fit into a lo-fi tape recorder aesthetic to be dictaphonic. Tape itself has many guises and many sounds of its own, and Mark E. Smith is obviously a fan. In his autobiography, Smith states:

> I used to take tape recordings of the original vinyl on tour with me. Record them
> in the kitchen on to tape. You get a bit of fuzz on it, but it sounds better than the
> CD. Tapes and vinyl are very underrated. It's like the difference between reading
> a book and reading something on a computer. (Smith 2008a, 197)

The Fall and 'The Studio'

Smith's relationship with 'The Studio' as an entity is complex. The music the group produces is often rich in sonic experimentation, yet Smith seems largely frustrated by the technicalities and egos of studio production: 'Thanks to all the engineers for the helpful obstruction' (sleeve notes to *Shift-Work*, 1991). When asked if he liked studios, Smith replied, 'No, fucking hate them' (Herrington 1996). As a recording group, they cannot avoid them but insist on using the most conventional studios: 'I never use hip studios. If I've got the money I make sure I use the straightest and best … In the end we used UB40's recording studio' (Smith 2008a, 195). Yet the results are frequently strange balances of instruments, unconventional textures and odd production techniques. It could be explained as a creative strategy designed to produce tension and conflict, a situation used frequently by Smith for creative ends. If you work with people less used to experimentation, you may need to fight harder for it. 'It's horrible how much people try to shape what you do' (Smith 2008a, 86).

Dictaphonics could be seen as a way in which The Fall have retained a distance from the studio sound and prevented the handing over of the authorship of a record's tonal shape to others. Whether clashing with an engineer, producer or record company executive, an artist who wants to be involved in the process and craft of studio recording often experiences conflict. While The Fall have used a variety of producers, Smith's disdain for the unthinking use of studio perfected sound has been constant. From the fuzzily recorded intro of barely decipherable rehearsal room banter to putting as sonically primitive a track as 'W.M.C.-Blob 59' (1980) on an album, there is a clear statement against the over-polishing of audio and against anyone forcing their will upon the group. Sometimes the sound quality says as much as a lyric can, as the press release for the *Grotesque* album put it in relation to the track 'W.M.C.-Blob 59'.[2] This ironic description of the track's sub lo-fi production characterizes The Fall's derision of the systems inherent in established recording methods. Although many Fall songs exploit the studio as a tool and even celebrate it (such as 'The Mixer' from *Shift-Work*), dictaphonic sounds are inherently against 'The Studio'.

The Fall's Dictaphonic Tracks

> I've been through six tape recorders in six months. They keep breaking, exploding on me. Because they're all assimilated into this computer rubbish. I've got a really good one that plays things about ten times faster than they should be. (Mark E. Smith, quoted in Herrington 1996)

There are many Fall songs which use dictaphonic sounds with around 50 songs appearing on their studio albums. We can see a number of patterns emerging in these tracks despite a diversity of approach. One technique is the use of musical and non-musical dictaphone sounds underneath a studio-sounding song to interrupt its acoustic homogeneity and rhythmic flow, essentially at odds with the studio recorded music. Typical examples would be 'Music Scene' from *Live at the Witch Trials* (1979), 'Who Makes the Nazis' from *Hex Enduction Hour* (1982) and 'Ibis-Afro Man' from *Are You Are Missing Winner* (2001). This transforms the music into a state of collision with the dictaphonic sounds breaking the separation and clarity of tone which is sought after in conventional rock production. In 'Music Scene', the taped effects growl away ignorant of the song's rhythm and balance of instruments, preventing any of the other instruments from developing into a solo. They are not distinct as sounds themselves but become a defined instrument in their own right, the tape recorder. The dictaphone's tonal characteristics dominate the sounds it has captured to the extent that it becomes more of an instrument than whatever generated them in the first place. 'Ibis-Afro Man' plays for much of its duration with two overlapping copies of the same song, out of time with each other. This disorientates the listener, the ear shifting from one version to the other as it tries to decide whether the dictaphonic or the 'clean' version is to be followed.

---

[2]   This description was cited in the previous chapter (see p. 72).

There is also the vocal injected into a song, bypassing the notion of re-recording words in the studio as lyrics – see 'North West Fashion Show' from *Cerebral Caustic* (1995), 'City Dweller' from *Middle Class Revolt* (1994) and 'The Acute' from *Are You Are Missing Winner*. In this instance, the dictaphone takes on the role of a second voice or personality within the song, chiming with Smith's lyrical preoccupation with multiple identities emerging from the same person: 'I wanted to explore, to put a twist on the normal. People think of themselves too much as one person – they don't know what to do with the other people that enter their heads' (Smith 2008a, 84). The dictaphone mirrors this splintering of personalities and characters in The Fall's songs from a tonal point of view, much like Philip K. Dick's multiple realities, which Smith is very familiar with. These voices cannot all exist in the tightly defined space of the track, forcing us to perceive them as multiple personalities, time slips or even realities leaked on top of each other. One version of Smith's voice can exist as a singer with the band, but an added dictaphonic voice becomes another filtered reality, separated by time or space. Conventional backing vocals remain anchored to the song because they obey the spatial rules of recorded music and are timed in confluence with the lead vocal. Dictaphonic vocals run free, unencumbered by the need to fit in with the lead vocal.

Field recordings or 'found sound' are also treated as a source of lyrical or melodic inspiration – see 'Symbol of Mordgan' from *Middle Class Revolt*, 'Clasp Hands' from *Fall Heads Roll* (2005), 'Last Commands of Xyralothep via M.E.S.' from *The Real New Fall LP* (2003) and 'Lost in Music' from *The Infotainment Scan* (1993). Here, the found sound has influenced the lyrics and delivery to the extent of becoming a backing singer in the group. 'Last Commands' begins with speech in a Lovecraft-inspired weird tongue, sounding as though from a dusty archive tape and which is treated as a text itself by the song. 'These are the Last Commands' comments Smith about these ancient words, as though they were not his own.

A number of Fall songs are recorded in a quality which would normally be considered less than that required for a demo – see 'Spectre vs. Rector' from *Dragnet* (1979) or 'W.M.C.-Blob 59' from *Grotesque*. 'Spectre vs. Rector' offers us two groups defined by their recording quality, 'The Fall' and a badly recorded 'ghost band', a dense and distant ensemble which plays from a separate space within the song. The intentional muddiness of the ghost band that Smith sings over in the first part of 'Spectre vs. Rector' is then wrenched away by the real band, an opportunity to use the claustrophobic squall of replayed sound to act like a character lurking in the space of the record. The fact that the two versions sit over each other uncomfortably adds to the song's dank atmosphere. The unflattering acoustic helps convey a sense of otherness because its tonal quality is outside of our expectations of a piece of music. 'New Puritan', a demo released as a part of the largely live *Totale's Turns* (1980), also derives atmosphere from its crunchy non-production, which adds to the sense of it being an audio message from a strange cult. If the song had been re-recorded in a studio it might have lost this powerful atmosphere.

Dictaphonic and studio perspectives are frequently cut or mixed between – see 'Paintwork' from *This Nation's Saving Grace* (1985), 'Sinister Waltz' from *Shift-Work* and 'Dog is Life' from *I am Kurious Oranj* (1988). 'Paintwork' could be the sound of a home cassette compilation gone wrong. We hear the dominant 'clean' version of the track interrupted by someone pushing record and randomly inserting fragments of living room TV sound into the song. The simple home keyboard chords and drums are repetitive and banal but the dictaphone wrecks the acoustic homogeneity. As such the song is inconceivable without it – tape has become an instrument that is a key part of the ensemble. The concept of erasing parts of your master tape with a home cassette recorder is an incredibly charged intervention: aesthetically, politically and in opposition to an industry whose prime asset is the master tape. It draws direct comparison with Brion Gysin and William Burroughs' tape cut-ups which randomly erase and interrupt narrative flow to generate meaning, acting as a crude technological analogy for the human brain's ability to switch from memory to present perception.[3] As one meaning is disrupted, a new meaning is also created.

'Dog is Life' does not switch from one acoustic to another; it travels seamlessly from megaphone to dictaphone, from close to far, from clean to scuzzy. This has the effect of moving us fluidly from one space to another, never sure of what we are hearing. The voice is Smith's, but it remains aloof, travelling through a non-environment, disembodied and unsettling without a comforting acoustic tether. Most common on dictaphonic Fall tracks is the intro or outro, a snatch of documentary band banter, a quick reading or just the live hiss of an open microphone in an empty room. These punctuating blasts of lo-fi have become a frequent technique, almost a convention in Fall records and there are many examples.

Dictaphonics as an Alienation Effect

> Even though it was the arse-end of punk, it wasn't the done thing for a studio
> to release something that sounded so wilfully alien to everything else. (Smith
> 2008a, 80)

In mainstream music and film, the conventional approach is for the sound's authors to use the recording, editing and mixing processes to create a result that mimics the way the brain processes sound information arriving from the ear. The sound of every instrument next to your ear has become the staple of rock and pop. It allows a small degree of acoustic imprint onto the sound but is essentially about the

---

[3]   Burroughs documents many variations on approaches to tape cut-ups in the epilogue to *The Ticket That Exploded* (1968).

intensity of direct (as opposed to reflected) sound. Sounds classified as not being part of the performance are usually eradicated, such as body movements, ambient noise and excessive amounts of echo and reverberation. When experienced at first hand outside of a recording, these 'noise' elements tend to be filtered by the brain. You might mentally turn down the sound of traffic when having a conversation next to a road, and reduce the amount of echo when conversing between two rooms. Your mental hierarchical preference for particular sounds affects how you perceive them, the mind constantly operating like a live sound mixer. These selective perceptions have defined the way mainstream music and film sound has been produced.

The diffuse acoustic blend of jazz, the direct power of rock and the powerful concert hall dynamics of classical music are mixed as we might perceive them in an idealized version of their performance. The recording process and subsequent mixing reject extraneous noise and clarify individual instruments in an attempt to bridge the gap between a recording and the actuality. Almost perversely, a recording that does not reduce and filter noise and attempts an objective representation is an alien sound to most listeners. A single pair of microphones recording a performance from one point in space is usually reserved for live bootlegs and is usually classed as an artefact for obsessives and not the true sound of a band. In reference to film sound practice, Michel Chion says:

> In other words, the processed food of location sound is most often skimmed of certain substances and enriched with others. Can we hear a great ecological cry – 'give us organic sound without additives'? Occasionally filmmakers have tried this like [Jean-Marie] Straub in *Trop tôt trop tard*. The result is totally strange. Is this because the spectator isn't accustomed to it? Surely. But also because reality is one thing, and its transposition into audiovisual two-dimensionality … which involves radical sensory reduction, is another. What's amazing is that it works at all in this form. (1994, 96)

The recording made 'without additives' does not perform the job of selective perception; of putting the instruments into a prioritized and homogenized whole divorced from excess acoustic reverberation and extraneous noise. This is why unprocessed and 'unproduced' field recordings seem more alien to us than a heavily produced rock studio sound or a skilful blend of voice, music and sound effects in film. Provided that the acoustic signatures presented to the listener in this conventional audio environment are both believable and largely homogeneous, the listener interprets the sonic picture as a close approximation of their own perceptive mechanisms.

In the same way, a codified system of film sound chooses where we should listen, prioritizing sounds and balancing them in place of our selective perception. Even highly complex perspective shifts can be used provided they are supported by images to explain them. We can follow the complex sound point of view shifts in Francis Ford Coppola's *The Conversation* (1974) because our listening has been conditioned by the grammar of the medium. We know that when we see a tape recorder, the sound should have a different tone to the characters we see. We know when characters are far away they will be quieter and more echoic. This film plays with our notions of what constitutes believable sound perspective, but always uses its images to direct these changes. It begins with a couple seen talking far away, but heard in close up. This is explained in the next shot by our seeing a sensitive microphone that is picking the sound up. Chion describes the filmic convention:

> Imagine a scene in a film where a man is listening to a taped interview. If the sound being listened to has technical qualities of directness and presence, it refers back to the circumstances of its original state. If it has aural qualities that highlight its 'recordedness' and if there is emphasis on the acoustic properties of the place where it is being listened to we tend to focus on the moment where the recording is being heard. (1994, 77)

Having firmly established the relationships of sound and image, *The Conversation* is able to take the audience back in time at will, simply by playing the recorded sound again and again with either an image from the original time and place or that of Harry Caul (played by Gene Hackman) hunched over a tape recorder listening for clues. We even hear commentary from the characters over the original recording, making the two spaces concurrent. However, *The Conversation* can only accommodate these multiple spaces in the specific circumstances it creates.

But when two markedly different acoustics are present concurrently in a piece of music, there is an awareness of the artifice and sharp dissonance created which prevents the listener from settling into a fixed space because the recording now does the opposite: it posits the listener quite unnaturally in more than one space and can therefore be viewed as interventionist. In narrative film, the visual image can easily motivate radical shifts in acoustic qualities. Film frequently traverses time and space, but music is much more rooted in one place and time. Its default mode of presentation is of a single performance that unfolds in linear time before the listener. When multiple spatial and temporal perspectives exist in a piece of recorded music, we are much less able to decipher them because they lack the visual explanation provided in film. When The Fall put two or more disparate acoustic signatures and voices into one song, the effect is often alienating because of this fragmentation of time, space and personality.

The Fall's Use of Tape in the Context of Other Artists

Of course The Fall were not the first rock group to use dictaphonic and tape compositions in their music. Captain Beefheart and His Magic Band's *Trout Mask Replica* (1969) has studio songs as well as stereo field recordings of the music being performed in the house the musicians lived in, trailing into conversations with neighbouring kids and barking dogs and some domestic tape tracks. Poems such as 'Orange Claw Hammer' and 'The Dust Blows Forward 'n' the Dust Blows Back' have a dictaphonic quality because of the audible blips and squeals between each line. No attempt is made to disguise these noises, and they can only be seen as intentional given that much of the LP was re-recorded in a studio at Captain Beefheart's (Don Van Vliet's) insistence.[4] 'China Pig' has a domestic tape sound which sets it apart from the rest of the LP acoustically and helps convey a sense of history and time passed – the song sounds old not just because of its delta blues style but because of its non-production. It could be seen as a precursor to The Fall's 'New Puritan'.

There is a crucial difference though: *Trout Mask Replica* largely isolates acoustics in the sense that they are not layered or combined within a song. The Fall's approach in contrast consists in combining different tonalities and acoustics for chaotic effect or shifting between them, which is both disorientating and attention grabbing. Van Vliet had his musicians create a meticulously rehearsed, structured musical chaos: Smith creates works with chaotic elements outside of the musician's control or remit, arrhythmic clashes and pitch mismatches such as the queasy wow and flutter church bells from 'The Birmingham School of Business School' from *Code: Selfish* (1992) or the spliced audio detritus in 'Music Scene' from *Live at the Witch Trials*.

The Beatles' use of tape effects, most notably on 'Tomorrow Never Knows' and 'Revolution 9' is most obviously influenced by the musique concrète of John Cage, Karlheinz Stockhausen and Pierre Schaeffer. The listener is placed in one introspective environment, because the diversity of sound sources and perspectives removes sounds from a sense of cause. The physical and spatial inferences normally made by listeners are removed by the sheer quantity of sound sources, forcing the listener to accept sound as sound because the brain is unable to decipher the causal relationships within the barrage of sounds. The effect is designed to imitate a psychedelic state.

However, The Fall use tape in a fundamentally different way, using two sound recorders, the studio's hi-fi and the singer's own lo-fi dictaphone. This allows the retention of a causal relationship because the listener can decode the fairly simplistic spatial relationships in the two distinctly recorded acoustics. This could be seen as opposite to Schaeffer's musique concrète, which placed most value on removing causality from a sound, abstracting it and removing associations with the physical world. The Fall use tape as an instrument to add more causality, more association. The physical world is made more present in the shuffles of footsteps and rustle of clothing picked up as human activity clouds the recording. Smith seems very fond of these uncontrolled audio events and their warts-and-all nature is key to his use of tape.

Pierre Schaeffer's definition of the acousmatic as 'a sound that is heard without its cause or source being seen' is expanded upon by Chion: 'Radio, phonograph,

---

[4]   The recording methods on *Trout Mask Replica* which combine 'field recordings' and the studio are documented in *Captain Beefheart* (Barnes 2000, 84).

telephone, all of which transmit sounds without showing their emitter, are acousmatic media by definition' (1994, 71). The majority of recorded music follows this definition, however it ignores the fact that the medium of transmission can become part of the source. But a sound can comprise a number of layered sources such as a phone left off the hook in a room or a PA system piping music into a shopping centre. A telephone may not show its listener, but its sound quality tells us they are remote and using a telephone. If you were to record birdsong in high quality and play it back to a blindfolded person, they might not be able to tell if it were a real bird singing to them or not. In the same circumstances, the recordedness of the dictaphone would be very apparent.

Dictaphonics reveals part of its source through clues within itself and could therefore be termed 'metaphonic'--a sound containing ciphers that suggest part of its origins. The click of the record button, the break-up of the cheap speaker and the nasal tone become obvious signifiers as to one of the sounds' origins, allowing the listener to visualize its specific source, even if the source is one stage removed from the original sound. It is working against its acousmatic nature to become partially visualized once more. Of course, at the same time it cloaks whatever this identified recorder originally captured in dictaphonic colouration making it less comprehensible and identifiable – even taking over and becoming the sound itself in some circumstances.

The Highs and Lows of Tape

Smith's politics are complex and changeable, but there are certain constants which are clear from interviews and lyrics: a lack of deference to conventional musical craft, a DIY attitude borne from if not allied with the punk movement and a distrust of established structures. The Fall's tape-based musical additions differ in a very clear way from Schaeffer and Cage's high art origins. This is not the academic musician who splices with conceptual and aesthetic precision; it is a democratized DIY sound injection from the most affordable of pocket recorders. The immediacy of a dictaphone is its appeal, not purity or fidelity. That said, there are clear lineages following on from the pioneers of tape music. John Cage was against improvisation, seeing it as a way in which musicians would fall back on existing musical patterns or interactions and hence old musical ideas, but believed firmly in chance and indeterminacy. Smith has a similar approach, as evident in the line, 'Don't start improvising for god's sake' from 'Slates, Slags, Etc.' (1981, *Slates, etc.*) randomly capturing and replaying sounds to add or incorporate into The Fall's music. This dictaphonic randomness is made more apparent when set against the repetitive structures of rock. Writing in 1954, at a time when the creative possibilities of magnetic tape were beginning to reveal themselves, John Cage said 'There are two great dangers for magnetic tape: one is music (all the history and thinking about it); and the other is feeling obliged to have an instrument' (1978, 179). Mark E. Smith and The Fall have avoided both of these dangers. Smith's early attempts to learn a conventional musical instrument seem to have ended with him taking up the tape recorder as an instrument. He is also acknowledging that the sanctity of music as an isolated experience set apart from the method of its reproduction or the acoustic of where it is played is an unattainable and irrelevant ideal.

The aesthetics created by lo-fi tape have formed a significant part of The Fall's sound and their contribution to the group's political stance can be seen through a defiant anti-establishment desire to interrupt the acoustic, spatial and temporal complacency of the established rock formula. When someone seeks to make music that confronts on many levels, having a small tape recorder at your disposal can be invaluable. The primitive tape recorder has become a site of creative tension capable of transcending its origins and adding to the abrasive power of the group's output.

Chapter Seven

'Let me tell you about scientific management': The Fall, the Factory and the Disciplined Worker

Owen Hatherley

Over the last few years two conflicting ideas about The Fall have come about, without ever really being recognized as contradictory. There's the old idea of Mark E. Smith and the group as grim Northern disciplinarians, prone to reactionary statements in interviews and a disdain for students and the work-shy; and another, which has been more common lately, which concentrates on Mark E. Smith as 'Prophet in Prestwich' (Bracewell 1997, 186), a kind of Lovecraftian psychic and seer opposing the technocratic rationalism of Factory records. However, this tension between an iron, workerist discipline, which can be heard in the grinding, repetitive sound, and the visionary revelations which pervade the lyrics, is best understood through management. Specifically, through the supplanting of nineteenth-century work norms with the more efficient, apparently scientific system imported from the USA after the 1910s, under the influence of the theorist Frederick Winslow Taylor, whose 'rationalization' paved the way for the assembly line and mass production.

First of all though there are the curious perceptions of the factory and industry in The Fall's early work. For all his professed workerism, Mark E. Smith's pre-Fall experience, after a time in a meat factory, was mostly as a dock clerk, outside of the site of production itself, followed by a spell of unemployment and assiduous reading. The factory is something observed, but not directly experienced – something studied and aestheticized to discover its effects. Accordingly, in *Live at the Witch Trials* (1979) industry features as a sinister presence, a centrifugal force sucking people in and spitting them out as valium-addicted, psychically and physically warped. 'Industrial Estate' admonishes that the company 'air will fuck up your face', creating something new and bizarre out of it. At this point, however, there is still a certain *flailing* element to The Fall's music, with the drums constantly clattering and falling about. There might not have been solos or displays of individual technique, but there was a certain sloppiness and franticness to The Fall that would soon be purged. Smith, too, was not sounding particularly enamoured by the English obsession with hard graft, bemoaning being 'tied to the puritan ethic' on the title track. However, a particular industrial obsession had already crept in on their first single, in 1978 – the importance of the 'Three Rs: Repetition, repetition, repetition' ('Repetition').

Of course this has to be seen in the context of British Industry, and of Britain and specifically Manchester as the first area worldwide to comprehensively transform itself into a purely industrial, purely urban and anti-rural economy – it should be noted that Smith uses 'peasant' as an insult in 'C'n'C-S Mithering'. The forcible remaking of the worker as an appendage to a machine was traced by Marx in *Capital* thus:

> To work at a machine, the workman should be taught from childhood, in order that he may learn to adapt his own movements to the uniform and unceasing motion of an automaton ... at the same time that factory work exhausts the nervous system to the uttermost, it does away with the many-sided play of the muscles, and confiscates every atom of freedom, both in bodily and intellectual activity ... it is not the workman that employs the instruments of labour, but the instruments of labour that employ the workman. (1946, 420–23)

This forcible simultaneous limiting and over-stretching of the body's capabilities is what becomes a feature of The Fall's records from *Dragnet* onwards. 'Spectre vs. Rector' was cited in the finest, most comprehensive analysis of The Fall's most creative period (see Fisher Chapter 8, this volume) as perhaps the first truly great Fall track, the first to showcase Smith's fractured, gnostic storytelling. This is true enough, but it is also intriguing what happens to the early Fall sound here. The song is dominated by a huge, ugly bass riff, repeating relentlessly and drawing everything (apart from Smith) into its pattern. The track resounds with repetitive clatter, evoking some kind of foundry or mill, something also evoked by the claustrophobic, noise-ridden production. *Dragnet*'s sleeve notes, meanwhile, evoke a city more post-industrial than industrial – 'up here in the North there are no wage packet jobs for us, thank Christ'. As with sleeves at the time such as that for 'How I Wrote "Elastic Man"', it's the ruined factory and its ghosts that are more redolent of the urban reality than Factory's seamless *Sachlichkeit*. The *Dragnet* sleeve features an excerpt from a conversation with dry-cleaners that evokes perfectly the romantic possibilities of the dilapidated, decommissioned city: 'How did your coat get so dirty Mr. Smith? What do you do for a living?' Answer: 'I hang around old buildings for hours and get very dirty in one of those hours.'

The Fall's definitive morphing into the merciless machine of *Hex Enduction Hour* (1982) was yet to occur, however. To go back for a moment to Taylor and Marx, there's a certain difference between the painful overexertion of the English factory system and American scientific management. Taylor writes in *Principles of Scientific Management* (1998) that there are two particular fallacies obstructing the efficient management of labour: one that places the accent on the naturally gifted individual and places the onus on extraordinary, voluntaristic excesses of labour – the Stakhanovite movement in the USSR is a fine example of this, straining to

achieve deliberately excessive targets – and another, where the workers' belief
that efficient labour will make their own jobs obsolete leads to slow, deliberately
obstructive working. Taylor writes that his intention is:

> to prove that the best management is a true science, resting upon clearly
> defined laws, rules, and principles, as a foundation. And further to show that
> the fundamental principles of scientific management are applicable to all kinds
> of human activities, from our simplest individual acts to the work of our great
> corporations, which call for the most elaborate cooperation. And, briefly, through
> a series of illustrations, to convince the reader that whenever these principles are
> correctly applied, results must follow which are truly astounding. (1998, 4)

This was achieved via the time and motion study, where the movement of the
worker was charted in minute detail and then evaluated by management to decide
the way in which he could produce the most in the least amount of time.

The earlier Fall, with its relatively scrappy inefficiency can be seen as a remnant
of the earlier principles of management, where the workforce essentially does its
own thing, leading to sudden sporadic increases in work and physical expenditure.
From around 1980 this becomes severely circumscribed by the dominance in every
song of Steve Hanley's bass riffs, which in their rumbling, metallic tone evoke
the humming of a brutally effective factory. The workers, the actual musicians,
are severely disciplined if they shirk the steady tempo or, even worse, decide to
express themselves: note the oft-quoted, 'don't start improvising, for God's sake'
on *Slags, Slates Etc* (1981). At around the same time, Smith's lyrics get both more
fantastical and more insistent on the need for pure, pared-down repetition and
exhibit much disdain for malingerers. While two years earlier the puritan ethic
was disdained, now a certain ambiguous identification with a Cromwellian ethic
could be found in his lyrics. Not just the threat of a 'New Puritan', but other
telling references creeping in – a healthiness gained through decidedly unhealthy
sources. 'Fit and Working Again' features Smith, over a steady, undemonstrative
chug, declaring 'And I feel like [the boxer] Alan Minter/I just ate eight sheets
of blotting paper/And I chucked out the Alka Seltzer' – shoving down industrial
products until they make him superhuman.

Taylorism is often associated with cybernetics, and the machine aesthetic that
the Fall have often deliberately stood against, the synthesizers and robots of the
early 1980s. But as much as it suggests, in the acclimatizing to simple, repetitive,
machine-like tasks, something beyond human, it also implies something before
the human. Antonio Gramsci's short study 'Americanism and Fordism' (1929–35)
(Gramsci 1971) reminds us that Taylorist management theorists, as with Smith's
description of musicians as cattle, were not particularly respectful of the human
subjectivity of their workers. Gramsci cites Taylor's term for the worker as 'the
trained gorilla' as 'expressing with brutal cynicism' what he describes as 'developing
in the worker to the highest degree automatic and mechanical attitudes, breaking
up the psycho-physical nexus of qualified professional work, which demands a

certain active participation of intelligence, fantasy and initiative on the part of the worker' (Gramsci 1971, 302). Gramsci sees this as a progressive development, eliminating the sentimentality and peasant spirituality from the working class, who will then be able to prepare for power. Taylor, meanwhile, insisted his system was fairer than the nineteenth-century's work norms, what he called 'the more or less open warfare which characterizes the ordinary types of management'. But in the Taylorist factory itself there would be absolutely no question about who was manager and who managed. He promised his system would not lead to unemployment but the Fordist modes of production could only guarantee full employment briefly. There would be slightly more job security than there would be in the service of The Fall, but not much.

Taylor and his disciples set themselves the task of obliterating the imagination and the fantastic. Smith's aim, meanwhile, seems to be the elimination of any desire for initiative and any ostentatious display of technique on the part of his musicians. This is, after all, a profession that tends, at least outside of classical music, to think of itself as creative and individualistic, rather than as a set of cogs in a disciplined machine. Accordingly, the turnover becomes enormous. But while deriding individualism in The Fall, the songs are far more ambiguous about the process of being subjected to the will of the machine and the manager. 'Fiery Jack' depicts a character whose repetitive job leaves him able to 'think think think' and 'burn burn burn', with no outlet – the wasting of human intelligence under the factory system, slack-jawed, living on pies, drunk for three decades. Yet this isn't a moralistic expression of sociological concern so much as admiration and identification for the speeding, simmering resentment that drives Jack. Although it is never a good idea to impart a definitive authorial voice to any Fall song, there's a definite undercurrent in several songs from the 1980–83 period that discipline and puritanism have done something awful to the psyche of the British. Frequently this is ascribed to the survival of a peasant residue, as on the atavistic horrors of *Grotesque* and the anti-rock mocking of how 'all the English groups act like peasants with free milk' (1980, 'C'n'C-S Mithering'). Elsewhere, though, this seems more a factory product. 'Kicker Conspiracy' details how by the early 1980s English football had become a grim slog, in which any individual talent was effaced for an amateurish, brutal limitation of possibilities, a place where 'flair is punished' – something which sounds a great deal like being in The Fall. However, there was always one person allowed to demonstrate flair, with Smith's indisciplined, fragmented, oblique and far from utilitarian textual/verbal collages roaming into the places which the rigours of the music blocked off.

In the live version of 'Cash 'n' Carry', Smith improvises that 'Even in Manchester, there's two types of factory there. One makes men old corpses. They stumble round like rust dogs. One lives off old dying men. One lives off the back of a dead man ... You know which Factory I mean', before declaring that in contrast 'I have dreams, I can see.' Factory Records and its protagonists have been comprehensively claimed by museum culture, with all the biopics, exhibitions and retrospectives that entails, and have even been cited as central to the 'regeneration' or gentrification of the city. The Fall have yet to be fully claimed by this history, and haven't been reduced to cliché quite yet. The nearest thing to that has been the *NME* caricature of Smith as grim foreman and pub bore, something to which the singer has himself played up. Discipline in the later Fall becomes nearer again to nineteenth-century production than the iron consistency of the Taylor system. Smith recently quoted Carlyle's aphorism 'produce, produce, produce, what else are you there for', though for much of the last decade or two what is produced often seems less important than the mere act of production itself. However, in The Fall's best work, the factory and production features as an ambiguous but utterly central motif. It warped a people, warps minds as much as bodies and rather than being in conflict with the weird and fantastical, itself produces the Weird.

PART III
The Aesthetics of The Fall

Chapter Eight

'Memorex for the Krakens': The Fall's Pulp Modernism

Mark Fisher

Maybe industrial ghosts are making Spectres redundant. (The Fall, *Dragnet* sleeve notes)

Scrawny, gnarled, gaunt: Smith doesn't waltz with ghosts. He materialises them. (Sinker, 1988)

Who can put their finger on the Weird? It has taken me more than 20 years to attempt this deciphering. Back then, The Fall did something to me. But what and how? Let's call it an 'Event' and at the same time note that all events have a dimension of the uncanny. If something is too alien, it will fail to register; if it is too easily recognized, too easily cognizable, it will never be more than a reiteration of the already known. When The Fall pummelled their way into my nervous system, circa 1983, it was as if a world that was familiar – and which I had thought *too* familiar, too quotidian to feature in rock – had returned, expressionistically transfigured, permanently altered.

I didn't know then that, already in 1983, The Fall's greatest work was behind them. No doubt the later albums have their merits but it is on *Grotesque* (1980), *Slates* (1981) and *Hex Enduction Hour* (1982) that the group reached a pitch of sustained abstract invention that they and others are unlikely to surpass. In its ambition and its linguistic and formal innovation, this triptych bears comparison with the great works of twentieth-century high literary modernism by James Joyce, T.S. Eliot and Wyndham Lewis. The Fall extend and performatively critique that mode of high modernism by reversing the impersonation of working-class accent, dialect and diction that, for example, Eliot performed in *The Waste Land* (Eliot 1969). Smith's strategy involved aggressively retaining accent while using, in the domain of a supposedly popular entertainment form, highly arcane literary practices. In doing so, he laid waste the notion that intelligence, literary sophistication and artistic experimentalism are the exclusive preserve of the privileged and the formally educated. But Smith knew that aping master class mores presented all sorts of other dangers; it should never be a matter of proving to the masters that the 'white crap' could be civilized. Perhaps all his writing was, from the start, an attempt to find a way out of that paradox which all working-class aspirants face – the impossibility of working-class achievement. Stay where you are, speak the language of your fathers and you remain nothing; move up, learn to speak in the master language and you have become a something, but only by erasing your origins. Isn't the achievement precisely that erasure: 'You can string a sentence together, how can you possibly be working class, my dear'?

For Smith, the temptation was always to fit into the easy role of working-class spokesman, speaking from an assigned place in a given social world. Smith played *with* that role, for example, through phrases like 'the white crap that talks back', as well as in the tracks 'Prole Art Threat' and 'Hip Priest', while refusing to actually play it. He knew that representation was a trap; Social Realism was the enemy because in supposedly 'merely' representing the social order, it actually constituted it. Against the Social Realism of the official Left, Smith developed a late twentieth-century urban English version of the 'grotesque realism' Bakhtin famously described in *Rabelais and his World* (Bakhtin [1965] 1984). Crucial to this grotesque realism is a contestation of the classificatory system which deems cultures and populations to be either refined or vulgar. As Peter Stallybrass and Allon White argued, 'the grotesque tends to operate as a critique of dominant ideology which has already set the terms, designating what is high and low' (1986, 43).

Instead of the high modernist appropriation of working-class speech and culture, Smith's 'pulp modernism' re-acquaints modernism with its disavowed pulp doppelganger. Lovecraft is the crucial figure here since his texts, which first appeared in pulp magazines like *Weird Tales,* emerged from an occulted trade between pulp horror and modernism. Follow the line back from Lovecraft's short stories and you pass through Dunsany and M.R. James before coming to Edgar Allen Poe. But Poe also played a decisive role in the development of modernism, via his influence on Baudelaire, Mallarmé, Valéry and their admirer T.S. Eliot. The fragmentary, citational structure of a story like Lovecraft's 'Call of Cthulhu', meanwhile, recalls *The Waste Land*. More than that, as Benjamin Noys argued in his unpublished essay, 'Lovecraft the Sinthome', the abominations from which Lovecraft's strait-laced scholars recoil bear comparisons with cubist and futurist art: Lovecraft, that is to say, turns modernism into an object of horror.

Yet Lovecraft's texts are exemplary of Weird, rather than straightforwardly gothic fiction. The Weird has its own consistency, which can be most clearly delineated by comparing it to two adjacent modes, fantasy and the uncanny. Fantasy, of which Tolkien is the key exemplar, presupposes a completed world, a world that, although superficially different to 'ours', with different species or supernatural forces, is politically all-too familiar since there is usually some nostalgia for the ordered organization of feudal hierarchy. Following Freud ([1919] 1990), we might say that the Uncanny, by contrast, is set in 'our' world, only that world is no longer 'ours', it no longer coincides with itself, it has been estranged: the strangely familiar, or the familiar become strange produces the charge of the 'unheimlich', which Freud saw at work, for example, in *The Tales of Hoffmann*. The Weird, however, depends upon the difference between two or more worlds, with 'world' here having an *ontological* sense. It is not a question of an empirical difference; the aliens are not from another planet, they are invaders from another reality system. Hence the defining image is that of the threshold, the door from this world into another and the key figure is the 'Lurker at the Threshold', which, in Lovecraft's mythos is called Yog Sothoth. The political philosophical implications are clear: *there is no world*. What we call *the* world is merely a local consensus hallucination, a shared dream.

Is There Anybody There?

'Spectre vs. Rector', from 1979's *Dragnet*, is the first moment – still chilling to hear – when The Fall both lay out and implement their pulp modernist methodology. 'Spectre vs. Rector' is not only a ghost story, it is a commentary on the ghost story. The chorus, if it can be called that, is a litany of pulp forebears: 'M.R. James be born be born/Yog Sothoth rape me lord' in which language devolves into an asignifying chant, into verbal ectoplasm: 'Sludge Hai Choi/Van Greenway/Ar Corman'.

Not coincidentally, 'Spectre vs. Rector' was the moment when The Fall really began to sound like themselves. Before that, The Fall's sound is a grey-complexioned, conspicuously consumptive garage plink-plonk punk, amphetamine lean and on edge, marijuana fatalistic, simultaneously arrogant and unsure of itself, proffering its cheap nastiness as a challenge. All of the elements of Smith's later (peripheral) vision are there on *Live at the Witch Trials* and on the other tracks on *Dragnet* – watery-eyed figures lurking in the corner of the retina, industrial estates glimpsed through psychotropic stupor – but they have not yet been condensed down, *pulped* into the witches' brew that will constitute Smith's vision.

On 'Spectre vs. Rector', any vestigial rock presence subsides into spectrality. The original track is already a palimpsest, spooked by itself; at least two versions are playing, out of sync. The track and it is very definitely a track, not a 'song', foregrounds both its own textuality and its texturality. It begins with cassette hum and when the sleeve notes tell us that it was partly 'recorded in a damp warehouse in MC/R' we are far from surprised. Steve Hanley's bass rumbles and thumps like some implacable earth-moving machine invented by a deranged underground race, not so much rising from sub-terra as dragging the sound down into a troglodyte goblin kingdom in which ordinary sonic values are inverted. From now on and for all the records that really matter, Hanley's bass will be the lead instrument, the monstrous foundations on which The Fall's upside-down sound will be built. Like Joy Division, fellow modernists from Manchester, The Fall scramble the grammar of white rock by privileging rhythm over melody.

Fellow modernists they might have been, but The Fall and Joy Division's take on modernism could not have been more different. Producer Martin Hannett and Peter Saville gave Joy Division a minimalist, metallic austerity; The Fall's sound and cover art, by contrast, was gnarled, collage cut-up, deliberately incomplete. Both bands were dominated by forbiddingly intense vocalist-visionaries. But where Curtis was the depressive-neurotic, the end of the European Romantic line, Smith was the psychotic, the self-styled destroyer of Romanticism. 'Unsuitable for Romantics', Smith will graffiti onto the cover of *Hex Enduction Hour* and 'Spectre vs. Rector' is the template for the anti-Romantic methodology he will deploy on The Fall's most important releases. After 'Spectre vs. Rector', there is no Mark E. Smith the romantic subject. The novelty of Smith's approach is to impose the novel or tale form as made explicit by the three part structure of 'Spectre vs. Rector' onto the Romantic-lyrical tradition of the rock and roll song, so that the impersonal author-function supplants that of the lyrical balladeer. There are parallels between what Smith does to rock and the cut-up surgery Eliot performed on the etherized patient of Romantic expressive subjectivity in his early poems. Smith chant-narrates, rather than sings, 'Spectre vs. Rector'.

The story is simple enough and on the surface is deliberately conventional: a post-*Exorcist* (1973) revisiting of the classic English ghost story. At another level, the narrative is generated by a Raymond Roussel-like playing with similar words: Rector/Spectre/Inspector/Exorcist/Exhausted. A rector is possessed by a malign spirit, 'the spectre was from Chorazina', which is described on the sleeve notes as 'a negative Jerusalem'. This is actually a reference to M.R. James' 'Count Magnus': 'Chorazin ... I have heard some of our old priests say that the Antichrist is to be born there (James 2005, 73); a police inspector tries to intervene but is driven insane. This is a real Lovecraftian touch, since the dread fate that haunts Lovecraft's characters is not of being consumed by the polytendrilled abominations but by the schizophrenia that their appearance often engenders. Both Rector and Inspector have to be saved by a third figure, a shaman-hero, an Outsider who 'goes back to the mountains' when the exorcism is complete.

The Rector stands for rectitude and rectilinearity as well as for traditional religious authority. The ontological shock that Lovecraft's monstrosities produce is typically described in terms of a twisting of rectilinear geometries. The Inspector, meanwhile, as Ian Penman conjectured in his 1980 interview with The Fall, 'stands for an investigative, empirical world view' (Penman, 1980). The hero, his 'soul possessed a thousand times' has more affinity with the Spectre, whom he absorbs and becomes, than with the agents of rectitude and/or empirical investigation: 'The spectre enters hero/But the possession is ineffectual.' It seems that the hero is driven more by his addiction to being possessed, which is to say dispossessed of his own identity – that was his kick from life – than from any altruistic motive and he has no love for the social order he rescues.[1]

In *Madness and Civilization* (2004), Foucault argues that the insane occupy the structural position vacated by the leper, while in 'The Ecstasy of Communication', Baudrillard describes 'the state of terror proper to the schizophrenic: too great a proximity of everything, the unclean promiscuity of everything which touches, invests and penetrates without resistance, with no halo of private projection to protect him anymore' (1983, 132). Baudrillard is of course describing the schizophrenia of media systems which overwhelm all interiority. Television brings

---

[1]   For these lyrics, please see 'Lyrics Parade' at The Fall Online: http://fall.byethost13. com/lyrics.html

us voices from far away and there is always something on the other side. For Baudrillard, there is an increasing flatness between media and the schizophrenic delirium in which they feature; psychotics often describe themselves as receivers for transmitted signals. And what is the hero of 'Spectre vs. Rector' if not another version of the 'ESP medium of discord' that Smith sings of in 'Psykick Dancehall' (1979)?

Smith's own methodology as writer-ranter-chanter echoes that of the hero-malcontent. He becomes nothing but the mystic pad on which stray psychic signals impress themselves, the throat through which a warring multiplicity of mutually antagonistic voices speak. This is not only a matter of the familiar idea that Smith 'contains multitudes'; the schizophonic riot of voices is itself subject to all kinds of mediation. The voices we hear will often be reported speech, recorded in the compressed 'telegraphic' headline style Smith borrowed from the Lewis of *Blast*. Listening to The Fall now, I am often reminded of another admirer of Lewis, Marshall McLuhan. The McLuhan of *The Mechanical Bride* (2002), subtitled *The Folklore of Industrial Man*, understood very well the complicity between mass media, modernism and pulp. McLuhan argued that modernist collage was a response to the perfectly schizophrenic layout of the newspaper front page and Poe, who in addition to his role as a forebear of Weird fiction was also the inventor of the Detective genre, plays a crucial role in *The Mechanical Bride*.

'M.R. James, be born be born'

Ten times my age, one-tenth my height. (The Fall, 'City Hobgoblins')

So he plunges into the Twilight World, and a political discourse framed in terms of witch-craft and demons. It's not hard to understand why, once you start considering it. The war that the Church and triumphant Reason waged on a scatter of wise-women and midwives, lingering practitioners of folk-knowledge, has provided a powerful popular image for a huge struggle for political and intellectual dominance, as first Catholics and later Puritans invoked a rise in devil-worship to rubbish their opponents. The ghost-writer and antiquarian M.R. James (one of the writers Smith appears to have lived on during his peculiar drugged adolescence) transformed the folk-memory into a bitter class-struggle between established science and law, and the erratic, vengeful, relentless undead world of wronged spirits, cheated of property or voice, or the simple dignity of being believed in. (Sinker 1986)

Whether Smith first came to James via TV or some other route, James' stories exerted a powerful and persistent influence on his writing. Lovecraft, an enthusiastic admirer of James' stories to the degree that he borrowed their structure (a scholar/researcher steeped in empiricist common sense is gradually driven insane by contact with an abyssal alterity), understood very well what was novel in James' tales. 'In inventing a new type of ghost', Lovecraft wrote of James, 'he departed considerably from the conventional Gothic traditions; for where the older stock ghosts were pale and stately and apprehended chiefly through the sense of sight, the average James ghost is lean, dwarfish and hairy – a sluggish, hellish night-abomination midway betwixt beast and man – and usually *touched* before it is *seen*' (Lovecraft 1985, 507). Some would question whether these dwarf-like figures, 'Ten times my age, one-tenth my height', could be described as 'ghosts' at all; often, it seemed that James was writing *demon* rather than ghost stories.

If the libidinal motor of Lovecraft's horror was race, in the case of James it was class. For James' scholars, contact with the anomalous was usually mediated by the 'lower classes', which he portrayed as lacking in intellect but in possession of a deeper knowledge of weird lore. As Lovecraft and James scholar S.T. Joshi observes:

> The fractured and dialectical English in which ... [James' array of lower-class characters] speak or write is, in one sense, a reflection of James' well-known penchant for mimicry; but it cannot be denied that there is a certain element of malice in his relentless exhibition of their intellectual failings ... And yet, they occupy pivotal places in the narrative: by representing a kind of middle ground between the scholarly protagonists and the aggressively savage ghosts, they frequently sense the presence of the supernatural more quickly and more instinctively than their excessively learned betters can bring themselves to do. (2005, xv)

James wrote his stories as Christmas entertainments for Eton schoolboys and Smith was doubtless provoked and fascinated by James' stories in part because there was no obvious point of identification for him in them: 'When I was at the Witch trials of the 20th Century they said: You are white crap' (sleeve, *Live at the Witch Trials*). *Live* at the witch trials: is it that the witch trials have never ended or that we are in some repeating structure which is always excluding and denigrating the Weird?

A working-class autodidact like Smith could scarcely be conceived of in James' sclerotically, stratified universe; such a being was a monstrosity which would be punished for the sheer hubris of existing; witness the amateur archaeologist Paxton in 'A Warning to the Curious'. Paxton was an unemployed clerk and therefore by no means working class but his grisly fate was as much a consequence of 'getting above himself' as it was of his disturbing sacred Anglo-Saxon artefacts. Smith could identify neither with James' expensively educated protagonists nor with his uneducated, superstitious lower orders. As Mark Sinker puts it: 'James, an enlightened Victorian intellectual, dreamed of the spectre of the once crushed and newly rising Working Classes as a brutish and irrational Monster from the Id: Smith is working class, and is torn between adopting this image of himself and fighting violently against it. It's left him with a loathing of liberal humanist condescension' (1986).

But if Smith could find no place in James' world, he would take a cue from one of Blake's mottoes adapted in *Dragnet*'s 'Before the Moon Falls' and create his own fictional system rather than be enslaved by another man's. In James' stories, there is, properly speaking, no working class at all. The lower classes that feature in his tales are by and large the remnants of the rural peasantry and the supernatural is associated with the countryside. James' scholars typically travel from Oxford or London to the witch-haunted flatlands of Suffolk, and it is only here that they encounter demonic entities. Smith's fictions would both locate spectres in the urban here and now and establish that their antagonisms were not archaisms.

> No one has so perfectly studied the sense of threat in the English Horror Story: the twinge of apprehension at the idea that the wronged dead might return to claim their property, their identity, their own voice in their own land. (Sinker 1988)

'The grotesque peasants stalk the land'

> The word *grotesque* derives from a type of Roman ornamental design first discovered in the fifteenth century, during the excavation of Titus's baths. Named after the 'grottoes' in which they were found, the new forms consisted of human and animal shapes intermingled with foliage, flowers, and fruits in fantastic designs which bore no relationship to the logical categories of classical art. For a contemporary account of these forms we can turn to the Latin writer Vitruvius. Vitruvius was an official charged with the rebuilding of Rome under Augustus, to whom his treatise *On Architecture* is addressed. Not surprisingly, it bears down hard on the 'improper taste' for the grotesque: 'Such things neither are, nor can be, nor have been,' says the author in his description of the mixed human, animal, and vegetable forms: 'For how can a reed actually sustain a roof, or a candelabrum the ornament of a gable? Or a soft and slender stalk, a seated statue? Or how can flowers and half-statues rise alternately from roots and stalks? Yet when people view these falsehoods, they approve rather than condemn, failing to consider whether any of them can really occur or not.' (Parrinder 1984, 8)

By the time of *Grotesque*, The Fall's pulp modernism had become an entire political-aesthetic programme. At one level, *Grotesque* can be positioned as the barbed Prole Art retort to the lyric antique Englishness of public school prog rock. Compare, for instance, the cover of 'City Hobgoblins' (one of the singles that came out around the time of *Grotesque*) with something like Genesis's *Nursery Cryme*. *Nursery Cryme* presents a corrupted English surrealist idyll. On the 'City Hobgoblins' cover, an urban scene has been invaded by 'emigrés from old green glades': a leering, malevolent 'kobold' looms over a dilapidated tenement. But rather than being smoothly integrated into the photographed scene, the crudely rendered hobgoblin has been etched, Nigel Cooke-style, onto the background. This is a war of worlds, an ontological struggle, a struggle over the means of representation.

Grotesque's 'English Scheme' was a thumbnail sketch of the territory over which the war was being fought. The enemies are the old Right, the custodians of a national heritage image of England, 'poky quaint streets in Cambridge' but also, crucially, the middle-class Left, who 'condescend to black men' and 'talk of Chile while driving through Haslingden'. In fact, enemies were everywhere. Lumpen punk was in many ways more of a problem than prog, since its reductive literalism and perfunctory politics, 'circles with A in the middle' ('C'n'C-S Mithering') colluded with Social Realism in censuring/censoring the visionary and the ambitious. Although much of *Grotesque* is an enigma, the LP's title gives clues. Otherwise incomprehensible references to 'huckleberry masks', 'a man with butterflies on his face' and Totale's 'ostrich headdress' and 'light blue plant-heads' begin to make sense when you recognize that, in Parrinder's description, the grotesque originally referred to 'human and animal shapes intermingled with foliage, flowers, and fruits in fantastic designs which bore no relationship to the logical categories of classical art' (Parrinder 1984).

Grotesque, then, would be another moment in the endlessly repeating struggle between a Pulp Underground, the scandalous grottoes and the Official culture. 'Spectre vs. Rector' had rendered this clash in a harsh Murnau black and white as expressed by lines such as 'I've waited since Caesar for this'; on *Grotesque* the struggle is painted in colours as florid as those used on the album's garish sleeve, which was the work of Smith's sister. It is no accident that the words 'grotesque' and 'weird' are often associated with one another, since both connote something which is out of place, which either should not exist at all or should not exist *here*. The response to the apparition of a grotesque object will involve laughter as much as revulsion. In his 1972 study of the grotesque, Philip Thomson argued that the grotesque was often characterized by the co-presence of the laughable and that which is not compatible with the laughable. The role of laughter in The Fall has confused and misled interpreters. What has been suppressed is precisely the co-presence of the laughable with what is not compatible with the laughable. That co-presence is difficult to grasp, particularly in Britain, where humour has often functioned to ratify common sense, to punish overreaching ambition with the dampening weight of bathos.

With The Fall, however, it is as if satire is returned to its origins in the grotesque. The Fall's laughter does not issue from the commonsensical mainstream but from a psychotic outside. This is satire in the oneiric mode in which invective and lampoonery becomes delirial, a (psycho)tropological spewing of associations and animosities, the true object of which is not any failing of probity but the delusion that human dignity is possible. It is not surprising to find Smith alluding to Jarry's *Ubu Roi* in a barely audible line in 'City Hobgoblins': 'Ubu le Roi is a home hobgoblin.' For Jarry, as for Smith, the incoherence and incompleteness of the obscene and the absurd were to be opposed to the false symmetries of good sense. But in their mockery of poise, moderation and self-containment, in their logorrhoeic disgorging of 'slanguage', in their glorying in mess and incoherence, The Fall sometimes resemble a white English analogue of Funkadelic. For both Smith and George Clinton, there is no escaping the grotesque, if only because those who primp and puff themselves up only become more grotesque. We could go so far as to say that it is the human condition to be grotesque, since the human animal is the one that does not fit in, the freak of nature who has no place in nature and is capable of recombining nature's products into hideous new forms.

On *Grotesque*, Smith has mastered his anti-lyrical methodology. The songs are tales but tales half-told. The words are fragmentary, as if they have come to us via an unreliable transmission that keeps cutting out. Viewpoints are garbled; ontological distinctions between author, text and character are confused and fractured. It is impossible to definitively sort out the narrator's words from direct speech. The tracks are palimpsests, badly recorded in a deliberate refusal of the 'coffee table' aesthetic Smith derides on the cryptic sleeve notes. The process of recording is not airbrushed out but foregrounded, surface hiss and illegible cassette noise brandished like improvised stitching on some Hammer Frankenstein monster. 'Impression of J Temperance' was typical: a story in the Lovecraft style in which a dog breeder's 'hideous replica … brown sockets … Purple eyes … fed with rubbish from disposal barges' haunts Manchester. This is a Weird tale, but one subjected to modernist techniques of compression and collage. The result is so elliptical that it is as if the text – part-obliterated by silt, mildew and algae – has been fished out of the Manchester ship canal which Hanley's bass sounds like it is dredging: '"Yes" said Cameron. "And the thing was in the impression of J Temperance."'

The sound on *Grotesque* is a seemingly impossible combination of the shambolic and the disciplined, the cerebral-literary and the idiotic-physical. The obvious parallel was The Birthday Party. In both groups, an implacable bass holds together a leering, lurching schizophonic body whose disparate elements strain like distended, diseased viscera against a pustule and pock-ridden skin: 'spotty exterior hides a spotty interior' ('C'n'C-S Mithering'). Both The Fall and The Birthday Party reached for Pulp Horror imagery rescued from the 'white trash can' as an analogue and inspiration for their perverse 'return' to rock and roll as also evident in the neo-rockabilly of The Cramps. The nihilation that fired them was a rejection of a pop that they saw as self-consciously sophisticated, conspicuously cosmopolitan, a pop which implied that the arty could only be attained at the expense of brute physical impact. Their response was to hyperbolize crude atavism, to embrace the unschooled and the primitivist.

The Birthday Party's fascination was with the American 'junkonscious', the mountain of semiotic/narcotic trash lurking in the hind-brain of a world population hooked on America's myths of abjection and omnipotence. The Birthday Party revelled in this fantasmatic Americana, using it as a way of cancelling an Australian identity that they in any case experienced as empty and devoid of any distinguishing features. Smith's 'r 'n' r' citations functioned differently, precisely as a means of reinforcing his Englishness and his own ambivalent attitude towards it. The rockabilly references are almost 'what if?' exercises. What if rock and roll had emerged from the industrial heartlands of England rather than the Mississippi Delta? The rockabilly on 'Container Drivers' or 'Fiery Jack' is slowed by meat pies and gravy, its dreams of escape fatally poisoned by pints of bitter and cups of greasy spoon tea. It is rock and roll as working men's club cabaret, performed by a failed Gene Vincent imitator in Prestwich. The 'What if?' speculations fail. Rock and roll needed the endless open highways; it could never have begun in Britain's snarled up ring roads and claustrophobic conurbations.

For the Smith of *Grotesque*, homesickness is a pathology, as borne out by the interview on the 1983 *Perverted by Language Bis* video, in which Smith claims that being away from England literally made him sick. There is little to recommend the country that he can never permanently leave; his relationship to it seems to be one of wearied addiction. The fake jauntiness of 'English Scheme' complete with proto John Shuttleworth cheesy cabaret keyboard is a squalid postcard from somewhere no one would ever wish to be. Here and in 'C'n'C-S Mithering', the US emerges as an alternative to the despair at the class-ridden Britain of 'sixty hour weeks and stone toilet back-gardens', the 'clever ones … point their fingers at America', but there is a sense that, no matter how far he travels, Smith will in the end be overcome by a compulsion to return to his blighted homeland, which functions as his poison and remedy, sickness and cure. In the end he is as afflicted by paralysis as Joyce's Dubliners.

On 'C'n'C-S Mithering' a rigor mortis snare drum gives this paralysis a sonic form. 'C'n'C-S Mithering' is an unstinting inventory of gripes and irritations worthy of Tony Hancock at his most acerbic and disconsolate, a cheerless survey of estates that 'stick up like stacks' and, worse still, a derisive dismissal of one of the supposed escape routes from drudgery: the music business, denounced as corrupt, dull and stupid. The track sounds, perhaps deliberately, like a white English version of rap. Here as elsewhere, The Fall are remarkable for producing *equivalents* to, rather than facile imitations of, black American forms.

'Body … a tentacle mess'

But it is the other long track, 'The N.W.R.A.', that is the masterpiece. All of the LP's themes coalesce in this track, a tale of cultural political intrigue that plays like some improbable mulching of T.S. Eliot, Wyndham Lewis, H.G. Wells, P.K. Dick, Lovecraft and Le Carré. It is the story of Roman Totale, a psychic and former cabaret performer whose body is covered in tentacles. It is often said that Roman Totale is one of Smith's 'alter-egos'; in fact, Smith is in the same relationship to Totale as Lovecraft was to someone like Randolph Carter. Totale is a character rather than a persona. Needless to say, he is not a character in the 'well-rounded' Forsterian sense so much as a carrier of mythos, an intertextual linkage between Pulp fragments.

The intertextual methodology is crucial to pulp modernism. If pulp modernism first of all asserts the author-function over the creative-expressive subject, it secondly asserts a fictional system against the author-God. By producing a fictional plane of consistency across different texts, the pulp modernist becomes a conduit through which a world can emerge. Once again, Lovecraft is the exemplar here: his tales and novellas could in the end no longer be apprehended as discrete texts but as part-objects forming a mythos-space which other writers could also explore and extend. The form of 'The N.W.R.A.' is as alien to organic wholeness as Totale's abominable tentacular body. It is a grotesque concoction, a collage of pieces that do not belong together. The model is the novella rather than the tale and the story is told episodically, from multiple points of views, using a heteroglossic riot of styles and tones: comic, journalistic, satirical, novelistic; it is like Lovecraft's 'Call of Cthulhu' rewritten by the Joyce of *Ulysses* and compressed into 10 minutes.

From what we can glean, Totale is at the centre of a plot – infiltrated and betrayed from the start – which aims at restoring the North to glory, perhaps to its Victorian moment of economic and industrial supremacy; perhaps to some more ancient pre-eminence, perhaps to a greatness that will eclipse anything that has come before. More than a matter of regional railing against the capital, in Smith's vision the North comes to stand for everything suppressed by urbane good taste: the esoteric, the anomalous, the vulgar sublime, that is to say, the Weird and the Grotesque itself. Totale, festooned in the incongruous Grotesque costume of 'ostrich head-dress … feathers/orange-red with blue-black lines … and light blue plant-heads', is the would-be Faery King of this weird revolt who ends up its maimed Fisher King, abandoned like a pulp modernist Miss Havisham amid the relics of a carnival that will never happen, a drooling totem of a defeated tilt at Social Realism, the visionary leader reduced, as the psychotropics fade and the fervour cools, to being a washed-up cabaret artiste once again.

'Don't start improvising for Christ's sake'

The temptation, when writing about The Fall's work of this period, is to too quickly render it tractable. I note this by way of a disclaimer and a confession, since I am of course as liable to fall prey to this temptation as any other commentator. To confidently describe songs as if they were 'about' settled subjects or to attribute to them a determinate aim or orientation, typically a satirical purpose, will always be inadequate to the vertiginous experience of the songs and the distinctive *jouissance* provoked by listening to them. This enjoyment involves a frustration, a frustration, precisely, of our attempts to make sense of the songs. Yet this jouissance, similar to that provoked by the late Joyce, Pynchon and Burroughs is an irreducible dimension of The Fall's modernist poetics. If it is impossible to make sense of the songs, it is also impossible to stop making sense of them, or at least it is impossible to stop attempting to make sense of them. On the one hand, there is no possibility of dismissing the songs as Nonsense; they are not gibberish or disconnected strings of non sequiturs. On the other hand, any attempt to constitute the songs as settled carriers of meaning runs aground on their incompleteness and inconsistency.

The principal way in which the songs were recuperated was via the charismatic persona Smith established in interviews. Although Smith scrupulously refused to either corroborate or reject any interpretations of his songs, invoking this extra-textual persona, notorious for its strong views and its sardonic but at least legible humour, allowed listeners and commentators to contain, even dissipate, the strangeness of the songs themselves. The temptation to use Smith's persona as a key to the songs was especially pressing because all pretence of democracy in the group had long since disappeared. By the time of *Grotesque*, it was clear that Smith was as much of an autocrat as James Brown, the band the zombie slaves of his vision. He is the shaman-author, the group the producers of a delirium-inducing repetition from which all spontaneity must be ruthlessly purged. 'Don't start improvising for Christ's sake', goes a line on *Slates*, the 10″ EP follow-up to *Grotesque*, echoing his chastisement of the band for 'showing off' on the live LP *Totale's Turns*.

Slates' 'Prole Art Threat' (1981) turned Smith's persona, reputation and image into an enigma and a conspiracy. The song is a complex, ultimately unreadable play on the idea of Smith as 'working-class' spokesman. The 'threat' is posed as much to other representations of the proletarian pop culture, which at its best meant The Jam and at its worst meant the more thuggish Oi!, as it is against the ruling class as such. The 'art' of The Fall's pulp modernism – their intractability and difficulty – is counterposed to the misleading ingenuousness of Social Realism. The Fall's intuition was that social relations could not be understood in the 'demystified' terms of empirical observation, the 'housing figures' and 'sociological memory' later ridiculed on 'The Man whose Head Expanded'. Social power depends upon 'hexes': restricted linguistic, gestural and behavioural codes which produce a sense of inferiority and enforce class destiny: 'What chance have you got against a tie and a crest?', Paul Weller demanded on The Jam's 'Eton Rifles' (1979) and it was as if The Fall took the power of such symbols and sigils very literally, understanding the social field as a series of curses which have to be sent back to those who issued them.

The pulp format on 'Prole Art Threat' is spy fiction, its scenario resembling *Tinker Tailor Soldier Spy* redone as a tale of class cultural espionage but then compressed and cut up so that characters and contexts are even more perplexing than they were in Le Carré's already oblique narrative. We are in a labyrinthine world of bluff and counter-bluff – a perfect analogue for Smith's own elusive and allusive textual strategies. The text is presented to us as a transcript of surveillance tapes, complete with ellipses where the transmission is supposedly scrambled: 'GENT IN SAFE-HOUSE: Get out the pink press threat file and Brrrptzzap* the subject. (* = scrambled)'. 'Prole Art Threat' seems to be a satire, yet it is a blank satire, a satire without any clear object. If there is a point, it is precisely to disrupt any of what Bakhtin ([1973] 1990) calls the 'centripetal' effort to establish fixed identities and meanings. Those centripetal forces are represented by the 'Middle

Mass', described as 'vulturous in the aftermath' and 'the Victorian vampiric' culture of London itself, as excoriated in 'Leave the Capitol'. This horrifying vision of London as a Stepford city of drab conformity, 'hotel maids smile in unison', ends with the unexpected arrival of Arthur Machen's tale, *The Great God Pan* last alluded to in The Fall's very early 'Second Dark Age', presaging The Fall's return to the Weird.

The Textual Expectorations of *Hex Enduction Hour*

> He'd been very close to becoming ex-funny man celebrity. He needed a good hour at the hexen school. '*Hex* press release' (*Hex Enduction Hour* cover notes)

Hex Enduction Hour was even more expansive than *Grotesque*. Teeming with detail, gnomic yet hallucinogenically vivid, *Hex* was a series of pulp modernist pen portraits of England in 1982. The LP had all the hubristic ambition of prog rock combined with an aggression whose ulcerated assault and battery outdid most of its post-punk peers in terms of sheer ferocity. Even the lumbering 'Winter' was driven by a brute urgency, so that, on side one, only the quiet passages in the lugubrious 'Hip Priest' – like dub if it had been invented in drizzly motorway service stations rather than in recording studios in Jamaica – provided a respite from the violence.

Yet the violence was not a matter of force alone. Even when the record's dual-drummer attack is at its most poundingly vicious, the violence is formal as much as physical. Rock form is disassembled before our ears. It seems to keep time according to some system of spasms and lurches learned from Beefheart. Something like 'Deer Park', which is a whistle-stop tour of London circa 1982 sandblasted with 'Sister Ray' style white noise, screams and whines as if it is about to fall apart at any moment. The 'bad production' was nothing of the sort. The sound could be pulverizingly vivid at times: the moment when the bass and drums suddenly loom out of the miasma at the start of 'Winter' is breathtaking and the double-drum tattoo on 'Who Makes the Nazis?' fairly leaps out of the speakers. This was the space rock of Can and Neu! smeared in the grime and mire of the quotidian, recalling the most striking image from *The Quatermass Xperiment*: a space rocket crashlanded into the roof of a suburban house.

In many ways, however, the most suggestive parallels come from black pop. The closest equivalents to the Smith of *Hex* would be the deranged despots of black sonic fiction: Lee Perry, Sun Ra and George Clinton, visionaries capable of constructing (and destroying) worlds in sound. As ever, the album sleeve, which was so foreign to what were then the conventions of sleeve design that HMV would only stock it with its reverse side facing forward, was the perfect visual analogue for the contents. The sleeve was more than that, actually: its spidery scrabble of slogans, scrawled notes and photographs was a part of the album rather than a mere illustrative envelope in which it was contained.

With The Fall of this period, what Gerard Genette calls 'paratexts' – those liminal conventions, such as introductions, prefaces and blurbs, which mediate between the text and the reader – assume special significance. Smith's paratexts were clues that posed as many puzzles as they solved; his notes and press releases were no more intelligible than the songs they were nominally supposed to explain. All paratexts occupy an ambivalent position, neither inside nor outside the text: Smith used them to ensure that no definite boundary could be placed around the songs. Rather than being contained and defined by its sleeve, *Hex* haemorrhages *through* the cover. It was clear that the songs weren't complete in themselves, but part of a larger fictional system to which listeners were only ever granted partial access. Smith's refusal to provide lyrics or to explain his songs was in part an attempt to ensure that they remained, in Barthes's terms, *writerly*.[2]

Before his words could be deciphered they had first of all to be heard, which was difficult enough, since Smith's voice – often subject to what appeared to be loudhailer distortion – was always at least partially submerged in the mulch and maelstrom of *Hex*'s sound. In the days before the Internet provided a repository of Smith's lyrics (or the best guesses of fans at what the words were), it was easy to mishear lines for years. Even when words could be heard, it was impossible to confidently assign them a meaning or an ontological 'place'. Were they Smith's own views, the thoughts of a character or merely stray semiotic signal? More important was the question of how clearly each of these levels could be separated from one another. *Hex*'s textual expectorations were nothing so genteel as stream of consciousness: they seemed to be gobbets of linguistic detritus ejected direct from the mediatized unconscious, unfiltered by any sort of reflexive subjectivity. Advertising, tabloid headlines, slogans, pre-conscious chatter, overheard speech were masticated into dense schizoglossic tangles.

'Who wants to be in a Hovis advert, anyway?'

'Who wants to be in a Hovis advert, anyway' Smith asks in 'Just Step S'ways', but this refusal of cosy provincial cliché – Hovis adverts were famous for their sentimentalized presentation of a bygone industrial milieu – is counteracted by the tacit recognition that the mediatized unconscious is structured like advertising. You might not want to live in an advert, but advertising dwells within you. *Hex* converts any linguistic content – whether it be polemic, internal dialogue or poetic insight – into the hectoring form of advertising copy or the screaming ellipsis of

---

[2]   Barthes (1990) opposes such texts, which demand the active participation of the reader, to 'readerly' texts, which reduce the reader to the passive role of consumer of already-existing totalities.

headline-speak. The titles of 'Hip Priest' and 'Mere Pseud Mag. Ed.', as urgent as fresh newsprint, bark out from some Vorticist front page of the mind.

As for advertising, consider the opening call to arms of 'Just Step S'ways': 'When what you used to excite you does not/Like you've used up all your allowance of experiences.' Is this an existentialist call for self re-invention disguised as advertising hucksterism, or the reverse? Or take the bilious opening track, 'The Classical'. 'The Classical' appears to oppose the anodyne vacuity of advertising's compulsory positivity, 'this new profile razor unit', to ranting profanity, 'hey there fuckface!' and the gross physicality of the body 'stomach gassssss'. But what of the line, 'I've never felt better in my life'? Is this another advertising slogan or a statement of the character's feelings? It was perhaps the unplaceability of any of the utterances on *Hex* that allowed Smith to escape censure for the notorious line, 'Where are the obligatory niggers?' in 'The Classical'.[3] Intent was unreadable. Everything sounded like a citation, embedded discourse, mention rather than use.

Smith returns to the Weird tale form on 'Jawbone and the Air-Rifle'. A poacher accidentally causes damage to a tomb, unearthing a jawbone which 'carries the germ of a curse/Of the Broken Brothers Pentacle Church'. The song is a tissue of allusions, such as to James' tales 'A Warning to the Curious', 'Oh, Whistle and I'll Come to you, my Lad' (James 2005), to Lovecraft's 'The Shadow over Innsmouth' (Lovecraft 1999), to Hammer Horror and to *The Wicker Man* – culminating in a psychedelic/psychotic breakdown, complete with a torch-wielding mob of villagers:

> He sees jawbones on the street
> Advertisements become carnivores
> And road-workers turn into jawbones
> And he has visions of islands, heavily covered in slime
> The villagers dance round pre-fabs
> And laugh through twisted mouths.

'Jawbone' resembles nothing so much as a *League of Gentlemen* sketch and The Fall have much more in common with the *League of Gentlemen*'s febrile carnival than with witless imitators such as Pavement. The co-existence of the laughable with that which is not laughable is a description that captures the essence of both The Fall and *The League of Gentlemen*'s grotesque humour.

'White face finds roots'

> Below, black scars winding through the snow showed the main roads. Great frozen rivers and snow-laden forest stretched in all directions. Ahead they could just see a range of old, old mountains. It was perpetual evening at this

---

3 A line that reputedly scuppered an impending deal with Motown records.

time of year, and the further north they went, the darker it became. The white lands seemed uninhabited, and Jerry could easily see how the legends of trolls, Jotunheim, and the tragic gods – the dark, cold, bleak legends of the North – had come out of Scandinavia. It made him feel strange, even anachronistic, as if he had gone back from his own age to the Ice Age. (Moorcock 1973, 86)

On *Hex*'s second side, mutant r 'n' r becomes 'r 'n' Artaud' as the songs become increasingly delirial and abstract. 'Who Makes the Nazis' is as lunar as *Tago Mago*, as spacey-desolated as King Tubby at his most cavernous. It is a TV talk show debate rendered as some Jarry-esque pantomime and composed of leering backing vocals and oneiric-cryptic linguistic fragments: 'longhorn breed … George Orwell Burmese police … Hate's not your enemy, love's your enemy/Murder all bush monkeys'.

'Iceland', recorded in a lava-lined studio in Reykjavik, is a fantasmatic encounter with the fading myths of North European culture in the frozen territory from which they originated. 'White face finds roots' Smith's sleeve notes tell us. The song, hypnotic and undulating, meditative and mournful, recalls the bone-white steppes of Nico's *The Marble Index* in its arctic atmospherics. A keening wind, on a cassette recording made by Smith, whips through the track as Smith invites us to 'cast the runes against your own soul', another James reference, this time to his 'Casting the Runes' (2005). 'Iceland' is rock as *ragnarock*, an anticipation or is it a recapitulation of the End Times in the terms of the Norse 'Doom of the Gods'. It is a *Twilight of the Idols* for the retreating hobgoblins, kobolds and trolls of Europe's receding Weird culture, a lament for the monstrosities and myths whose dying breaths it captures on tape: 'Witness the last of the god men … A Memorex for the Krakens'.

Chapter Nine

Language Scraps: Mark E. Smith's Handwriting and the Typography of The Fall

Paul Wilson

> I like the cover to reflect what's inside ... I think rock artwork has gone right down the drain ... I do all my own. Like, I love all those misspelt posters – a graphic designer would never get it right in years! My attitude to the sleeve is the same as my attitude to the music. (Smith in Robertson, 1982)

> [Writing] ... is not merely a mechanical task, a simple matter of putting speech down on paper. It is an exploration in the use of the graphic potential of a language, an act of discovery. (Crystal 1992, 212)

Mark E. Smith's handwriting has become a typographic signifier of and for The Fall. This essay attempts to situate Mark E. Smith and The Fall, not in a history (or context) of music or of sound, but in terms of a broad coalition of visual communicators and designers/typographers: those whose creative and critical focus is upon an expressive visualization and articulation of writing and the written word.

As he has acknowledged, Smith's attitude towards the development and articulation of a visual identity for The Fall, and in particular the use of his handwriting, reflects his position towards The Fall's sonic identity. Further, his ambivalence towards contemporary technologies (of sound recording, communication and graphic design), together with his fascination with the idea of creative unwinding (or as he often calls it 'unlearning') continually relocates The Fall's aesthetic tending towards an idealized primitivism. This essay aims to explore this particular parallel history of The Fall, in which Smith's design and typography 'has ceased to be a quiescent channel for orderly, sequential argument and become an active visual medium for the complexity of [his] thought' (Poyner 1999, 73).

The Trap of Scription and 'The Twelve Pound Look'

> To me, a song's never finished and it's never good enough, that's why I don't write lyrics down ... Tthey are completely fluid ... lyrics change shape and meaning all the time. (Middles and Smith 2003, 272)

In *The Grain of the Voice* (1991) Roland Barthes discusses what is lost in the process of articulating speech into writing, which he referred to as 'scription'. Among the casualties, he identifies the impulsive, unpremeditated and unrehearsed 'innocence' of speech. Through writing, therefore, our self-image commits us to processes of editing, where we erase the dangers of spontaneous speech: 'we censure or delete our blunders, our self-sufficiencies (or our insufficiencies), our irresolutions, our errors, our complacencies ... speech is dangerous because it is immediate and cannot be taken back' (Barthes 1991, 4).

For Smith, the act of committing his lyrics to scription is indeed a trap. It becomes an act of provocation, replacing abstract fluidity with concrete permanence. Smith seemingly seeks to continually challenge fixed positions and/or sensibilities, an idea to which he seems most antipathetic. His fascination with ambiguity underpins a contrarian streak in his character and helps explain his strategies for constructing The Fall as both an oral and a visual experience.

> Typography has one plain duty before it and that is to convey information in writing. No argument or consideration can absolve typography from this duty. A printed work which cannot be read becomes a product without a purpose. (Emil Ruder, as quoted in Weingart 2000, 270)

Smith's apparent willingness to embrace abstraction is clearly at odds with Ruder's Modernist definition of typography which emphasizes ideals of clarity and makes plain that typography exists as a clear and purposeful vehicle for communication. It is a rejection of these notions of formality and of a pleasing aesthetics for its own sake. However, Smith's use of typographic language within a graphic design context reflects a deeper ambivalence to the very existence of such a prescriptive approach. Typographer Wolfgang Weingart rejected Ruder's set of inherently limiting professional practices and sought to redefine typography's conceptual possibilities. Like Smith, Weingart continually returned to his own handwriting as a means of self-definition and as deliberate rejection of perceived conformity and the commodification of his craft.

> Crawling like an old grouch, struggling like a seven-year old, writing with the uncertainty of a blind person, scribbling like someone who is impatient, or writing with the grace of a calligrapher. I've collected samples of my handwriting since the late forties, but there is no evidence of a mature or lasting hand. (Weingart 2000, 124)

Rather than clarity, one of Smith's overriding aesthetic strategies appears to centre on non-linearity, contradiction, chaos and juxtaposition, each a property or aspect of collage and/or montage. This is particularly apparent on the cover to *Hex Enduction Hour* (1982).[1] At this point in The Fall's career, Smith has acknowledged that there was an overabundance of words within The Fall's sound and *Hex Enduction Hour* bears out this assertion with phrases erupting chaotically onto the surface of the cover. A sense of tension exists between the visual order of the design's top third and the collaged free-for-all of the other two-thirds. This arrangement of the visual motifs, title and typographic treatment of the group's name seem to be an attempt at marking out some kind of quiet(er) space, a pause or silence before the typographic deluge, the apotheosis of Mark Smith's handwritten cover design: an overload of aphorisms, visualized using a range of tools, approaches and styles. This multiplicity of voices reflects *Hex Enduction Hour*'s musical content: apparently structureless, repeated chaotic interruptions marked by sudden shifts in tone.

A brief overview of those individuals who have made use of the tactic of deliberate and often destructive or disturbing interventions into an otherwise linear, creative process highlights a number of intriguing approaches: John Cage's utilization of the I Ching to aid decision-making, Brian Eno's 'Oblique Strategies' cards to suggest lateral solutions to particular problems and George Perec's lipogrammatic novels.[2] Such techniques are apparent both in The Fall's music such as the accidental edits retained in 'Paintwork' (1985) and, as noted above, in Smith's use of a seemingly chaotic, visually collaged typography on their album covers. Describing the recording of *Hex Enduction Hour*, Smith stated: 'I was trying to get the group to play out of time ... taking musicians out of their comfort zone, getting them to think about timing in a distorted way' (Smith 2008a, 115).

The role of the typewriter as a tool for the production of both lyrics and typographies featured on Fall covers is apparent from the group's earliest recordings. 'The Twelve Pound Look' is the title of a J.M. Barrie play written in 1910. It describes the independence offered to a new generation of typewriter-enabled/emancipated women, when the technology and activity of typewriting created 'the largest female workforce in history, the monstrous regiment of typists' (Riddell 1975, 10). A more obscured cultural history of the machine is its role as a writing technology for the production of abstract visual typographies: from its earliest days it seems the typewriter was employed as a tool of cultural and creative production.

H.N. Werkman's 'typeprint' experiments, which took place between 1923 and 1929, mark a point when this tool of business began to be utilized as a means to

---

[1]   Reproductions of this and other album covers mentioned in this chapter can be found at The Fall Online, Discography, Singles and Albums, at http://www.visi.com/fall/discog/singlesalbums.html

[2]   Brian Eno's 'Oblique Strategies' were a series of aphoristic statements printed on over 100 cards, the use of which was meant to help the owner sidestep creative deadlock. George Perec employed techniques of constrained writing in novels such as *A Void* (1994) and *The Exeter Text: Jewels, Secrets, Sex* (1996). *A Void* was written without the letter 'e' and *The Exeter Text* used 'e' as the only vowel in the text.

exploit 'the abstract visual rhythms of the keyboard's signs and letters' (Riddell 1975, 11). The typewriter's use by practitioners of concrete poetry in the 1950s and 1960s embraced its relatively unique potential for combining the verbal with the visual and actively explored strategies for the communication of poetic and semantic content. Smith's use of the typewriter, however, seems to recall his career as a dock-working clerk, in which lists and other formal or prescriptive systems for visual organization and graphic expression are employed in the making of a seemingly formalized and organized visual language. The use of a mono-spaced font, such as that found on the typewriter, also imbues Smith's text with an authority that handwriting does not, in that it echoes a more formal, machine-made typography conveying aspects of power and status. The consistency of letter-forms and baseline alignment provide an immediate visual sense of authority whereas the slanted, compressed and cursive handwritten letters imply variation and characteristics that could only be arrived at by hand (Walker 2001, 45).

Room to Live (1982) seems to superficially continue the visual approach of *Hex Enduction Hour* but actually replaces its deliberately chaotic, over-wrought textual landscape with a more sober and apparently visually ordered sensibility. The typewriter's use immediately regulates the majority of the cover's typography. The patterns of Salfordian brickwork seek to locate Smith and The Fall within a particular cultural geography. Two photographs are set together in white space with a trace of the same brickwork in each, alluding to the domestic and to personal, private spaces; the homeliness and domesticity of a back garden. The album's title screams out in one moment of disordered exclamation but, other than that, an air of near sobriety and surprisingly measured visual tone hangs over the cover and its typography.

Alongside the typewriter, Smith's writing instrument of choice is often the pen, in particular the ballpoint pen. Popularly known as a 'biro' after Lazslo Biro, the inventor of the modern ballpoint, its grainy scribbles run across a range of Smith's typographies, most notably *Hex Enduction Hour*. Biro in Hungarian means 'judge', an occupation that seems to fit neatly alongside Smith's other authoritative alter egos, in particular the 'Hip Priest' introduced on *Hex Enduction Hour*. The selection of these writing technologies, the cheap pen and the battered typewriter, can be linked with Smith's notions of the primitive and the everyday, which seem to appear within any discussion of The Fall. Since their earliest days he has continually defined The Fall in this way, largely in terms of their sound with the use of repetition, simplistic instrumentation and overtly non-professional playing.

Typographically this can be defined in terms of the relationship and correspondence between hand skills and physical materials: both visible in Smith's vision for design and for typography. His dismissive attitude towards the embedded practice of learnt professionalism, in both music and graphic design, is apparent in his typography: the fondness for handwritten and superficially ugly, unprofessional and inappropriate textual arrangement, horizontal and vertical incoherency and misplaced capitalization. It is also clear in terms of the album covers he has himself designed over the course of The Fall's career. As this essay will show, the earliest handwritten covers seemed to be mindful of certain prescriptive or learnt practice: horizontal alignment and composition, for instance, whereas later handwritten covers seemingly lose all apprehensions regarding notions of legibility or visual organization in the sense that Emil Ruder might understand them.

Branding, Authenticity and Authority

> A person's handwritten mark ... holds a special place in society. It is required for legal agreements, and its forgery can be illegal. Likewise a person's general handwriting conveys identity: no two people's writing is the same in every respect. (Crystal 1992, 189)

The handwritten/handmade has become a means to visually distinguish certain elements of craft, authenticity and the notional 'real' within design's predominantly digital working methods that have emerged over the last 20 years. Certainly, within typography, a shift towards handwriting and letter-forms with an explicitly hand-rendered sensibility can be regarded as an attempt to stylistically equip certain information with an aura of honesty, legitimacy, authority and individuality.

Mark E. Smith's voice is The Fall's defining characteristic and Smith's handwriting can perhaps be best understood as an analogue to the voice. Any translation of sound into letters and words relies upon a number of (typo)graphic conventions and Smith makes use of a number of effects and techniques to establish a particular 'tone of voice' for his handwriting's appearances on Fall covers. This consistency of tone and the visually distinctive qualities of his handwriting helped quickly establish aspects of The Fall's 'brand' identity. Core values that we might associate with Smith's use of handwriting as a method for branding were embedded within the designs for the covers of The Fall's first run of singles: 'Bingo-Master's Break-Out!' (1978), 'It's the New Thing' (1978), 'Rowche Rumble' (1979) and on the album *Totale's Turns* (1980).

Each cover is defined by its relative simplicity: a pared-down and minimal use of typography within white space. Smith's handwriting signifies a visual approach and identity for the group, its paradoxical 'anti-image' defined together with the direct, graphic styling of the words themselves. The use of a single colour (black on white) becomes a statement of honesty through visual simplicity. Regardless of financial constraints, this lack of colour is a unifying factor that helps define The Fall's earliest, meaningful, visual identity. This ideal of a consistency of approach (in terms of both the limited use of colour and maintaining Smith's typography as an essential aspect of the group's image) often spans decades. 'Marquis Cha-Cha' (1983) presents a relatively abstract refinement of what had previously appeared chaotic (*Hex Enduction Hour, Room to Live*), and seems to be in the process of shifting from text and language towards a more abstract, graphic symbolism. 'Theme from Sparta FC#2' (2004) explicitly echoes 'Marquis Cha-Cha', as it references this particular visual approach and graphic style within a seemingly knowing self-pastiche.

Smith's use of his own handwriting on Fall covers can be regarded as an explicit reassertion of his, and the group's distinct identity. In the eighteenth century, handwriting was subject to a deliberate process of standardization when it 'underwent a gradual but significant shift to the impersonal, a shift that involved a move away from calligraphic, somatic models of design to rational, mathematical models' (Thornton 1996, 26). The Palmer Method, developed in the United States in the late nineteenth century, was a further attempt to promote a handwriting acquisition that was 'practical and consistent … devoid of personal characteristic or excessive flourishes' (Papaelias 2004).

Such reform of so-called 'penmanship education' sought to use handwriting as a mechanism for the creation of 'good workers … [promising] … to do so by neutralizing the will and transforming the body into a machine' (Thornton 1996, 165). Edward Johnston's Print Script attempted to aesthetically standardize the (hand)written word under the pretence of a return to a idealized and 'purer' alphabetic form following centuries of what was regarded as needless decoration. With UNESCO's recommendation in 1969 that Print Script should be introduced throughout the Western world, handwriting itself became thoroughly systematized, rationalized and commodified.

Papaelias (2004) argues that handwriting manages to retain qualities of authenticity and individuality when used in a commercial context (such as advertising or record cover design), maintaining that 'simulated handwriting represents authenticity just as well as the original'. Further, digital handwriting fonts 'mimic the "uniqueness" of handwriting by standardizing personality'. So, following the attempted rationalization of handwriting's formal aesthetic we arrive at a situation where its conceptual, cultural and semiotic associations can be regulated and controlled. How we might read handwriting, it seems, has become as processed as how we might write it.

Within what might be regarded as The Fall's earliest stage of being branded via Smith's design and typography there seems to be an intuitive use of elements in white space, in terms of generating pleasing and aesthetically balanced design. 'Bingo-Master's Break-Out!' shows evidence of a compositionally structured approach and the alignment of elements presenting a simplistically ordered visual space. The instigation of a primitive Fall logotype appears in evidence with a furtive stylization of the word's appearance and with the lower-case 'h' and 'll' seeming particularly adjusted. 'It's the New Thing' seems to introduce an element of decoration within its typographical design, with each letter-form slightly more considered in terms of its construction and with The Fall's nascent 'logo' reappearing with its consistently adjusted letter-forms. 'In My Area' marks the appearance of a more formal, non-handwritten logotype with the use of the 'Frutiger Black' typeface. The punctuation of track titles – each ending with a full point – presents each song as a definite statement and an interjection into the cover's visual narrative. *Totale's Turns* pares back the use of handwritten text in white space to an almost absolute minimum, with white space to the fore, and a rigid sense of typographic composition and alignment in evidence. The repeated, exclamatory punctuation appears to allude to or, perhaps, parody the excited and excitable language of advertising.

Contradictions: Professionalism and the Ordinary

> Graphic designers only know how to use a computer – they're the visual equivalent of an audio typist. (Smith 2008a, 50)

Smith's antipathy to the formalities, technologies and questionable professional status of graphic design and designers is more than apparent in the above citation. In particular, he seems singularly unimpressed with design's shift towards a fully digitized work environment and the subsequent lack of any signs of human intervention or involvement within the design itself. For Smith, the notion of the commercial artist bent over a drawing board assembling a collage of cut and paste camera-ready artwork, an image of graphic design pre-desktop publishing, might be perhaps closer to his writerly model; something that bears the imprint and impressions of human activity and presence:

> My idea was just to get people's heads going, because they don't fucking read. But also with computer graphics coming in, it became quite impossible to do that. If you're on a major label you can't do this [he arranges the contents of our table – notebooks, scraps of paper fag packets, beermats – into a hasty collage], you can't do that and say: that's the back cover. The computer graphics and the art department can't handle it, because it doesn't fit on the bloody computer, does it? (Herrington 1996, 29)

This description of a seemingly organized constellation of objects with its arrangement of fragments and objects from everyday life certainly recalls Kurt Schwitters' 'Merz' collage experiments and attempts to describe a creativity stemming from an imaginative treatment of otherwise nondescript items. As an illustration of ordinariness as a statement of creative and aesthetic intent, the interior cover of *Interim* (2004) lays bare a portrait of Mark E. Smith's working methods and how contemporary record company/artist communications can take place via the corner-shop fax machine.

Ostensibly a reconstructed faxed message, here Smith's handwriting and the surface upon which it's written become everything. Stretched to the full length of the inlay, almost as if they were emerging from the fax machine, Smith's handmade typographies do nothing other than describe the musical content and the band's line-up. Gone are the para-textual aphorisms, jokes and riddles from earlier (handwritten) Fall covers. Instead, marker pen numerals dominate, alongside biro annotation upon the almost grey-white space of the painterly fax-paper.

One paragraph appears to be voiced by Smith himself in the role of narrator: telling of the recording's context and challenging the listener to be anything other than pleased with its content. The freewheeling nature of the typographic design, with little or no mind for a narrative within the insert itself, again mirrors the content of the recording. *Interim* is just that: a moment of marking time, of pausing and presenting work-in-progress.

As discussed earlier, Smith's apparent professionalization of The Fall via the development of the group's brand identity (on the covers of their earliest singles) gives some indication of a contradiction between his unhidden ambivalence to prescribed rules that determine supposed professional practice and his desire to present a coherent aesthetic of combined sound and image. Smith's description of his working relationship with Pascal Le Gras perhaps illustrates another of his roles within the group: as art director/visual editor. This is very much evident upon the *Interim* cover.

> He [Le Gras] never moans about me messing about with his stuff. Of course I mess about with things, change the angle and things like that. But I'm just his editor or something. (Smith in Kessler, 1993)

Here, he seems acutely aware of The Fall's brand and aesthetic, going to such lengths as re-appropriating Le Gras' original image to suit his own intentions. Smith is adamant that 'routine is the enemy of music' (Simpson 2008, 19), a belief further expressed in his bitter disregard for the middle class who have come to represent the 'mediocre average', standardization and conformity: 'The worst thing is a sanitized society ruled by the middle class … It's the middle you need to look out for' (Smith 2008a, 154).[3]

This indifference is reflected within what might appear a contradictory impulse: Smith's stated attraction towards cultural artifacts from the so-called 'high' 'and 'low' ends of the spectrum: the primitive *and* the avant-garde. Smith's notion of unlearning (in terms of attempting to strip away what he regards as unnecessary, predetermined attitudes and techniques of playing) reflects his stated ideal of and for music: 'I always thought the pure essence of rock and roll was a completely non-musical form of music. Rock and roll is surely not a "music" form' (Smith 2008a, 117). His reductive approach to music idealizes an authenticity that stems from simplicity (the focus on repetition, for instance; the treatment of improvisation as a form of bourgeois 'showing-off') and is a deliberate rejection of any form of unnecessary decoration or stylization: 'You can work at things too much, do too many takes, make it too clear. Strip it of its mystery' (Smith 2008a, 66).

Within his discussion of what is lost in the trap of scription, Roland Barthes identifies 'scraps of language' as being one significant casualty of the technological shift from speech to writing. These fragments he regards as 'one of the great

---

[3]   Smith's antipathy towards the middle class is perhaps best represented in the track 'Middle Mass' (*Slates*, 1981).

functions of language, the phatic or interpellant function' (Barthes 1991, 4). This social glue of conversation, these almost meaningless, decorative expressions that serve no purpose other than to affirm the location of another within social interactions, act as 'appeals, modulations ... through which a body seeks another body' (Barthes 1991, 5). These seemingly off-hand locational devices are apparent within Smith's typographies and reflect a vital aspect of Smith's approach to how his writing and The Fall's aesthetic more generally should reflect the everyday and the ordinary.

The idea of such fragmented shards of language serving a broader purpose within dialogue and linguistic exchange reflects Smith's fascination with notions of the everyday and the use of the found or recovered lyrical object within The Fall's sound. Certainly, Smith's continued reinforcement of his own class position locates him within the 'ordinary', which he regards as allowing him a degree of camouflage and invisibility or transparency when acting as an interlocutor, observing his immediate environment. Similarly located in the everyday and evidence of the fragmentary or fragmented nature of urban spaces, Paul Elliman's 'Bits' typeface collects objects that resemble letter-forms (through accident or design): scraps and discarded splinters of the city. To Elliman, these shards from the surface of urban space are legible to those who wish to look, find and collect. Like Smith, he is fond of repetition but wary of repeating himself: within the typeface each letter-form is only ever used once and then archived. Another character is collected to replace each one used. The superstructure of the alphabet allows for multiple permutations of each character but they are only ever guaranteed one public airing.

Similarly, Czech artist Jiří Kolář's collages are constructed through an obsessional piecing together of found fragments from the almost constant churn of textual and typographic production in everyday life: newspapers, magazines, books and bibles. In parallel with Smith, Elliman and Schwitters, Kolář reconstitutes 'incomprehensible fragments of texts in foreign languages and scripts, individual letters of the alphabet, musical notes, Braille characters, hieroglyphic doodles ... [becoming] the potential elements of this vocabulary of an "unknown culture"' (Buchler and Lingwood 1990, 13). Kolář's deliberate methodologies for confusing and twisting the materiality of language have parallels in Smith's seemingly contradictory use of abstraction as a strategy employed in a range of his visually articulated typographies.

'How I Wrote "Elastic Man"' (1980) marks Smith's first attempt at presenting a seemingly illogical, abstracted visual juxtaposition using a mix of illustration and photography. *Are You Are Missing Winner* (2001) reorients this aspect of The Fall's visual history within a resolutely ugly, impactful image that seems fitting for such a raw, clumsy and abrasive Fall-sound and is perhaps an attempt to recall an earlier, more primitive aesthetic (both sonically and visually). *The Twenty-Seven Points* (1995) presents a literal and conceptual unravelling, as the image of disgorged cassette tape captures the sense of a band unwinding. The marker-penned, handwritten titles (band and track names) are rendered with a crudity which appears to communicate anger, frustration or a deeply embedded sense of laissez-faire. Chaos and verité dominate with a 'warts-and-all' honesty and a refusal to exclude mistakes, crude edits and overlap within the hastily assembled presentation of visible language scraps. Information is blasted into fragments, elements collaged into a thick-edged visual aesthetic and The Fall's brand identity (slowly shaken apart over the intervening years) appears to be emerging from the cracked tape's guts. Letter-forms, slides, coins and a range of other objects are scattered across the cover's surface, reflecting a world of tourist debris and international travel exhaustion that's both visually and conceptually distinct when compared to some of The Fall's earlier, distinctly (sub)urban cover images and associated typographies.

Elliman's channelling of the visual characteristics of urban space and the idea of a city transmitting encoded messages to its citizens recalls Smith's experiences as city-dweller, where he articulates his city's streets and transforms the everyday into fodder for an audiovisual transcription of Manchester, Salford and their outlying districts. Like Paul Auster's doomed author-as-walker in 'City of Glass' (Auster 1988), Smith's trajectories through and across his streets write unique historiographies onto physical space. The use of photography on 'How I Wrote "Elastic Man"' (1980) and *Grotesque (After the Gramme)* (1980) reinforces this, locating The Fall as particularly (sub)urban in their portrayal of events, spaces and textures. *Grotesque* crunches together a collage of layered scenes into one image dominated by hard (visual) edits, with architectural detail(s) juxtaposed alongside fragmented, familiar social scenarios.

Conclusions

Mark E. Smith's handwriting has played a central part in establishing The Fall's visual identity and in cementing both his characteristic approach to music and The Fall's position as a cultural 'artifact'. This use of handwriting signifies spontaneity, informality and non-standardized or informal production: all features of a notional 'primitive' to which Smith is seemingly continually drawn. A chronology of Mark E. Smith's typographical design reveals three particular and distinct thematic and aesthetic periods reflecting differing levels of engagement with the creation and control of The Fall's visual identity. Within the earliest covers, Smith's handwriting is employed within a formal, visually structured and tentatively branded context. His use of handwriting is then further developed and explored, becoming increasingly linguistically chaotic and with semantic content driving the design: the covers themselves becoming a distinct readerly experience. Later, a form of 'descriptive chaos' is employed with the cover design itself being more ordered but with little written content apparent other than details of the recording.

> It's important that you get it right with covers, that they really reflect what's contained within. The Light User Syndrome and the American version of

Reformation are the only two that I can think of that I reckon should have been done again. (Smith 2008a, 149)

While reiterating his belief in the key function of The Fall's covers, Smith's unhappiness with two in particular highlights a reason for their perceived failure: his own lack of involvement.

More recently, he has seemingly been content to allow others to 'design' The Fall while maintaining as he acknowledges a quasi-editorial role. Any handwritten participation is largely that of an occasional cameo via periodic typographic intervention into an otherwise orderly design. Smith's handwriting, therefore, serves to remind the viewer of his presence and of a link to The Fall's essence through this writerly reminder. With his handwriting now available for digital download, computer-users across the world have become enabled to produce their own texts in Smith's hand. His typography has become dislocated and decontextualized, appearing on a range of websites, promotional literature, not always with a Fall connection, and assorted media artifacts. Like a self-referential shorthand, Smith's handwriting bestows authority via association, unhooked from the man himself and adrift in a wider cultural landscape.

.

Chapter Ten

'Humbled in Iceland':
On Improvisation during The Fall

Robin Purves

This essay attempts to find a means to comment usefully upon a song, 'Iceland', by The Fall, the tenth track (of eleven) on their 1982 album *Hex Enduction Hour*. The song has drawn sporadic but favourable comments from several writers since its recording but mainly for aspects of its perceived lyrical content or for the relatively unusual circumstances pertaining to its composition. By carefully listening to the reciprocal referencing that takes place between the various elements of its sound world, I hope to establish a plausible analysis of 'Iceland' as a coherent and complex musical structure that nevertheless retains something miraculous and therefore irreducibly inexplicable about it.

The initial approach to the song, via theories of improvised music, was selected because 'Iceland' apparently incorporates sound elements which derive from group improvisation. Accounts of the recording session from which 'Iceland' emerged suggest that although a proportion of what we hear when we listen to the song may well have been worked out in advance by certain members of The Fall, significant parts of it were not. Some or all of the lyrics could have been generated on the spot and no one on the recording knew quite what the other members were going to do. Most importantly, what the recording records is the first time that the musicians in The Fall had heard the singer (and group leader) Mark E. Smith's contribution to the song and it is likely to have been the first time that he had heard theirs.

The attempt to say something about 'Iceland' takes a detour through many of the available writings on improvisation and if I want to establish what I can use from those writings, I first need to dispense with some of the more problematic stories that improvisation's practitioners and fans tell about it. The first of these stories is that improvisation is the fundamental, inaugural process of music-making, which was catastrophically ousted from its historical prominence by the evils of the written score and recording technology.

Derek Bailey, perhaps the most well-known and celebrated musician of the improvisational tradition until his death a few years ago, Cornelius Cardew, composer and musician, and Eddie Prévost, ex-drummer with veteran pillars of group improvisation AMM, have all provided variants on this first claim in published books or essays. Bailey, in his book *Improvisation*, makes the claim that, 'Historically, [improvisation] predates any other music – mankind's first musical performance couldn't have been anything other than a free improvisation' ([1980]

1992, 83). The first part of this assertion is only weakly supported by the second's uncorroborated insistence on the lack of alternatives. This insistence, however, has to be qualified or withdrawn if we question whether or not there could have been or had to be one, single and generative 'first musical performance' and whether or not the notions of music and performance could have developed out of a take on rhythmic (or otherwise expressive) behaviour which eschews repeatability and concerted action in favour of singularity and the simultaneous articulations of individuals refusing to act in concert.

It would be easy enough to demonstrate the vulnerability of the theorists of improvisation to the operation Derrida performs on Rousseau in *Of Grammatology*, since improvisation's discourses are often startlingly Rousseauesque. For example, both Bailey and Cardew attempt to forestall accusations of elitism in their field by claiming that 'free improv' – as it is often called – is a democratic space. Although Bailey claims that from its practitioners it demands more 'skill ... devotion, preparation, training and commitment' ([1980] 1992, xii) than any other musical genre, it is open also

> to use by almost anyone – beginners, children and non-musicians. The skill and intellect required is whatever is available. It can be an activity of enormous complexity and sophistication, or the simplest and most direct expression: a lifetime's study and hard work or a casual dilettante activity. ([1980] 1992, 83–4)

Cardew, in his essay 'Towards an Ethic of Improvisation', states in the same vein that his ideal performers would be a 'collection of musical innocents' (1971, xix). The demand made by both writers is either to know everything (in order to transcend your knowledge) or to know nothing whatsoever, one of the most familiar themes in the aesthetic ideology which claims the summit of art to be artlessness. The theme is implicated in the alleged primordiality of improvisation: the child and primitive man are united in their enviable and aboriginal virtue and simplicity and are united in turn, across what would normally appear to be an impossible gulf, with the superlative musical creator who can utilize his or her mastery in order to dispense with it, effortlessly achieving the deathless qualities of honesty, purity and clarity. The inclusiveness of these gestures is suspect, working as it does to exclude anyone falling in between the categories of virtuoso and ingénue or pygmy.[1] Bailey's description of the characteristics associated with 'ethnic' instruments, even as it critiques the patronizing Western musicians who

---

[1]   Cardew's essay illustrates this exclusivity neatly when, at the end of a tortuous piece of reasoning, he comes to the conclusion that his 'most rewarding experiences' when recruiting players to perform his work *Treatise* has come from working with 'people who by some fluke have (a) acquired a visual education, (b) escaped a musical education and (c) have nevertheless become musicians, i.e. play music to the full capacity of their beings' (1971, xix).

make a show of adopting them, appears to agree that these instruments 'have a fixed, very limited capability and that very little instrumental skill is needed to play [them]' but that nonetheless authentic ethnic music has an aural 'directness and dignity' which Western imitators could never replicate: we are not far here from the troubling ethnological concept of the noble savage ([1980] 1992, 101, 102). At other moments, the regression to early stages of development touches base with the wellsprings of the life-force itself: 'Improvisation is a basic instinct, an essential force in sustaining life. Without it, nothing survives' (Bailey [1980] 1992, 140). No doubt this point is true if we take 'improvisation' in the broadest sense but if we narrow that focus by choosing any particular example of 'free improv' to test the thesis, it is difficult to see where the evolutionary advantage might lie in someone skronking away at the 'wrong' bits of a cello, or simulating a difficult flatulence with the detached mouthpiece from a tenor sax.

The connections with Rousseau multiply since, like Rousseau, many writers on improvisation claim or assume that the music first produced by means of improv is a linguistic phenomenon, 'born of voice and not of sound' (Derrida 1976, 195). This unadulterated vocalese is later hobbled by the encroachments of grammar and writing in general which, most damagingly as the score in music, artificially impose on what ought to be a natural and passionate effusion. Ben Watson writes that free improv is a kind of 'repartee', but should you listen correctly, it divulges 'glimpses of a world where pure intuition could speak, transcending vocabulary and grammar' (2004, 192). Can *anything* be said to *speak*, without recourse to a vocabulary or a grammar (of some sort)? When it comes to establishing what, if anything, is being said, free improv seems to say much the same sort of things as more conventional musics, or would do if it could. Watson describes a particular recording of a group improvisation in the following way:

> On 'Improvisation >>5010<<,' Guy answers Rutherford's trombone snuffles with a brilliant vocabulary of bass rattles and plunks. 'Improvisation >>5020<<' is again a miniature, but like a copperplate by William Blake, it has a concentrated energy lacking in the gestures of public art. There's a resigned and haunting section of bowed-bass harmonics, Salvation Army brass melancholy, the guitar notes strained and scrapy. Notes are sounded with drama and decisiveness, but linger strangely. The listener has an edge-of-seat intimation that the musicians have broken into new vistas of emotional resonance with no plan ... and no route back. (2004, 165–6)

With a 'brilliant vocabulary' at their disposal, all the players are apparently able to do is allow the listener to guess at a rough idea of how they feel (resigned, haunted, sad or decisive) though we cannot know why they feel that way and why they have chosen this oddly indirect way of letting us know. This seems to be the musical equivalent of autism, not because free improv is inherently self-absorbed or withdrawn but because the insistence on the music-is-language metaphor inevitably makes it appear as such. Adorno has written a salutary warning against just this kind of insistence. He writes that:

> Music resembles a language. Expressions such as musical idiom, musical intonation, are not simply metaphors. But music is not identical with language. The resemblance points to something essential, but vague. Anyone who takes it seriously will be seriously misled. Music resembles language in the sense that it is a temporal sequence of articulated sounds which are more than just sounds. They say something, often something human. (Adorno 1992, 1)

Music, then, can have a syntactic extension amounting to something like a narrative but Adorno goes on to explain that 'the identity of … musical concepts lay in their own nature and not in a signified outside them' and that to 'interpret language means: to understand language. To interpret music means: to make music. Musical interpretation is performance, which, as synthesis, retains the similarity to language, while obliterating every specific resemblance' (1992, 2, 3). His argument is not that musical concepts have no 'signified outside them' but that in the sounding of a chord in its sequence, or in the chordal sequence itself, there is no useful distinction to be made between signifier and signified, because instrumental music has no demonstrably necessary relation to what it is held to signify. This would hold true even in cases where composers may have deliberately organized the elements of their compositions into symbolic orders analogous to certain kinds of discursive systems, so that their music is said to *resemble* a philosophical theory or argument. Adorno's point about the interpretation of music being musical performance begs the question of where the listener who does not perform might find a place in this scheme. What might she be doing when she listens, if the activity is not interpretation as Adorno conceives it? If we are to be permitted to listen to music and to think about it without actually making it, perhaps that listening and thinking could be considered a type of performance which makes music mean something, as long as that something can be shown to resist its comprehension in linguistic terms, for example by a persuasive verbal paraphrase.

If free improv were a language, it would be one inflected by the infantilizing or primitivist assumptions of its enthusiasts; for example Bailey describes the goal of one of his assemblies of improvising musicians as constructing 'a language that would be literally disjointed, whose constituents would be unconnected in any causal or grammatical way' ([1980] 1992, 107). This model of deliberated inarticulacy, which tries to 'get back' before the effect of grammatical order in order to explore pre-grammatical energies doesn't stop Watson considering Bailey's interactions with his fellow improvisers to be nothing less than Socratic dialogues where the eminent guitarist would appraise his fellow players' 'musical utterances', a characterization which surely takes for granted that these exchanges are intelligible in significant ways (Watson 2004, 137).

The third claim in many treatises on improv that I want to distance myself from is the notion that it is politically significant. The idea comes in a variety of modes including the tentative and vague suggestion that improvised music has a content which does not correspond to or revel in the prerogatives of the present day philosophical/political hegemony. This claim, that a radically ambiguous, sometimes utterly disarticulated and ad hoc 'language' is oppositional in a progressive and meaningful way, requires more proof if it is to be convincing. To say that it doesn't reflect or celebrate dominant ideologies may suggest only that improv views itself as standing serenely apart from them. Ben Watson's admirable avoidance of the tentative and vague sweeps him along to a more unhinged set of slogans, that 'Free Improvisation … is the manifestation of socialist revolution in music', or that it is 'no more recuperable by class society than revolutionary Marxism' (2004, 143). Class society may well be as interested in recuperating revolutionary Marxism as it is in recuperating the act or sound of someone dropping metal washers onto a piano's strings while someone else hits a harp with a plastic golf club. On one page in the same volume Watson claims that free improv is like a polite and interesting conversation; if there is a discordance between the overweening claims for improv's seditious potential and the more mundane comparisons Watson sometimes reaches for, they come together most remarkably in the claim that 'the kind of virtuosity proposed by Bailey is so shockingly physical that the listener is forced to think of such acts as armpit-scratching and nose-picking. Its return of music to the physical act debunks civilization itself' (Watson 2004, 149–50). We can only speculate just how much more debunked civilization would be if Bailey had walked onstage one evening and *actually* picked his nose. With his guitar.

One of the elements I want to take from the discourses on improvisation, in order to begin discussing 'Iceland' by The Fall, emerges from Derek Bailey's differentiation between what he calls 'idiomatic improvisation' and his own, preferred brand of non-idiomatic or 'free' improvisation ([1980] 1992, xi). Bailey's references to idiomatic improvisation condemn it because it is alleged to be too attached to a pre-established sound world, any sound world which can be identified with a particular genre, whether it is jazz or anti-folk or anything else, and bound up also to the institutions associated with the genre, so that they cannot embody all the advantages which writers commonly associate with free improvisation. Free improv's advocates tend to consider generic markers and any acknowledged formal musical inheritance as restrictive and/or disciplinarian and thus are free to represent their own practice as protean, evanescent and liberating, though in practice, since performers such as Bailey are constrained by the need to *avoid* all conventional or familiar idioms, they are inclined merely to select their gestures from a different set of sequences which advertise their permanent (idiomatic) evasion of melody, harmony and narrative. At some point during a gig, for example, a guitarist will rattle his house-keys or some other object round the rim of his guitar's f-hole, if it has one; a violinist will stroke her bow against the tuning keys or ignore her instrument altogether and whip her bow through the air.

It is odd that there is hardly any recognition in the world of free improv that before you turn up to a gig you know exactly what is going to happen and what the gig is going to sound like because the circumvention of the obvious always takes a set of obvious routes and because players have an uncanny knack of making most instruments, no matter how different, sound indistinguishable from one other. The utter indifference Bailey displays to virtually all music apart from what he himself happens to be playing while he is playing it is understandable in the circumstances but becomes an issue in his book, *Improvisation*, when the sole authority asked to account for improvisation in rock music is Steve Howe of the abysmal prog band Yes. Howe's story of how the virtuoso player's pretensions coincided happily with the commercial exploitation of the albums market towards the end of the 1960s appears in the first edition of the book, published in 1980, and appeared again in the second edition in 1992 without revision or expansion by more recent voices, despite the intervening years producing bands who did much to extend or productively narrow the possibilities for guitar-based rock music, such as Public Image Ltd, Black Flag, Bad Brains, Sonic Youth, Boredoms, Fushitsusha and The Jesus and Mary Chain, to name just a few.

For me, 'Iceland' is an example of idiomatic improvisation concerned with expressing the idiom of rock music in an often remarkably beautiful, conflicted and valuable way; the song assumes its identity by unapologetically representing recognizably 'rock' sounds without being particularly reminiscent of the noise any other band tends to make. Its hammered two-note piano motif carries an extraordinary amount of variation inside its relentless repetition by slight fluctuations in the pressure applied to the keys and by minute discrepancies in the rhythm of the repetitions which make the intervals between the notes fluctuate by microseconds. Certain details could conceivably bring to mind Can's 'Mother Sky' or, more distantly, several tracks by The Velvet Underground including the introduction to 'All Tomorrow's Parties', the musematic repetition of riffs in 'Black Angel's Death Song' and 'European Son', but none of these comparisons are remotely persuasive enough to take any of the songs as a model for 'Iceland'. I borrow the term 'musematic' from Richard Middleton who uses it to describe the extended repetition of short musical units. In 'Iceland' this applies to the piano and, to a lesser extent, the bass and drums. Middleton associates this kind of repetition with trance-inducing, ego-dissolving hymns to desire and death and discriminates musematic from 'discursive repetition', which is 'the repetition of longer units, at the level of the phrase' and is said to be identified with 'the ego and the self' (2006, 17, 20). 'Iceland' incorporates discursive repetition by the refrains in longer sequence of banjo, electric piano and voice, and the interplay of musematic and discursive repetitions along its course provides a kind of ground or backdrop for the differently elaborating variables which come in and out and move around this dubiously supportive surface.

In free improv terms, however, 'Iceland' is not 'free' because it has a fairly 'regular pulse', the polyrhythmic percussive piano riff and its interactions with the rhythm section would be said to be confined by 'the dogma of the beat', to borrow a phrase from Tony Oxley, a drummer who has worked alongside Bailey (Oxley in Bailey [1980] 1992, 87). The idea that its syncopation might count as sufficient grounds for the dismissal of a song such as 'Iceland' is a strange one to have to come to terms with; perhaps it is enough to point out that its rhythms are actually far from inflexible, especially when compared to the arbitrary authoritarianism that would elevate the bypassing of regularity to the status of an article of faith.

The aim now is to go a little deeper into the interior of 'Iceland', to try to say what it is about and why I think it is good, bearing in mind what we think we know about the way it happened. Colin Irwin, in a *Melody Maker* article on the recording session which produced 'Iceland', gives the following account of its genesis:

> Mark then announces they will try a new song. Craig patters out a tune on the piano, Marc Riley starts to play banjo, making it sound like a sitar, and you suddenly recognise the abstract tinkering they'd done earlier. 'Is he going to sing?' asks the engineer. Kay didn't know. Grant goes to find out. 'He's going to play a cassette first, and then he's going to sing,' says Grant. The engineer scarcely blinks. 'I see,' he says. 'A cassette. I do like these easy sessions.' [...] Mark plays his cassette – of the wind howling against his hotel room window – and launches into the verbals... [...] 'No, we didn't know what he was going to do either,' says Riley, in a state of euphoria later. 'He just said he needed a tune, something Dylanish, and we knocked around on the piano in the studio and came up with that. But we hadn't heard the words until he suddenly did them. We did "Fit And Working Again" on "Slates" in exactly the same way. Yeah, I suppose it is amazing really.' (Irwin 1981)

When we come to listen to the track, the music begins and proceeds, initially at least, liberated from the necessity of accompanying any particular lyrical content but in the expectation that something will happen. The first moments of the song are scoured by crudely recorded and replayed wind noise and fragments of unintelligible speech. The wind sounds like feedback, but signifies the condition of exposure to the elements. When the music takes over as the noise from the cassette fades out and stops, the dominant mood is ominous, tense, expectant. The musematic irresolution of the initial sounds, and the sounds themselves, are fittingly baleful, as it turns out, since the first spoken line speaks of an omen, signalling the out-of-jointness of this particular time: 'A plate steel object was afired.' 'Afired', if that is the word used and it's not simply Mark E. Smith's idiosyncratic pronunciation of the word 'fired', is perhaps a coinage so the meaning is that 'A plate steel object had been on fire.'

If we take Richard Middleton's categories and their connotations seriously, the interplay between the instruments on the track, including the cassette recording, already writes 'Iceland' as a song which concerns and enacts the struggle of a threatened and singular first person, the ego or self encountering the possibility of the loss of self. The words as they come confirm this reading, as the 'I' disappears after the spoken opening to the song in order to be therapeutically recast or submerged in the 'you' that emerges now and then throughout the rest of the lyrics. The spoken section, as it replaces the instrumentation as the focus of attention, introduces the need for a different kind of listening attuned to the reception and evaluation of information: the voice-over arrests, but nevertheless also takes its cues from and prompts, for a short while, the development of the instrumentation. It immediately confesses to a pathological lack of fellow-feeling for those who are of the same country: either the British people in general or their immediate representatives, the rest of the band who accompany him on this trip to a Reykjavik studio. His numbed alienation is a consequence of the speaker's self-hatred, which arises in turn from his awareness of a lack of resolve or ability making it impossible to achieve what he can nevertheless tormentedly envision. If the spoken words describe a previous condition, the bulk of the song, delivered in Smith's very casual take on *Sprechgesang* indicates a current condition and it is notable for my reading of 'Iceland' that the shift from speaking to (almost) singing is prompted by the vocals borrowing the shadow of a melodic arc from Marc Riley's banjo refrain: at this point the lyrics can no longer be considered independently of the music, as sense and sound will echo each other and therefore, to a certain extent, generate each other.

Two brief accounts of 'Iceland' have been written by the music journalists Simon Reynolds and Mark Fisher. Reynolds suggests an inappropriate metaphor for the sound of the song, lazily derived from a picturesque detail of its production: 'The track "Iceland" was improvised in a Reykjavik studio with lava walls, the band oozing out a drone of two-note piano cycles and banjo that sounded like sitar, topped with incantations from Smith about casting "runes against your self-soul"' (2005, 196). And his brief interpretation is seemingly clinched by a comment which more or less labels the population of Iceland as superstitious cretins: 'The culmination of The Fall's fascination with the supernatural came with 1982's *Hex Enduction Hour*, half of which was recorded in Iceland, a country where most of the population still believes in elves' (Reynolds 2005, 196). Mark Fisher's reading (in this volume) is more sustained and inventive, focusing on a reading of the track as a frozen warning of the impending disappearance of manifestations of what he calls the Weird: goblins, Krakens and whichever creature ('What the goddamn fuck is it?') might have played 'the pipes of aluminum'.

To read the song in this way, and only this way, as partaking of an exotic or otherworldly landscape, ignores the immediately familiar occurrences and locations, thoughts and sentiments that populate the song too: falling over in a café aisle, drinking coffee, underpants … it might even amount to doing what the singer of the song does himself; that is, submitting to a mixture of shame and mystification in the presence of an unfamiliar but attractive milieu. If the peculiar force of the Weird arrives with the realization that, in Fisher's words, '*there is no world.* What we call *the* world is merely a local consensus hallucination, a shared dream', we can go along with the statement as long as we bear in mind its indispensable contrary position: in truth, that there *is* a world (p. 97, this volume).

Some of the song's lyrics conform to conventions associated with the travel writing genre such as the speaker's bafflement at the alien environment he finds himself inhabiting, and a perceptible admiration for the alluring appearance, self-possessed behaviour and well-organized culture of the indigenous population. But a productive line of enquiry with respect to 'Iceland' might chase up a more troubling aspect to the humbling that the protagonist undergoes, by way of the crabbed note to the song provided on the album sleeve: 'Valhalla brochure bit White face Finds Roots, boys don't even notice – & look for games machines.' The note mischievously suggests that Smith finds his own racial equivalent to the recently televised *Roots* series (from Alex Haley's bestselling books) among the Viking complexions in Reykjavik bars and streets. The liberal-baiting is more overt in Colin Irwin's contemporary *Melody Maker* interview where Smith is careful *not* to say that he likes or supports right-wing Oi! bands though he does declare a preference for them over the Marxist group Gang of Four.

The boys (in the band) who, much to their own credit, are more interested in playing Space Invaders than in conjuring their own epiphanies of ethnicity are key to the song and to its success. The sound of the song exactly characterizes the state of the rapport between the singer and the rest of the band; the lyrics comment upon their relations; 'Iceland' is about the intra-group tensions and alliances and it enacts them in a way that is immeasurably more nuanced than the familiar descriptions of Smith as a martinet and the rest of the group as hapless drones. A typical example of such a description, filtered through the author's pulp science fiction frame of reference, can be found in Mark Fisher's essay, 'Memorex for the Krakens' in this volume.

> By the time of *Grotesque*, it was clear that Smith was as much of an autocrat as James Brown, the band the zombie slaves of his vision. He is the shaman-author, the group the producers of a delirium-inducing repetition from which all spontaneity must be ruthlessly purged. 'Don't start improvising for Christ's sake', goes a line on *Slates*, the 10″ EP follow-up to *Grotesque*, echoing his chastisement of the band for 'showing off' on the live LP *Totale's Turns*. (p. 106, this volume)

Fisher's mishearing of the line, since Smith actually says/sings, 'Don't start improvising/For God's sake', masks a marginally more serious misreading. On the song in question, the band have been playing a murky and furious locked groove for several minutes and there is no audible evidence that anyone has tried, is trying, will try to improvise. Smith's comment is, in fact, more of a wry memo to himself. When, in 'Iceland', his lyrics borrow a fragment of a tune from Marc Riley's banjo, they are no longer independent from the music that the band performs; the meaning of the lyrics is altered and, if some or all of the lyrics are being improvised in real time, their sense may well emerge from the dictation Smith hears in the performance of his fellow members.

There are uneasy undercurrents to the song but the ambivalence of the attachments between singer and band also introduce the remote possibility of a therapeutic side to the performance. What I mean by that is that the intense and novel kinds of concentration involved in the activity of group improvisation lead to a performance that is more than just collaborative, more than just keeping your head down and playing your own part. I think that the music is alert and inventive and dynamic at every phase of its course and the act of listening and playing, the listening that I can *hear* when I listen to 'Iceland', for example at the line 'Make a grab for the book of prayers' where the banjo exactly mimics Smith's vocal pattern (which had more crudely taken its cue from the banjo when it first began breaking towards song), signals the potential rediscovery of fellow-feeling in the actions and reactions of the group.

The process of being 'humbled in Iceland' might have to do with the apprehension that the island's inhabitants have much to be admired, but when the speaking voice steps out of the wind at the beginning of the song and, with the encouragement of its accompaniment, moves into a sheltered space to sing, and when, around halfway through the song, everything suddenly accelerates and gets louder and more discordant, what sounds like self-assertion turns away from this purpose and will announce itself as abnegation: 'What the goddamn fuck is it/…/That induces this rough text'? What brings this turbulent, discordant, unfinished and astonishing text into existence? 'Iceland' half-solicits an answer to this question and half-states its own singular mode of being in the moments where melody tentatively becomes a function of harmony even if never quite enough to suggest or speak of resolution. Shortly afterwards, the singer recedes back into and out of the precinct of improvising musicians with some fading sibilance … whistles … If the I of the spoken opening is self-condemned, rocked by its alienation, it has momentarily been rocked back towards a new condition in humility and sent on its way. The singer is granted the opportunity to weather the risk of exposure in the act of improvisation and then to slip almost unnoticed from the track, as the group begin to conclude their agreement to improvise a new ground in an extended instrumental passage of harsh beauty and sensitivity unlike any other in the entire corpus of The Fall. It is tempting to cite Ben Watson's heart-warming statement on the central risk of free improv here, that its 'wager is that any roomful of humans can find community, whatever their linguistic or musical systems, simply by the act of listening and playing' (2004, 375), but my own interpretation of 'Iceland', of the riveting tensions and temporary rapprochements across its duration, doesn't find anything as stable and supportive and long-lasting as a community there.

Chapter Eleven

The Fall, Mark E. Smith and 'The Stranger': Ambiguity, Objectivity and the Transformative Power of a Band from Elsewhere

Martin Myers

'Good evening, we are The Fall'

The niche that Mark E. Smith and The Fall have created for themselves within the Manchester, British and international music scenes has always been distinct and different to that of other bands. Despite both their longevity and their changing of musical styles across three decades, they have retained a coherent and distinct persona and voice. While much of this rests upon the personality and vocal talents of Mark E. Smith himself, the musicians who have worked within The Fall have also produced music which fans of The Fall would understand to sit within a single continuum. In short, despite the many changes of personnel, the fickleness of sales figures and the ups and downs of Smith's personal life, The Fall have produced a body of work that is both recognizably their own and distinct. Their distinct otherness has not spawned a movement or a scene and attempts to mimic the qualities or style of the band tend to fall flat, as Alex Kapranos noted in BBC 4's *The Fall: The Wonderful and Frightening World of Mark E. Smith* (2005):

> I don't think you can compare any other bands to The Fall. 'Cos nobody really sounds like The Fall, and when bands do sound like The Fall, you just kind of go, 'you're trying to rip off The Fall, fuck off.'

This essay will examine the 'otherness' of The Fall and its creative potential, and, taking Georg Simmel's figure of 'the stranger' as a starting point it will consider Smith and The Fall's continuing ability to distance themselves from cultural norms while at the same time sitting intimately among them. Describing the 'stranger' as 'the man who comes today and stays tomorrow', Simmel (1971, 143) highlights how the role of the outsider intensifies and unsettles those around him by his continuing presence. This essay argues that The Fall's ambivalent relationship with the world mirrors the relationship between strangers and the wider community; and that just as Simmel notes the creative value that can be derived from the presence of the stranger, so too this relationship is used by The Fall to great creative effect to transform local and comfortable knowledge into something altogether more unsettling and alien.

Otherness on the Dance Floor

'Otherness' as a distinctive feature of the persona and character of musicians is in many ways one of the most commonplace markers of what makes an audience sit up and take notice of a pop or rock band. A trademark quality or unique selling point will often be a significant factor in the promotion of a band, featuring heavily in its advertising material and the media coverage generated around it. Such 'otherness' can take many different shapes and forms; though often there is a suspicion that even when it stems from a musician's roots, the 'otherness' in question is fine-tuned by the promotional departments of record labels. So, for example, while it cannot be denied that Bob Marley and the Wailers sprung out of the Trenchtown ghetto as representatives of a downtrodden, underclass, when Island Records marketed Bob Marley to international, predominantly white audiences, it did so using the 'otherness' of Marley's Jamaican past in relation to his new audience and wrapped it up within the packaging of a Western, white, rock record label. Bob Marley performing in the dancehalls of London or New York throughout the 1970s to large numbers of white people represented a distinct 'otherness', but it was essentially an echo of Marley's roots within the Kingston music scene; an echo of something distanced by time and by space. Marley's own importance within the Jamaican music scene itself was of course also considerably diminished during this process (Bradley, 2000), even if his political, cultural and personal importance became hugely important on the island.

A corollary to some extent of the difference that marks out some musicians is a prevalence of other groups who promote an altogether more comfortable 'sameness' about their persona and origins; they are the boys and girls next door. This is perhaps marketed in its purest form through Reality TV programmes such as *Popstars* (2000, 2001) which allowed a degree of audience participation to manufacture a band. Describing the 2001 winners Girls Aloud, Caroline Sullivan noted that:

> What's immediately evident is that, attractive as they are, these are girls-next-door-made-good rather than bred-in-the-bone stars. Despite having trained for showbiz careers almost since they could talk, they have no aura to distinguish them from other women in the room. (2004, 8)

While it would be tempting to consider an axis that stretched from the most way out and different performer at one end to the most weak and watery comfortable musician at the other, in which the high-minded avant-garde occupy one pole diametrically opposite the commercially oriented slush of puppy love pop on the other, penniless poets in the red corner versus over-pampered, overpaid pop stars with nothing to say in the blue corner, this is not, however, quite the case. Rather 'sameness' and 'difference' are characteristics of many different performers; sometimes the same performer might exhibit both of these qualities. The Happy Mondays were perhaps a typical example of a band who were both like their fans and sprung from among them, while also representing an 'other', different and at odds with much of the world. What is more, avant-gardists, anarchists and intellectuals have all made their way onto *Top of the Pops* at one time or another and their 'otherness' has not always been as apparent or as 'other' as might have been anticipated (anyone who lived through the commercially lean years of the anarchist squatters Chumbawamba would probably have fallen off their armchairs in shock to see them hammering out a good time drinking song on *Top of the Pops*; it wasn't so much that the song lacked the band's political edge but more disturbing was that band and audience members seemed locked in a routine that could have graced a Friday night Butlins' cabaret).[1] 'Otherness' to some degree is materialized in the work of all performers, even if it is only a distancing by celebrity or success and even if this barely registers in the personae that make up a group such as Girls Aloud.

The Otherness of The Fall

The 'otherness' of The Fall has been an unmissable and consistent hallmark of their work that seems of a different order and a greater complexity to that encountered elsewhere in the music industry. Unlike the Clash, U2 and David Bowie respectively, The Fall's otherness is not defined by their being a gang, by their promotion of ostensibly radical political ideas or by flirting with artsy avant-gardism. If in some part this derives from a lack of career stability, for example The Fall have not been subject to a consistent 30-year marketing strategy, it also derives from the roots that have remained between Mark E. Smith and The Fall and the locality of Salford/Manchester, from the image the band and Mark E. Smith in particular project to the outside world and from the type of work that has been produced under the name of The Fall. These last three elements, which have remained under the control of the band and its leader, often seem to pitch a degree of intimacy and everydayness into the more generally anticipated behaviours of rock outsiders. In doing so the band and their work generate a degree

---

[1]   This is undoubtedly unfair to Butlins, Chumbawamba and the *TOTP* audience (who were probably only doing what they were told to anyway). The great success of Chumbawamba was to engage in both a politicized struggle and a great love of the world and all its anomalies around them including the joy of genuine popular culture, for example going to Butlins. Their great failure was to disengage from their fan base by signing up to a major label and then produce a successful drinking song.

of ambivalence that resonates with the unsettling nature of Simmel's stranger (1971).

According to Simmel the ambivalence of the stranger is ultimately derived from his alien occurrence within society; he is an immigrant figure, a literal outsider but one who chooses to settle among the natives. His presence is unsettling because the stranger represents the remoteness of a culture that comes from beyond the boundaries of settled society. By remaining within the community, rather than passing by or returning home, the stranger creates an ambiguous relationship underlined by the closeness felt by the stranger's presence amid society opposed to the distance felt in cultural understandings. Zygmunt Bauman (1991) develops the notion of the stranger within the context of the nation state, by making a distinction between the society of friends, that is the insiders, the natives of the nation state, and the society of enemies, that is those people beyond the spatial and cultural boundaries of the nation state. In this context the appearance of the stranger creates a deeply troubling and unsettling relationship:

> There is hardly an anomaly more anomalous than the *stranger*. He stands between friend and enemy, order and chaos, the inside and the outside. He stands for the treacherousness of friends, for the cunning disguise of the enemies, for fallibility of order, vulnerability of the inside. (Bauman 1991, 61)

The Fall have always been adept at maintaining their distance from the fads and fashions of the music industry while at the same time Mark E. Smith is clearly a man ensconced in its workings who has made his living from the industry throughout his life. The band has always been associated with geographical territory; with the North generally, with Manchester and with Salford/Prestwich in particular. And, yet they rarely reflect back established off-the-shelf stereotypes of Northern life or Mancunian musical tropes. The sense that The Fall are close to these worlds and adroit at managing a livelihood among them is tempered by the sense that they remain perennial outsiders on the margins, producing a body of work that is alien to these worlds. In Bauman's terms the spatial connections of The Fall might suggest they are the 'enemy within'.

Simmel goes on to consider how the sensation of individuals and groups being both close to each other and similar, while at the same time distanced and unalike is reflected throughout other relationships within society. In doing so the stranger he describes transcends its genesis in an immigrant figure and becomes a more general 'type' of figure. A figure characterized by the dual sense of remoteness and nearness and the ambiguity that flows from that relationship; it includes an ability to bring other qualities into the community and in this sense to possess a capability of being original, to generate ideas outside of the norm; this originality in part is informed by a sense of objectivity that results from the stranger being detached, though as Simmel notes: 'objectivity does not simply involve passivity and detachment; it is a particular structure composed of distance and nearness, indifference and involvement' (1971, 145).

Something of this objectivity is to be found within the work of The Fall. In 'English Scheme' (*Grotesque*, 1980), for example, a list of near-stereotypes and English tropes is used to nail down a class-based analysis of the structure of English (British) social life, which as Smith notes provides a very recognizable view of British society,

> English Scheme was one of the few songs I've written that have sparked off genuine reactions. Boys I'd known for years on and off but never talked to would come up and proclaim its accuracy. (1985, 28)

However, while 'English Scheme' restrains itself to the distinctive and recognizable features of society, elsewhere on *Grotesque* similar images abound but within far more complex and unrecognizable accounts. In 'New Face in Hell' there is the recognizable view of British society in the world of a 'wireless enthusiast' gossiping with his neighbour on 'cream porches', but this falls within a paranoid and disturbing account of surveillance, murder and mayhem at the hands of 'servant[s] of government'. Similar collisions of the recognizable and the everyday with very unsettling and distanced imagery appear throughout The Fall's back catalogue; 'Jawbone and the Air-Rifle' (1982), for example, pits a narrative account of marital breakdown within a gothic horror story and 1993's *The Infotainment Scan* seemingly unravels agonizing British nostalgia across nightmarish readings of European history and current affairs, transforming them both into a coherent yet disturbing world view. The Fall's ability to produce work that seemingly remains both close to its subject matter and distanced at the same time produces ambivalent and unsettling material that is in Simmel's sense highly objective. It is work that very creatively transforms original and at times quite mundane material into something altogether more disturbing. Objectivity for Simmel is determined in part through a sense of freedom that is not afforded society at large, which, in contrast, is essentially constricted by its own social mores and values, unlike the world of the stranger. In bypassing the cultural restraints of the dominant society The Fall often produce startlingly recognizable imagery and accounts of society but in new ways that do not sit comfortably within stereotypes or anticipated accounts.

As well as work that reinvents the world around them The Fall have a long-standing ability to produce very intimate work. A number of songs appear to focus sharply on the domestic and personal life of Mark E. Smith and this somehow feels unexpected within the wider alien landscapes that define The Fall's output, which is often characterized by a degree of aggression. Such unexpected intimacy certainly adds to the ambiguity experienced when listening to The Fall and it also echoes something of Simmel's later discussions of the stranger's relationship with society. Simmel suggests that the stranger is treated with a degree of openness and with the confidences of society (in part because of his objective stance). The small but surprisingly personal revelations of married life (to Brix E. Smith) that appear in songs like 'Paintwork' and 'My New House' (both 1985) for example, also carry with them a shock of intimacy. When Smith notes (of his new house), 'according to the postman/it's like the bleeding Bank of England', it's an extraordinarily engaging comment and one that we would expect to hear from a friend or close acquaintance not from the lead singer of a difficult and awkward rock band.

Just as Simmel's stranger is at once very close and very distant, so The Fall also seem prepared to offer a similar arrangement. Mark E. Smith rarely seems close or chummy with his fans, neither, it should be noted, is he dismissive or disdainful of them, preferring to keep them at arm's length. Within this relationship the intimacies he does share seem startling and somehow a little discomforting. His updated lyrics book *vII* (Smith 2008b) continues the trend for unexpected intimacies being shared both between himself and his public but also, apparently closer to Simmel's understanding, in the confidences a war veteran shared with Smith. The book includes a photograph of Charles Walter Thomas a veteran of the Burma campaign in the Second World War and close friend of Mark E. Smith's father, reproductions of two poems he wrote during the war and the lyrics for The Fall's 'Scenario' (from *Reformation Post TLC*, 2007) which draw heavily upon the poems, in particular one about Thomas' mother. There is a great clarity in Smith's delivery of the song, which seems to draw out the full emotional clout of young men at war thinking about their mothers and in later life thinking about their comrades. The song sharply contextualizes these emotions within a society that has lost touch with a generation of people whose world was defined by the Second World War. It's an unfashionable subject for an avant-garde rock band but The Fall deliver extraordinary sympathy to ensure it is a subject treated respectfully and without cheapening the original material. The intimacy and depth of feeling exhibited make for another unsettling moment in The Fall's work

Sitting Between Two Stools: The Ambiguous Worlds of The Fall

Beyond being materialized within their recorded output, the 'otherness' of The Fall seems, unsurprisingly, connected directly to the working practices of The Fall including the relationships between band members and with record labels and the overwhelming ethos of the band. Often this 'otherness' seems to fall outside of the routines and image-making associated with other musicians; The Fall do it differently, they exceed the parameters anticipated for rock 'outsiders'. They do not sit comfortably within a typical dichotomy of rock stars' lives that might on the one hand simply embrace a celebrity lifestyle, or on the other play to an image of outsiders defined by their sense of rebellion and rejection of societal values. The Fall clearly do not occupy the same spaces that provide a home for the Spice Girls and Madonna, or in which the stadium rock of U2 can flourish. Such spaces are constructed within a package of glamour, success and the ascription of the label of 'celebrity' that is at once at odds with the work of The Fall. At the same time the otherness of The Fall is not situated within the youth or class-based rebellion of artists like the Sex Pistols, Happy Mondays or

Oasis; The Fall's often antagonistic approach to the world does not sit happily among such more readily encountered expressions of otherness and rebellion.

One reason for this difference is The Fall's seeming ambiguity in the face of almost any given situation relating to their musical and artistic practice. Some examples of these are discussed in greater detail below, and what these demonstrate is the tendency of The Fall to sit *between stools*, that is to occupy spaces and operate in ways that mark out their difference from their peers and from the music industry. In many of the choices they make, about record labels for example, and in many of the standpoints they assume such as their positioning in relation to prevailing musical trends they neither fully associate nor disassociate themselves with a consistent style. Instead they adopt a position of discomfort; one that not only makes people around them uncomfortable but also works to make their own working lives uncomfortable. Despite their persistent presence on the music scene The Fall have remained estranged from the industry itself by producing a body of work that is not readily classifiable, by the behaviour and persona of Mark E. Smith, and by working practices that include the management and control of social relations between band members in tandem with usual band activities (such as touring and recording), all of which maintain the distance between The Fall and everyone else. The ambiguity that is produced is defined by their being both insiders and outsiders at the same time; like Simmel's stranger The Fall maintain their distance from their working world and yet are wrapped up within it. Deliberately maintaining an ambivalent relationship to the music scene has ensured the otherness of The Fall is freighted with an ambiguity that unsettles those around them by not being obviously understandable.

Even the genesis of The Fall and their appearance amid the Manchester music scene of 1976 lacks a definitive account. This is perhaps unsurprising given the reinventions of the histories of Manchester music following the well-known live appearances of the Sex Pistols at the Lesser Free Trade Hall and the impact these had in kick-starting punk bands and later post-punk bands in the city. Witts, in this volume, demonstrates how the Pistols' live performances, the successes of Factory Records and the revitalization of the city, musically, culturally and socially, have become linked within a mythologized narrative in which Tony Wilson, Joy Division/New Order and Oasis come to encompass the saving of Manchester's soul. The Fall neatly sidestep this narrative, Smith's own accounts of the Sex Pistols' gig (Smith 2008a) tending to emphasize The Fall's different trajectory, which in the first instance materialized within the looser music/art/poetry world of the Manchester Musicians' Collective and only delivered actual vinyl product quite late in the day.[2]

Later, The Fall never signed to Factory Records, underlining their growing distance from much of the city's cultural impetus particularly during the glory days of 'Madchester'. In 2010 the distance is still firmly in place and The Fall remain

---

[2]   The Fall's first EP, 'Bingo-Master's Break-Out!' was recorded in 1977 but not released until the summer of 1978.

antagonistic and apart from the centre of the city's musical and cultural worlds. Despite such distancing from the Northern cultural circuit, within the media (the music press in particular) the discomfiture of The Fall is often glibly linked to a gloomy Northern outlook, with Smith in particular singled out as a morose misery guts. Newspaper copy unfailingly associates Smith's name with obligatory adjectives such as 'curmudgeonly' or 'grumpy' and in some part this derives from Smith's own production of his image.[3] The germ of an idea of Northernness remains though it is subverted in the context of cultural understandings of Manchester. In a sense Smith uses a certain aloofness to retain his distance and generate an ambiguous image of himself, his group and its relation to the music scene. Such distancing reiterates the near/far relationship of the stranger, but the strangeness it engenders is perhaps made even more ambiguous by the media account's assumption of a clear-cut Northern sensibility.

The distancing from the Manchester music scene is not a new phenomenon in the history of The Fall. In the late 1970s and early 1980s they signed to Rough Trade Records, on two separate occasions. This was a record label associated with a very eclectic approach shaped in the moments when punk mutated into what would later be categorized as post-punk or indie music. Most importantly it was distinctively the record label associated with an alternative London music scene, but despite this geographical association with the capital, Rough Trade Records was hugely astute at identifying, promoting and releasing regional and international music. It was a label driven by a hippy bohemianism that was almost the antithesis of The Fall's own stance. At the same time the other increasingly successful UK independent label, Factory Records, itself based in Manchester, was ignored by the band. While there were no doubt many good reasons for The Fall not to sign to Factory, it still seems odd that The Fall should avoid a local and successful label in order to sign up not once but twice to Rough Trade. The attachment to an uncomfortable working environment at Rough Trade always seemed doomed to end badly – which it did, twice – but on both occasions it produced some of The Fall's most creative and exceptional work.

One measure of the ambiguity in the working relationship between The Fall and Rough Trade is the band's first release on the label, *Totale's Turns* (1980), a live album of The Fall antagonizing an '80% disco weekend mating audience' (Smith as Totale, 1980) at various working men's clubs in a succession of Northern towns. To all intents and purposes this record documented an alien and incomprehensible world to London ears in 1980; these were gigs that sounded shockingly off kilter when compared to the experience of going to watch other Rough Trade bands in London at the time. It is hard, however, to imagine other potential labels based in the North at the time being willing to engage with such recorded output or to

---

[3]   This is satirized nicely in The Fall Press Kit: a resource for bastard lazy journalists by 'International Megastar' Mike Major. The kit provides journalists with all the tools necessary to discuss The Fall knowledgeably without the need for originality, accuracy or straying from the usual stereotypes.

successfully find a market for it; at the time the lo-fi, antagonistic slice of life that is *Totale's Turns* sat successfully as part of the eclecticism of Rough Trade where its very alien nature made it an attractive proposition and one that stood out. Within working relationships such as those with record labels an ambiguous and uncomfortable relationship is regularly considered a perfectly satisfactory option and it certainly does not detract from the quality of work produced.

The ambiguous positioning of The Fall has been maintained throughout the group's history. The 1980s saw the regular appearance of the drag artist Alan Pellay on stage and also the long-standing involvement with the ballet dancer Michael Clark which has included two full-scale ballet productions with The Fall involved as musicians and participants. Such work attracted a degree of discomfort and slight bewilderment, particularly because it appeared at a time when homophobia was more apparent. There was a sense in which the stereotypes within which The Fall should be operating, that is within an archetypal understanding of the white northern working classes, was undermined by an attachment to art that openly connected with homosexuality rather than heterosexuality, art forms of the middle rather than the working classes and musical intent that was determined intelligently from the head rather than the heart. There was also plainly a degree of predetermined antagonism involved in the use of such ambiguities. Kay Carroll, manager of The Fall and Smith's girlfriend at the time, describes the reaction towards Pellay: 'The audience and media didn't know what to make of it, but that was the intention, we wanted to push their posingness into their faces' (quoted in Ford 2003, 100).

Meanwhile, the lives of The Fall, of Smith, his wives, friends and colleagues particularly from the 1980s onwards became entangled in a continuing soap opera whose sustained dramatic highs and lows would not disgrace an episode of *EastEnders* or the pages of *Hello!* magazine. The 1981 American tour, for example, saw Smith leave for the States in a relationship with the group's manager that fell spectacularly apart while on tour. He then returned to the UK with his future wife and Fall guitarist Brix Smith. The appearance of Brix, who 'in marked contrast to her husband ... took pride in her glamorous appearance' (Edge 1989, 67), was one reason The Fall became a more interesting proposition for the media. She was also almost the antithesis of a Fall musician: American, peroxide blonde, glamorous and commercially minded; as Steve Hanley noted, 'She was like a bit of fresh air for five miserable blokes from Manchester' (quoted in Ford 2003, 124). This was the first very public demonstration of the soap opera that is The Fall, something that post-Brix has continued in the incident strewn accounts of Fall musicians coming and going and indeed Mark E. Smith's wives coming and going. It is also useful to note that Brix's arrival while contributing to some commercial successes, did not detract that greatly from the ambiguity and otherness of The Fall more generally. In many ways her unlikely appearance in the company of The Fall disrupted the anticipated image of the band in a similar fashion to the appearance of drag artists or ballet dancers on stage.

Reconciling Ambiguity

Bauman suggests that the ambiguity of strangers and the discomfort that surrounds their presence amid society is a disruptive pressure on the native population's understanding of its boundaries. However, this discomfort is also in many ways the stranger's great strength; it distinguishes the stranger from the dominant culture and instigates a reinterpretation of the cultural landscape. Reconciling the worlds of strangers and natives, that is reconciling both the near and the far, is a creative process. In a 1983 interview Smith describes something of his relationship to a Britishness, in which he outlines an attachment to the local world:

> You get this guilt thing where you think you've come so far and when you look around you've not come far ... we never set out to be a British band. I just thought that's what bands should be like and that's one of the things why The Fall were formed and I thought people weren't being particularly true to their roots and stuff and I thought it was a shame some groups sounded like they could have come from anywhere in the world and you could never pin it down (The Fall, 1983)

This suggests an attachment of Smith to the local, which in many ways is not borne out by the product itself. The interview was part of the *Perverted by Language Bis* (1983) video, and much of The Fall's material at this time appears quite un-British, certainly not easy to pin down as a British musical experience. At the same time one or two songs in particular have what might be more readily understood as an Englishness about them. 'Eat Y'self Fitter' from *Perverted by Language* is regularly described as typical of a quirky English culture and 'Kicker Conspiracy' (1983) tackles English football head-on, while remaining unlike any other football song. Other material at the time sounds entirely alien to Britishness: 'Hotel Bloedel' or 'Smile', for example, also from *Perverted by Language*. There's a similarly alien feel to the video sequences in *Perverted by Language Bis*; the interiors of homes and their scratchy cats, of clubs and pubs appear with a seeming nod to the local world that is undermined by cheaply generated but disturbing effects. Even Smith's disco dancing has a grotesque character to it, but one that does not resonate with a British grotesque. It is material that clearly reflects and has its roots within a local knowledge but is ambivalently positioned within work that is more complex and rooted far beyond the local. By being both recognizable and alien simultaneously, both distant and near, The Fall produce work that is uncomfortably strange.

The success of The Fall's transformation of the local into something altogether new and strange is perhaps borne out by the recognizablity that can be found throughout their work. Sara Ahmed (2000) argues that in many ways the term stranger is counter-intuitive; *strangers* are in fact wholly recognizable figures within society. When we encounter a stranger we are not fooled into not knowing who they are, rather we are all too fully aware of who the stranger is and their potential.

The world that is found within the work of The Fall is disturbing because despite being difficult, uncanny or uncomfortable in outlook, it remains a recognizable vision of the social world. Such recognizability is driven by the objectivity that is to be found within the role of the stranger. It is this objectivity that essentially reconciles the ambiguity and discomfort at play; the objective voice of Mark E. Smith and The Fall reveals the world.

The stranger generates new and objective commentaries on society as it stands and in doing this it has a certain transformative power to rethink cultural and social norms. The creativity of The Fall can be located within such transformative power. Local knowledge is transformed in their work not into an internationally marketable product in the way Bob Marley's local roots became reinvented as a global phenomenon. Rather The Fall produce something that is traceable to the local, to Mark E. Smith and The Fall and their everyday lives, but is turned into something odd and different. It provides an objective commentary on the world inhabited by The Fall but for much of the time not an easily understandable commentary. The deliberate ambiguities that lace so much of The Fall's work suggest a reading of society in which the band appear comfortable with their position despite producing accounts that are themselves decidedly uncomfortable. By using their role as outsiders they can maintain the distance needed to provide an objective and creative view of the world.

PART IV
The Fall, the Media
and Cultural Politics

Chapter Twelve

'The Sound of The Fall, the Truth of this Movement of Error': A True Companion, an Ambivalent Friendship, an Ethic of Truths

Angus McDonald

A Note on Method

It can be taken for granted that an academic treatment of The Fall will draw fire from both sides, both from academics who may consider The Fall too trivial a cultural object to address from an academic perspective, and from Fall enthusiasts who, taking their lead from Smith, may consider an academic perspective pretentious and irrelevant. The first risk is less certain than formerly, with Cultural Studies having established the space for analyses of popular culture; the latter risk is certain. This need not give us pause for thought, but ought to at least provoke a defence in response: what is to be gained by the encounter of an academic perspective with The Fall? The priority ought to be that an encounter indeed take place; there is a risk of a merely journalistic approach if Fall fans predominate, and of an over-emphasis on the academic framing of the object where the fact that it concerns The Fall becomes almost an afterthought, if academic theorization predominates. What is required is a dialogue between the two camps, a dialogue which gives equal weight to both sides, such that the academy and The Fall potentially destabilize each other's certainties. The task is to produce not just knowledge of The Fall, or a reflection of Fall experience, but *Fall knowledge*: something surplus to both the academy and The Fall, but created by their encounter. This need not be a dialogue with Smith, but with the cultural practice that he has created under the name The Fall. By a forced juxtaposition, with neither perspective in control, a new perspective may emerge. Such, at least, is the intent of the attempt made here, in three stages: by a reading of the Mark E. Smith persona, of the social form of The Fall and of the nature of the quest which drives The Fall to continue.

The Mark E. Smith Persona: A True Companion

Who is Mark E. Smith? Who could presume to answer that question; particularly, try to answer it via critical/postmodern theory rather than empirically? Yet this is what this piece attempts. Not by interviews with Smith (there is, after all, *Renegade* (Smith 2008a)) or his many associates and former associates, nor by a career overview (there are several, for example Ford 2003), nor even by a tight focus on the art, but by a speculative confrontation between critical and postmodern theory and the phenomenon. An unlikely project, perhaps, but no more unlikely than its subject:

> Now my words have a purpose. They have the purpose, obviously, of silencing the laughter, of avoiding judgement personally, though there is apparently no escape. Is not the great thing that stands in the way of our escaping it the fact that we are the first to condemn ourselves? Therefore it is essential to begin by extending the condemnation to all, without distinction, in order to thin it out at the start ... No excuses ever, for anyone; that's my principle at the outset. I deny the good intention, the respectable mistake, the indiscretion, the extenuating circumstance. With me there is no giving of absolution or blessing. Everything is simply totted up ... I am for any theory that refuses to grant man innocence and for any practice that treats him as guilty. You see in me, *tres cher*, an enlightened advocate of slavery. (Camus 1957, 96–7)

The first indication that The Fall were something different lay in the step sideways implicit in the adoption of 'The Fall' rather than the 'The Outsiders' as a group name: if resort to the novels of Camus was fairly predictable, the former was more oblique than the more obviously punky latter. In an already clear rejection of rock 'n' roll romanticism, The Fall recognizes that there is no innocent 'outside' from which the condemnation of 'inside' might be launched, no escape from participation in corruption. Camus' judge-penitent, the narrative voice of the novel, defends a bleak realism of universal guilt, justifying universal condemnation. 'No excuses ever, for anyone' encapsulates the extreme puritanism that punk and its consequences found to be the only justifiable attitude to the world and the pop culture in which it found itself, and to which it reacted. The world view Clemence describes in the novel is a fall from innocence produced by a relentless unblinking clarity of perception, combined with an ungenerous lack of sympathy and forgiveness. That Smith realized this persona would fit him perfectly at the outset of a career now extending beyond 30 years, and still be apt, is quite remarkable. 'He was exactly what he was always going to be as soon as the first Fall played their first show' (Morley 2008, 32). Smith took punk nihilism to its logical conclusion. Blanchot's review of Camus' novel delves deeper into the persona:

> The grim movement of a satisfied man who, by dint of adopting a virtuous and happy ego, finally abandons himself to this power of discontent and destruction that is also in the ego. It is dangerous to be too attentive to oneself. This attention is first a spontaneous and happy adhesion that forgets everything, both others and oneself; but the attention becomes reflection; the amiable gaze with which

one caresses oneself becomes a suspicious gaze; one is wounded precisely where one thought oneself loved; the wound is clairvoyant in finding everything that wounds; and everything wounds. Lucidity does its work in the end. It judges everything, and it condemns everything – ironically, without seriousness, and without respite, with the cold flame that it has kindled in the ego. (1997, 202–3)

Clemence/Smith's persona is on the one hand that of the scathing critic who sees too clearly, whose lucidity judges and condemns, but on the other hand, as Blanchot reminds us, the rancour is the product of an antecedent contentment. Smith's conservatism is an essential satisfaction with family, community, locality, class and habitat, a solid tradition from which to launch attacks on the new, the progressive, the absurd. The amiable persona who charms journalists and acquaintances produces the suspicious gaze of the lyricist who scripts the voice. Also, there is a lack of seriousness, an irony, because, after all, this is an aesthetic not a political practice. Smith is not going to *do* anything about the world he observes, criticizes, castigates, except perhaps change the way his audience looks at that world. Smith, ultimately, has found his calling, and is content to carp.

'To carp', fault finding and petty nagging is perhaps too dismissive: what Clemence/Smith is engaged in is *judgement* and *condemnation*. This judgement approaches self-reflexivity, also condemning the 'family, community, locality, class and habitat' which is its own basis on occasion, but stops short of self-scrutiny in Smith's case: this distinguishes him from Clemence, who condemns also himself. Smith always exonerates himself, in interview or autobiography, and limits his participation in his scenarios to narrator and observer, in lyric. This may be a hypocrisy, but the restraint from self-examination is a strength in the context of a pop culture whose truth is almost always the painfully sincere truth of the ego *who thinks he is more interesting than the world*. Smith's avoidance of the first person confessional mode of lyric writing opens up a broader range of possibilities than the rather tired tropes of the personal.

But Blanchot rejects, for *The Fall*, the notion that 'its purpose is to teach us discontent, the uncomfortable truth and necessary anxiety' (1997, 203). For, Blanchot says, 'it guards against teaching us anything. This is the grace of irony' (1997, 203). The lack of seriousness which irony produces, contrary to sincerity, has, paradoxically, a final grace, the grace, the covert generosity of the Smith voice, that the listener is treated as an equal, capable of working out meanings for themselves, not patronized, hectored or lectured, not taught, but *shown* how things are. Instead ('Is there anybody there?' 'Yeah!'):

Speaking is essential here. This speech is itself without end, like The Fall. It is the sound of The Fall, the truth of this movement of error, which speech has as its object to make one hear and to perpetuate, by revealing it without betraying it. Here, rather than the monologue of a man who is fleeing the world, the deceptive consideration, the false virtue, the happiness without happiness, I hear a monologue of The Fall such as we might perceive it were we able for a moment to silence the chatter of the stable life in which we maintain ourselves out of necessity. The character who speaks would willingly take on the figure of a demon. What he murmurs grimly behind us is the space in which we are invited to recognize that we have always been falling, without respite, without knowing it … At certain moments we realize that The Fall greatly exceeds our capability and that we have in some sense further to fall than we are able … we split ourselves off, becoming, for ourselves, the companions of our fall. But sometimes we are fortunate enough to find beside ourselves a true companion with whom we converse eternally about this eternal fall, and our discourse becomes the modest abyss in which we also fall, ironically. (Blanchot 1997, 207)

Because of this equality – and in this is the point of the ordinariness, the refusal of the pedestal, the embarrassment at any recognition of the achievement – there is a conversation between the Smith voice and the listener. A one-way conversation, surely, a monologue, but a monologue which does not impose upon the listener a passivity, but provokes an intelligent engagement. The achievement of the Smith voice is to create a persona which in turn has created an audience. That the size of this audience is inconsequential in a pop culture calibrated towards filling arenas is irrelevant, it is a bearing witness to a more ambitious possibility latent in pop culture but rarely achieved.

Smith is not merely his political attitude; he has after all *created*. The body of work that is the oeuvre of The Fall is part of a 'movement of error': first because of the error common to commentators of misreading aesthetic practices directly as political strategies, second, because post-punk's confused aims, of critiquing industry practices in an industry the critics still nonetheless wished to succeed in, were doomed to achieve only paradox. The Fall do, however, become 'the truth of this movement of error', by constituting a different relationship of non-condescension.

People are often so taken aback when someone powerful and great arises from among them that … they forget their daily work and stand around the deserted spot with weighty words and empty gestures … if a … field-general … puts forth a potent will, the others will feel unburdened and relieved of their duty. For they are convinced at heart that it was, after all, they who raised the hero out of themselves. (Rilke 1997, 84)

Rilke's phrase, 'a pupil who has done the homework for the entire class' (1997, 84) summarizes the Smith achievement; homework the class did not even realize they had been set has nonetheless been done, the potent will expressed in a powerful work ethic has given rise to an unburdening, a relief, that someone noticed this work needed to be done, and did it. This is the resolution of the conundrum which divides those who get Smith from those who do not: did you realize this work needed to be done? Once you do, you join those 'fortunate enough to find beside ourselves a true companion'.

The Social Form of The Fall: An Ambivalent Friendship

'True companion' might seem the least apt description of Smith's dealings with his group and his audience, the often shabby behaviour and often shabby product being legendary. But Smith needs colleagues, and needs an audience. Taking the question of the group first, the question of the band, the pack, it is clear that Smith cannot abide musicians, but cannot do without musicians either. The performance of the persona needs a platform. One of the clearest markers of difference in The Fall is in the particular sense of group dynamic projected. The nature of the social bond which makes a group requires analysis. We are used to a number of versions of the pop or rock group in pop culture. The Fall is something different again.

Two group formats can be readily identified: the 'gang of mates' paradigm and the 'corporate employees' paradigm. On this opposition can be predicated a series of polarities. The 'gang of mates' is generally associated with the procedures of independent, anti-corporate, white rock, where it is valorized as spontaneous, authentic and organic, with a line-up fixed early on in the career. The 'corporate employees' model is, by contrast, more associated with black soul and R & B music – think of Motown and James Brown – and seen as rigorously trained and planned, put together by a manager (who may also be a performer), structured (maybe with a studio band backing a group of singers), well-drilled, choreographed and perhaps with a turnover of members.

The pop group as gang of mates is above all a creation not of the first American rock 'n' roll generation associated with Elvis, but of the first serious British generation, associated with The Beatles and the Rolling Stones. Real groups, as opposed to industry manufactured idols, had to be a gang of mates, in it for fun, self-reliant and complementary (the quiet one, the cute one and so on). It became important that cover versions reflected a group sensibility, and eventually that material was group composed. The gang of mates notion was not challenged directly by punk: the Sex Pistols, the Clash, even with a degree of managerial manipulation, still embodied the same idea. The notion is also expressed in a variation by the idea of brothers in groups: The Kinks, The Jesus & Mary Chain, Oasis.

This model on occasion condescended to the other, and vice-versa. The issue here is professionalism. Stanley Booth described the matter well in *Rythm Oil* (1991). The period is the late 1960s and the culture clash is between the different expectations of different audiences and performers. Black (soul) audiences expect a show, a choreography, tightness; anything less would be an insult. White (hippy) audiences expect authenticity, spontaneity, looseness; anything less would be an insult. The hippies would find a slick show phony; the soul crowd would find a performer who didn't perform because they weren't in the mood unprofessional. Booth uses this contrast to explain why Janis Joplin's debut in Memphis at the Stax Volt party was a disaster:

> The Bar-Kays did the Pony, they boogalooed, stomped, hunched, screwed each
> other with guitars, did the 1957 Royales act at triple the 1957 speed, were loud,
> lewd and a general delight ... The crowd at the Fillmore, East or West, expects
> to see a band shove equipment around the stage for ten minutes or more, 'getting
> set up' – not being showbiz, in that context, is accepted show-biz practice. But in
> Memphis, this is not what people come to see. (1991, 104)

The conflicting expectations ended in confusion.

In relation to this contrast, The Fall, beyond a very early stage where the 'gang of mates' model applied (although, even then, the gender mix disrupted easy expectations) might appear to be more in the 'managerialist' camp, with Smith hiring and firing, and imposing strict discipline. However, it is this strict discipline which often falters in relation to his own performance. James Brown was as ferociously professional as he expected his band-employees to be. Put mildly, this has not always been the case with Smith. Quite deliberately on occasion, and helplessly on others, Smith has sabotaged performances. For the group, the need to perform by the rule book or be sacked is an imperative, albeit there isn't much 'putting on a show' beyond the music. Smith by contrast abrogates to himself the unruly authenticity of someone who will do what he wants, including arriving late, leaving the stage during the set, disturbing group members' attempts to be professional, summarily concluding a set or a song and so on. Smith's own performance, in other words, is committed to the rock ideology of authenticity and spontaneity, while that of the group is governed by the opposite values of conformity with predetermined rules and intense discipline.

Looking for an analogy to this polarity in critical theory, Deleuze and Guattari's development of the contrast between the pack-like war-machine and the hierarchic state-form strikes some echoes:

> this [thought], Kleist says [in the text 'On the Gradual Formation of Ideas in
> Speech', source not given] ... proceeds like a general in a war machine ...
> like a body charged with electricity, with pure intensity. 'I mix inarticulate
> sounds, lengthen transitional terms, as well as using appositions when they are
> unnecessary.' Gain some time, and then perhaps renounce, or wait. The necessity
> of not having control over language, of being a foreigner in one's own tongue,
> in order to draw speech to oneself and 'bring something incomprehensible into
> the world.' (1988, 378)

This could pass as a formula for Fall praxis.

However, we have observed already that The Fall are *both* models, not just the war machine, but also the state-form, with Smith as dictator. In Deleuze and Guattari's work, between the war machine which describes the nomadic life and the state-form which describes the sedentary life, there is an anomalous figure, neither one nor the other, associated in the development of culture with the artisan-metallurgist. There is serendipity in the name given to this figure:

the smith is simultaneously honored, feared, and scorned – more or less scorned among the nomads, more or less honored amongst the sedentaries ... it is necessary to evaluate the smiths themselves as Other; as such they have different affective relations with the sedentaries and the nomads. (Deleuze and Guattari 1988, 413)

The affective relations of the smith: here is the question of the social bond which defines The Fall. *The Frenz Experiment* coincided with Derrida's seminar on *The Politics of Friendship*, in 1988–89; the latter provides a classification of friendships which provides a key to one of the innovations in form performed by The Fall.

Derrida's typology of friendship, derived from Aristotle, consists of three kinds: 'three kinds of friendship, respectively founded ... on (1) *virtue* (this is *primary friendship*); (2) *usefulness* (for example, political friendship); and (3) pleasure. Other distinctions are made; one concerns us: the distinction of political friendship into *legal* political friendship and *ethical* political friendship' (1997, 203). The 'gang of mates' is a friendship founded on pleasure, characterized by impermanence, about which Derrida says, 'friends part and bonds unravel once the enjoyment has run its course: the friends have had their delight, they have given, received, offered; they have had, and do not request anything more' (1997, 205). This corresponds to Deleuze and Guattari's nomads. Many groups might be characterized thus and perhaps The Fall in their early days, but not recently.

The friendship founded on virtue, a sovereign friendship, arises from honour, and would attach to the model of 'corporate employee', where the employee sought out the employer/boss because of respect and honour for their standing. This is a friendship Smith has often rejected; notoriously, he wants no Fall fans in the group – prefers members who haven't even heard the records, maybe best of all, members who haven't even heard of The Fall. This would correspond to Deleuze and Guattari's sedentaries. This leaves the friendship based on usefulness, and this would seem to correspond to many editions of The Fall. A friendship of usefulness is perfectly capable of being virtuous and pleasurable too, but its reason is the use the friends make of each other. Derrida subdivides the category. The difference between legal political friendship and ethical political friendship is:

When it is grounded on consent, consensus, convention, this friendship is at once political and legal. It is, then, a matter of a homology of reciprocity, as in the case of a contract, an agreement between two subscribing parties. When, on the other hand, the parties leave the matter to each other's discretion, in a sort of trust without contract, credit becoming an act of faith, then friendship 'wants to be' moral, ethical and of the order of comradeship. (Derrida 1997, 204)

The ethical form often 'deteriorates' into the legal form, at the stage in which group members want their due specified in writing, when the question of the division of receipts and income arises. The inevitable history of many groups, from rehearsal room to courtroom, is caught in this declension:

> why is it that in this latter case recriminations and grievances abound? ... Indeed, those who associate themselves in this way wish to have both friendships at once, one in the service of interest (based on usefulness) *and* one appealing to virtue (the reliability of the other), friendship of the second type *and* primary friendship. (Derrida 1997, 204–5)

The complicated dealings of Smith with members of The Fall, delicate matters, seem to exemplify the tensions in these misrecognized friendships. While rejecting the friend who pays homage to virtue, Smith nonetheless expects 'a sort of trust without contract ... an act of faith' from new recruits, while on his side treating the friendship as one of a legal character, to be terminated when usefulness expires. These theoretical reflections can be employed to characterize The Fall practice, and attempt a kind of sociology of a specific sociability. This is to speculate concerning the social form constituted by The Fall, in terms not of empirical work on the dynamic of Smith and other members, glimpsed in the various biographies, the autobiography and the ex-members' testimonies, but rather in terms of formal relations, an ideal-typology which might make sense and have explanatory value without reliance upon the subjectivities of those involved.

The Quest of The Fall: An Ethic of Truths

Much as Smith needs The Fall, The Fall needs an audience, and just as 'a sort of trust ... an act of faith' may be required by a member of the group, a similar pledge may be demanded of the audience. The Fall fail to satisfy many of the presumed requirements of the entertainment industry – not just the occasional unreliability of the product, recorded or live, but something more fundamental. Paul Morley, explaining why it was Joy Division he became fixated upon, has observed, 'Mark E. Smith didn't provide me with the idea of change, of rebirth, that I was looking for ... did not point me towards intellectual and emotional salvation' (2008, 32) And therein lies the difference.

That Morley, the theorist of a post-punk Manchester sensibility, chose Howard Devoto, then Ian Curtis rather than Mark E. Smith as his totem shows how deep the identification of pop with escapism goes. Even to this most politicized, theorized scene, The Fall seem more akin to Henry Cow in the insistence on making a critique of the form, not just a better brand of pop star.

Wilson's Factory predicted, maybe even made, the new Manchester of style bars and loft-living. Smith *prefers* shabby working-class pubs and terraced streets. It is when one imagines Smith rather than Wilson as the lodestar for urban regeneration that one glimpses the bathos. To Smith, there was *nothing wrong* with the Old North (and everything). To be sure, there is an edge of irony to the Smith perception that would not allow him the sentimentality of a Morrissey, but the essential perspective remains one where, so to speak, 'moaning about it' is just the icing on the cake. Against escapism, it is his fatalism (*But it will turn out wrong*) which triumphs.

Change, rebirth, salvation – what Morley sought in post-punk, newly vulnerable, as he now tells us, in the context of his father's suicide: these are the ambitions of perhaps all dissatisfied, ambitious adolescents, the audience for the music. The Fall offered something else – not identification with a first person narrator, the usual short-cut for emotional empathy in the milieu, allowing a community of outsiders, but imaginative transformation of the world immediately surrounding you; not escapism, but intensification of the here and now.

This was achieved in three ways. One was by a writing of narratives, a third person storytelling tales of distinctly non-'pop' characters, from the bingo master to the container driver. Second was a breach of the convention that the only relationship that existed was between performer and audience. Smith breached this by a direct referencing of other bands on the scene, a bitching and sneering put-down of others with no precedent apart from the feuds of reggae DJs. This Brechtian acknowledgement of the cultural field and the cultural work was supplemented, thirdly, by an attempt at a different relationship with the audience: one of harangue, of distance, of non-acknowledgement. Not your 'mate', 'possibly the angriest thing you would ever see in your life' (Morley 2008, 53) in the early days, maybe the most contemptuous later on; a clear ban on group members communicating with the audience, after the formality of 'Good evening, we are The Fall', very little direct speech from the singer, little eye contact, some pointing. It is clear that The Fall, as a cultural practice, challenges the norms of the pop group, assumed norms which perhaps only become visible and questionable when the example of The Fall arises as a challenge. It might be argued that such norms were challenged in the era of punk; however The Fall's challenge is distinct from the punk challenge, sometimes pushing it further, sometimes presenting an unexpected variable.

There is little sense of an alternative community animating The Fall (one of the tensions with Rough Trade), little obvious 'fun', no rebel posturing, no dressing up for the stage, clear rejection of a whole panoply of rock 'n' roll clichés, no embracing of fan enthusiasm. There is instead a sense that this is work. Why does he do it? Why do they (the group members) do it? Why do we (the audience) do it? Is there a renunciation required here? What belief is required of him, them, us?

> A crisis of fidelity is always what puts to the test, following the collapse of an image, the sole maxim of consistency (and thus of ethics): 'Keep going!' Keep going even when you have lost the thread, when you no longer feel 'caught up' in the process, when the event itself has become obscure, when its name is lost, or when it seems that it may have named a mistake, if not a simulacrum. (Badiou 2001, 79)

The call of this ethical maxim: it is clear Smith has heard it, The Fall has heard it, the audience has heard it. And so all keep going. Something is being honoured here, something neglected elsewhere. There is a project, a quest, which locates truth even in 'this movement of error'.

To understand the significance of this we turn, finally to Badiouian ethics. Badiou has argued that an ethical practice responds to the above call to 'keep going' in a quite specific sense. Human being, Badiou argues, is between the animal and the immortal, and it is in being 'called upon to enable the passing of a truth along its path' (2001, 40) that humanity rises to an ethical practice. The prerequisite is the prior experience of, the being witness to, an *event*, a concept given a central role in the theory. For Badiou, discussing the transformation from being an object in the world (the human animal) into becoming a subject (the immortal), 'a *subject*, which goes beyond the animal ... needs something to have happened, something that cannot be reduced to its ordinary inscription in "what there is". Let us call this *supplement* an *event* ... which compels us to decide a *new* way of being' (Badiou 2001, 41). His examples, among others, are the French Revolution of 1792, a personal amorous passion and Galileo's creation of physics. A heterogeneous series, evidently, and one to which we might add, in the case of Smith and many of his generation (including the present writer), punk. This might seem a ponderous claim to make for a change in the mode of the music, but to many, punk *was* such an event, a possibility of questioning how one responded to the dominant mainstream and alternative culture of the time in the mid-1970s. It was a turning point which put scepticism to the fore, suspicion that the audience had been lied to, cheated, thus creating the demand for a new practice of culture which might be purified and, in a sense, ethical.

Badiou puts the decision the event demands of you this way: 'the decision to relate henceforth to the situation *from the perspective of its eventual supplement.* Let us call this a fidelity' (2001, 41). This fidelity is made manifest in the recognition that one cannot continue to practise culture in the same way one did prior to the event. The subject that practises this new fidelity to the event 'is not the artist ... In fact, the subject-points of art are works of art. And the artist enters into the composition of these subjects (the works are "his") without our being able in any sense to reduce them to "him"' (Badiou 2001, 44). Ultimately, it is the works, not the persona, that matter. An ethic of truths is, then, a maxim of consistency: 'Do all that you can to persevere in that which exceeds your perseverance. Persevere in the interruption. Seize in your being that which has seized and broken you' (Badiou 2001, 47). The alternative to this is stark: it is 'the temptation to *betray* a truth. Betrayal is not mere renunciation ... I must always convince myself that [the event] *never existed* ... For ... if I recognize its existence, [it] calls on me to continue' (Badiou 2001, 79). Is it not evident that this is the duty that animates Smith in the continuing quest which is The Fall? *HAVE A BLEEDIN GUESS.*

Chapter Thirteen

'I think it's over now': The Fall, John Peel, Popular Music and Radio

Paul Long

I want to begin with the assertion that any comprehension of the wonderful and frightening world of The Fall would be incomplete without recognition of the relationship of this band with the much-mourned BBC broadcaster John Peel. The nature of this relationship is, I think, important for an understanding of both parties situated within the practices and meanings of a wider popular music culture. When seen from a British perspective, such is Peel's continued reputation and standing in the history of radio and popular music culture, that one forgets that he needs some introduction for international readers. Thus, in unpacking my assertion, I'll outline Peel's importance as well as some of the issues around thinking about radio and music, exploring some of the homologies in the practices of band and DJ and the reciprocal manner in which the status and meanings of both have been cemented. Finally, I will offer some thoughts about this association in the light of the death of Peel in 2004.

After a stint in US radio, Peel established his reputation as a pop music DJ on Radio London. This was one of the many offshore, unlicensed stations broadcasting to the UK during the 1960s that challenged the monopoly and restrictive practices of the BBC at that time (see Chapman 1992). When the BBC established Radio 1 in 1967 as its own station dedicated to pop programming, Peel was an obvious figure for recruitment, albeit employed on a temporary contract that proved to be the condition of employment for the rest of his career. He quickly established a particular space for himself, when compared to the majority of his colleagues, through his genuine enthusiasm for the medium and for music per se – his catholic tastes. Peel's apartness from DJ culture can be illustrated by the way in which throughout his career, and as his wife lamented, colleagues with daytime shows on the same radio stations would tend to recommend evening television viewing for their listeners – that is, when Peel's own shows and other dedicated music slots were scheduled (Peel and Ravenscroft 2005, 358). Likewise, Peel regarded the many awards he won for broadcasting 'not as an accolade to himself, but as a "terrible indictment" of the other DJs' (Rimmer 1986, 65).

Peel's significance and role became defined as that of 'the BBC's own alternative taste-maker' (Hebdige 1987, 108). As a champion of the new, the left field, the overlooked, marginalized and generally ignored in popular music, Peel appeared to be a maverick when he believed himself to be faithfully fulfilling the brief of public service broadcasting. As Mark E. Smith generously commented in 1999:

> In the flow and jetsam of modern society, only John Peel stands out as the modicum of 'respectability-alternative'. Without John, all children would be weeping – their kindred looking towards heavens for signals, none apparent.
> (Quoted in Easlea 2005, 11)

Inevitably, the relationship of this broadcaster and The Fall was most immediate and pronounced for British fans of the band; they had longest direct access to Peel's BBC Radio 1 show in the pre-digital era. This relationship as broadcast began with the band's first session in June 1978 and the unveiling of the track 'Futures and Pasts', and ended with the final show's playlist of 14 October 2004 which featured the recorded version of 'Powder Keg'. With a less parochial purview, we could acknowledge Peel's presence too on the BBC World Service and Forces Network where his pleasure in the band reached a wider geographical audience, with German listeners proving to be as receptive to Peel's shows as they have been to The Fall.

While The Fall has a wider established international reputation as a recording and touring band, any significant role for Peel in its meanings seems less apparent for those without direct access to his broadcasts. Certainly, The Fall's extensive discography has been punctuated by the release of some material recorded especially for Peel's shows – the Peel Sessions, so-called – but here the DJ's role is merely titular.[1] Seen from these various angles, some of the basic nature, if not the full extent, of this relationship seems banally obvious, although Smith has commented recently that 'We never depended on John Peel for our livelihood. I don't put my career down to him' (Smith 2008a, 103).

Whatever Smith might say, however, it is difficult to conceive of The Fall without Peel. On one level, Peel's function in this relationship relates simply to the way in which radio is seen to serve as a cheap promotional tool for the music industries (see Rothenbuhler and McCourt 1992). Nonetheless, Peel's role in supporting the economy of 'alternative' music and the independent sector in the UK, wherein the band have been located for the majority of their career, has yet to be assessed in any meaningful manner. In the mid-1980s *The John Peel Show*, as it was then, scheduled at 10pm–midnight from Monday to Thursday, claimed 200,000 regular listeners (Devoy 1989, 11). This is a significant figure for a show focused largely on bands whose releases sold at best in tens of thousands of units, at worst in mere handfuls (see Devoy 1989; McKay 1996; Reynolds 2005). On the other hand, Peel was instrumental in giving initial exposure to acts whose success was more considerable. Managers of artists as diverse as Mike Oldfield to The Smiths have expressed an appreciation of the role that airplay on Peel's

---

[1]   For a comprehensive discography see Stefan Cooke and Conway Paton's indispensable The Fall Online at http://www.visi.com/fall/index.html

show played in their progress. In this sense, and in tandem with the 'serious' UK music press – the *NME*, *Sounds* and *Melody Maker* for instance – Peel indubitably contributed to the economic value of The Fall as an entity of the music business. In his enthusiasm, and out of a sense of public service in exploring and spreading his good taste, he advertised tours, new releases and indeed continuing interest in the band over the three decades of their association. This was during a period when The Fall rarely gained airplay elsewhere on the BBC, let alone across UK radio, even when signed to major label, Fontana, an arm of Phonogram.

Further to the economic function of his programmes to the music business, Peel's role in making 'the underground' available to his sizable audience suggests an immeasurable but qualitative influence on British popular music culture. In fact one could in part ascribe the tastes of a figure such as Smith to his tutelage under Peel, as a listener to the shows of the early 1970s. Ever eager to support his image as a self-sufficient, proletarian original, Smith suggests that he was never a huge fan, although 'I preferred it in the early 70s. I heard a lot of unusual reggae records through it' (Smith 2008a, 103). Music journalist and cultural analyst Paul Morley pursued this point in the 2005 BBC documentary *The Fall: The Wonderful and Frightening World of Mark E. Smith*, suggesting that The Fall's is a sound that was made *for* Peel, for the reason that it was partly forged out of listening to his presentation of bands such as The Stooges, The Velvet Underground, Can, all those reggae bands and so on. Certainly, Peel's show, as an outlet for such artists, was vital to listeners; it is difficult to appreciate the level of dedication it took to be a fan of certain types of music in the UK in the past. For instance, as Smith commented, 'you can't imagine how hard it was to get hold of Stooges LPs in those days. I'd harass every record shop in town when I was nineteen to get The Stooges. I'd keep going in every week, take a day of work, post off for it – anything' (Smith 2008a, 67).

I have argued elsewhere that, while important, such insights relegate Peel's role to that of a gatekeeper and do little to adumbrate his particular qualities as a broadcaster and how these qualities inflected his relationship not only with The Fall but with all of his preferred material (see Long 2006). What I have in mind here relates to the manner in which Peel's distinctive broadcast practices problematize both of the two main ways in which radio, and music radio in particular, is dealt with in the critical literature. Firstly is the characterization of radio as a 'secondary' medium, filling our background as an 'aural wallpaper in a way that even the blandest of speech cannot be' (Hendy 2000, 106). Secondly, and in spite of the dominance of music radio across the sector, it is speech that is the medium's primary code. In addition to these ideas is that of radio as primarily acoustic in nature: it operates as a mere vessel for conveying the tunes played (Crisell 1986, 51–5). Such a conception can be found in the idea of radio's promotional role in, for example, Keith Negus's characterization (1996) of the role of music radio stations as one of mediation – operating between discrete poles of production and consumption. Peel himself best summarized the sense of discreteness between these two poles in his usual, and in this context unhelpful, 'self-deprecating' fashion in a 1969 piece published in *Disc and Music Echo*. Here he commented on the 'parasitic' nature of radio DJs, as a group neither creative nor productive (albeit with a few exceptions):

> We have, however, manipulated the creations of others (records) to provide ourselves with reputations as arbiters of public taste ... These musicians have made you aware of, and appreciative of, their music – not J. Peel. (quoted in Peel and Ravenscroft 2005, 6)

The argument I have advanced builds upon Peel's distinctively simple and yet radical act (at least in the historical context of much of UK radio practice) of prioritizing music qua music. But even this is not to suggest that Peel's role was ultimately secondary either. What this means can be understood in a counter-argument to the dominant ways of thinking about radio, itemized above, in which it is suggested that the distinctions between the record and the entertainment industry are overdone. Tim Wall, for instance, argues that 'radio broadcasts of records are one of the ways the meaning of popular music is created, not how it is changed' (2003, 108). For our specific purposes, this posits that a recording by The Fall had particular meta-textual meanings when heard in the context of Peel's show and all that that entailed. This contextual quality and its importance to Peel's listeners can be illustrated by a widespread and perennial practice which involved taping and exchanging copies of his shows in their entirety as opposed to edits of the material he played. Although this was partly due to the rarity and obscurity of this material, as discussed above, it is also a testament to the nature of his presentation and the importance of that context. The extent of this practice and its value for listeners is manifest in an impressive collective job of recovery and sharing of these resources online.[2] Above all, for anyone seeking evidence of the central place of The Fall in these shows, there exists online a diverting montage derived from such tapes: DJ intros and 'outros' from hundreds of broadcasts of Fall recordings, from different occasions over the years.[3]

To hear recordings by The Fall on Peel was to hear these recordings as part of the wider practices of popular music culture – a type of performance of taste and the ways of being a popular music consumer. In making sense of this reading of Peel and his relationship with The Fall therefore, I have found it useful to enlist the Foucauldian notion of discourse, as 'practices that systematically form the objects of which they speak' (Foucault 1972, 49). As Roy Shuker relates, while discourse

> is embedded in organizational and institutional practices ... discursive practices are real or material, as well as being embodied in language, and function as a form of ideology. They help constitute our personal, individual identity, our subjectivity. (1998, 99)

---

2   See, for instance, http://johnpeeldotnet.wordpress.com
3   See http://x818.com/peelfallintros

For many of us, there is nothing more material or real than the music we consume and define ourselves through and all of the ways in which we define it and consume it – collecting, rating, categorizing, arguing, 'appreciating', differentiating and so on. For instance, I 'know' that the best song by The Fall is 'Wings': it is important that this song is the B-Side of 'Kicker Conspiracy', that I know this fact and, indeed, I can demonstrate this knowledge in tandem with my evaluative assertion. Then again, maybe the best song is 'Bill is Dead' from the album *Extricate* (at least this week), and whatever anyone else says is simply and categorically wrong (unless you agree with me, of course). Why and how I think this, why it matters and how it is made to matter can be turned into the object of scrutiny without getting bound up in whether anyone disagrees with me and the normative nature of such arguments (I'm still right of course!). Thus, a concept of discourse seems to me to offer a useful means of stepping outside of these common-sense but vital ways in which we both make, and make sense of, popular music.

It seems an obvious but necessary point to make then that The Fall came to be a defining feature in Peel's identity as a music fan and in his status as a popular music broadcaster. For instance, in his retrospective celebration of the music of the twentieth century – *The Peelenium* – he traced each year with a representative four tracks. The Fall contributed eight tracks with Mark E. Smith appearing on a further two. The Fall's work featured in annual end of year listener polls – the so-called 'Festive 50s' for over two decades, while 'Eat Y'Self Fitter' featured in Peel's selection of his favourite records for the Radio 4 biographical programme *Desert Island Discs* alongside more renowned luminaries including Handel and Roy Orbison.[4] Moreover, The Fall became a yardstick by which Peel consciously measured himself in terms of his taste and his commitment to music. In one interview he reflected upon how 'a lot of the stuff I used to play, in the early 70s in particular – James Taylor and stuff like that – I now find *agonizingly* embarrassing' (quoted in Rimmer 1986, 69). In comparison he predicted that 'I know in ten years time The Fall will still sound terrific to me even if they don't sound terrific to anybody else' (Rimmer 1986, 69). They served as a means of avoiding a general condition that he identified in the fact that 'Most people of my age, their tastes atrophied 20 years ago... I genuinely dread the idea of that happening to me. I can't bear the thought' (Rimmer 1986, 69). There is a homology here with Smith's own desire to move forward: 'The Fall are about the present, and that's it' (Smith 2008a, 54). Typically caustic when asked about plans for any celebrations of the band's longevity and suggested retrospectives, as if such a move might preserve them in aspic, Smith has said that

> I do hate looking back in the sense of glorifying the past, but I do think you have to be aware of the fact that The Fall have always been ahead of their time,

---

[4]   See Garner (2007, 195–9) and http://www.bbc.co.uk/radio1/johnpeel/ for a full list of Peel's choices.

because it's that which gives us the impetus to move forward. (quoted in Middles and Smith 2003, 221)

In his autobiography Smith has one complaint about his fans, which is their tendency to reminisce in contrast to his own aversion to looking back 'They seem to have different eyes from me, fondly reminiscing about Karl Burns, about the original line-up, the purity of punk' (Smith 2008a, 82–3). This ethos and Smith's practices represent constant renewal and innovation, qualities akin to Peel's own ever-changing playlist.

I want to turn here to a group of related practices that come under a broad category that can be labelled 'authenticity'. As one recent study has it

> the aesthetic of the 'authentic musical experience', with its rejection of music that is labelled contrived, pretentious, artificial, or overly commercial, has played a major role in forming musical tastes and canons. (Barker and Taylor 2007, ix)

In fact, I would argue that authenticity is the *central* value of popular music culture. Initially, we can comprehend the discourses of authenticity by seeing how it works in a binary fashion. One of the key determinants in understanding popular music culture in this way derives from the economic distinctions between major labels and independents and a not always accurate paralleling of aesthetic descriptions of 'mainstream' and 'alternative' practices. The issues arising here are summarized by Wall who has suggested that a discursive binary opposition is constructed between, on one hand, the 'safe', 'distant' majors, driven by 'profit', and, on the other, the independent labels, as associated with the new, the innovative and radical. The former are understood to pursue commerce, the latter a form of art untainted by such worldly concerns (Wall 2003, 96–106; Frith 1988, 11). Thus Wall observes that this sense of a polarization 'has placed independent companies in a romantic position as champions and guarantors of authenticity in popular music' (2003, 99).

Of course, labels such as Rough Trade, Artful, Kamera and Step Forward have provided homes to The Fall, the apotheosis of the original products of the independent labels championed by Peel. Their core appeal in this sense may be best summarized in his famous and oft-repeated characterization of their sound as 'always different and always the same'. The Fall continually satisfied his desire for the new and in this sense they are here understood to be *sui generis*, akin perhaps to the kind of modernism identified by Fredric Jameson, 'predicated on the achievement of some unique personal style that could be parlayed out to the subject of genius, the charismatic subject, or the supersubject' (quoted in Stephanson 1988, 21). If pursued, this quality is certainly something to be tied to Mark E. Smith's dogged and consciously proletarian self-reliance, curmudgeonly outsider status and unwillingness to compromise aesthetically. He has commented, on his ethos, that

I always thought the pure essence of rock and roll was a completely non-musical form of music. Rock and roll is surely not a 'music' form. I hate it when people say, 'Oh but the production's so bad on it and I can't hear the lyrics properly.' If they want all that they should listen to classical music or Leonard Cohen … I'm not about that … There's no fire or danger there, because they've thought all of it out. (Smith 2008a, 117)

This desire for differentiation is partly behind his complaint that the association of the band with Peel was an inhibiting one. His essential objection seems to be that at the start of The Fall's career an appearance on Peel was perceived to be a conventional move into a 'rock' career: bands stepped out of Peel's late night show to progressively earlier slots and thus to wider audiences and conventional roles. He laments too that in the end 'we never went that far from Peel, and ultimately that was a limitation for us. You become known as a "Peel group"' (Smith 2008a, 104).

Charles Guignon reflects on the close relationship of authenticity and integrity in the identity of the individual. For him, integrity is 'understood as involving an ability to form an integrated self through wholehearted commitments, that is, through standing for something' (2004, 155–6). One way in which Peel demonstrated his integrity and what he stood for – a commitment to new music and public service broadcasting – was in his response to a regulation limiting the amount of records that could be played on air. 'Needletime' limits were the result of an agreement between UK broadcasters, record company representatives and the Musician's Union that meant that for the first 20 years of Radio 1 over 60 per cent of musical output came not from records, but from pre-recorded live sessions (Garner 2007, 18). Peel took full advantage of this situation in order to commission contributions from the bands he favoured. Over his 37-year tenure at the BBC, in which he became the network's longest serving DJ (at the end he was the station's oldest broadcaster but had the youngest listener demographic), Peel and his producers commissioned 4,400 original sessions. Often, these recordings would be by bands with no record deal to speak of, perhaps with no discernible industry interest, no experience of recording and sometimes with members who did not even own their own instruments. As Garner observes, 'It's one thing to be obligated to hire musicians. It's quite another to use such a system to invite new bands to contribute to the output of a national public broadcasting corporation almost the moment they emerge' (2007, 18). Others on the network booked bands but none matched Peel's 'curiosity, industry and obsession with the new' (Garner 2007, 18). Nowhere is this more pronounced than in the prodigious fruits of his patronage of The Fall – and I think the term 'patronage' is an apposite and resonant one here.

Consider The Fall's recordings for Peel's show as an extended musical artefact. In total they number 24 sessions and 97 songs recorded over 26 years, representing an incredible commitment from both parties, paralleling but also diverting from commercial releases, and exploring and exploding the band's career and status.

Biographer Mick Middles, who suggests that The Fall may be understood as 25 years wrapped in these recordings, pinpoints the centrality of the collected Peel Sessions to the band's mythology. For him, everything that has happened to them 'every album, every band member, every gig, every bust-up, absolutely everything, is all punctuated by a John Peel Session' (Middles and Smith 2003, 140).

It would be misleading to suggest that these recordings were not an important part of the economic value of The Fall – that they remain part of the business of music. However, in the context of this system of patronage from a public service broadcaster there is a sense that this practice provided a space free from the encroachments of commerce and its demands. The integrity of his music is certainly something of importance to Smith, who has said in his reflections on the nature of the music business that

> I understand that it's always been about money; that's a given. But there's something inhuman about the way in which it's put into practice … And the swiftness of it all! From idealistic punks to moneyed indie chappies. I prefer to stay away from it all. (Smith 2008a, 100–101)

Most important here for thinking of the space afforded by Peel's patronage in this way is Middles' rumination on the curious nature of the sessions as music phenomenon, 'a timely kickback at the encroaching trend of artless overproduction; a live studio-blast – give or take the odd cosmetic overdub – that would, more often than not, simply shimmer with freshness' (Middles and Smith 2003, 141–2). Herein were opportunities for works in progress, revisions, reflection and, occasionally, faltering portents of exhaustion but also renaissance. As Daryl Easlea has written in his comprehensive notes to the official CD release of the entire sessions, this is where Smith's material was worked through, 'reviewed and put into context … an artist's notebook, the work is a collection of sketches waiting for the final moment where definition can be added' (2005, 9).

The idea of patronage is worth pondering here for a moment in relation to the way in which the BBC has afforded creative space to bands. We can think of how the great patrons of the European Renaissance cleansed their often ill-gotten material wealth through the cultivation of great artists and their works dedicated to a greater spiritual glory. Sequestered from obvious taint of commerce, Peel did this in the oasis of his show with bands like The Fall benefiting from the exigencies and opportunities provided by the session. There is also the reciprocal benefit for the patron here in terms of the construction of his authenticity and distinction. Smith's own position in this sense relates to the security of his 'prole-art' credentials, Northern working-class tones, love of beer, fags and football, 'plain' speaking, self-belief and dogged endurance. Denied such apparently 'essential' qualities, Peel had to work at his position, moulding middle-class public school tones and a cultural orbit into what Holly Tessler (2006) calls a 'stylised scouseness'. I would argue that through his patronage of The Fall, Peel's allegiance and appreciation played no small part in the construction of the meanings of his persona as a 'man of the people'.

The Fall and Peel both consistently defined themselves against 'the industry', mocking and avoiding playing its self-indulgent and self-important promotional game as well as scorning the unearned privilege and coterie nature of celebrity: 'You've got to realize and accept that you're never going to be on *Top of the Pops* every week if you're in The Fall, that's not what The Fall's about; The Fall's about hard work' (Smith 2008a, 26). Twenty-seven studio albums support this work ethic, at odds with the glamorous image of the indolent artist. Middles recalls Smith's reservations not only about the Fall appearing on Peel's show when they began, but also about music magazine coverage, and pursuing or even gaining any media exposure in general (Middles and Smith 2003, 103–5). This approach and the mutual integrity of both in this respect can be illustrated above all in noting Smith and Peel's personal connection over the years. As Peel's wife Sheila Ravenscroft reports:

> The strange thing is that John and Mark never exchanged more than a few words over the years. Their friendship involved little more that a mumbled greeting and an occasional punch on the shoulder or squeeze of the arm. That was all John needed from Mark. (Peel and Ravenscroft 2005, 311)

Telling too was Smith's voice among the obsequies upon the occasion of Peel's death, most noticeably in a curious performance on the BBC 2 current affairs programme *Newsnight* (26 October 2004). The programme ran interviews with Smith and Michael Bradley of The Undertones, writers of Peel's favourite record 'Teenage Kicks'. In comparison with the appreciative tones and respectful decorum of Bradley, Smith's behaviour in the interview seemed eccentric, bizarre even: fidgeting and chewing repeatedly. Smith seemed nonplussed by presenter Gavin Esler's gushing and hyperbolic approach to his subject. While Smith has since explained this situation as the result of BBC technical problems and a subsequent lack of communication, he did respond clearly but guardedly to Esler's suggestion that The Fall were particularly privileged to have gained Peel's favour: 'Me and John had an agreement, you know, we never were friends or anything like that, you know … this is what I admired about him, he was always objective – people forget that.'

By way of concluding this specific exploration of the relationship between band and broadcaster, a relationship which, I think, is suggestive for how we might conceive of the wider popular music culture and its practices, we should ponder the relationship's literal conclusion with Peel's death in 2004. Less prosaically, I am prompted in part by the serendipity of the opening lines of the first album by The Fall to be released after Peel's death; *Reformation Post TLC* begins with the announcement that 'I think it's over now, I think it's ending.' We can place this alongside Daryl Easlea's observation that the final session recorded by The Fall for Peel ended with a cover of The Move's 'I Can Hear the Grass Grow' (transmitted

12 August 2004), echoing the fact that this band provided the opening record for Radio 1 in 1967. Easlea asks 'Is this some sort of spooky closure?' (2005, 37).

This conceit is worth pursuing and expanding in relation to the idea that the sense of an end to popular music has been an ongoing and integral part of popular music culture. This was pronounced in reactions to Peel's passing, that his death has left an unfillable gap in popular music broadcasting, but this in itself is a recurring motif: journalists Julie Burchill and Tony Parsons were writing the obituary of rock and roll in 1978 (Burchill and Parsons 1978). In 1988 Simon Frith announced the 'end' of the record era, 'of a function or aspect of pop "as we know it"' (1988, 12). Another argument for the death of popular music was advanced by the late Ian MacDonald who suggested that 'in terms of form, pop has almost come to a halt, displaying few originalities in structure, metre or melody over the last ten years' ([1994] 1997, 340). Such stances are of course articulated partly for effect. However, something in the nature of how popular music has been practised and sought meaning in terms of its production, dissemination and consumption has certainly changed. As critic Sean O'Hagan has recently written, in an obsequy for, among other things, mix-tapes and album covers:

> In the past few months, I have read several articles about the demise of vinyl and the accompanying death of the record shop. It seemed to be that I had read these articles, or variation of them, several times in the past couple of decades. I had read them when the Sony Walkman was supposed to sweep all before it in the early Eighties and when the CD was almost certainly going to sound the death knell of the album and the single later in the same decade. This time around, though, the context is dramatically different. (2007, 8–9)

This context is, of course, the digitization institutionalized by the MP3 format, the organizing principle of the digital library and the consumption interface offered by the iPod (or less iconic variations thereof). Thus, we can consider how a number of things – artefacts and practices – are indeed effectively 'finished': cassette recordings, the sequencing of albums, A-sides and B-sides of singles. In fact, one could claim that as in other media forms, the central 'defining' textual object of the recording is transmuting, diluting and dying out. Many bands make their work available on MySpace, meaning that many have access to multiple versions of the 'record' of which there is no definitive version. While some of the discourses of popular music may endure (its persistent ending for instance), the context that Peel and The Fall have, in part, constructed through their relationship and practice is no more.

However, it is foolish to suggest that The Fall as a band is 'over' with Peel's passing, even if the band is unlikely to be afforded anything like the same attention from any other broadcaster. Nonetheless, subsequent releases have seen the band's stock at a premium, now greater than ever. With Smith's 'autobiography', published and partially serialized in *The Guardian*, he looks suspiciously like the kind of 'national treasure' Peel himself became. Certainly, as suggested by Smith's ideas and practices, as outlined in that book, there is much about him and his idea of the band which is 'past' as he now seeks to lead The Fall in middle age and uncharted territory. Nonetheless, and in the light of this characterization, perhaps the final word – and challenge – should come from Smith himself, in the guise of a song from the 2008 album *Imperial Wax Solvent*: 'I'm a fifty year old man/And I like it.'

Chapter Fourteen

In Search of Cultural Politics in a Fall Fanzine

Chris Atton

Shortly after the abstracts for the conference on which this book is based were posted on the web, I received an email from Ken Sproat, who had been a regular contributor to The Fall fanzine, *The Biggest Library Yet*.[1] In my abstract I wrote that my paper would examine how Fall fans constructed ideology and cultural politics through the music of The Fall. Ken wrote that he was 'amused at my subject matter' and was 'a bit alarmed that what were essentially "throwaway" articles are up for academic dissection'. He might be being modest: as we shall see later, in many instances Ken's work is far from 'throwaway'. Whether through Janice Radway's pioneering work on readers of romance fiction ([1984] 1991) or Henry Jenkins' explorations of fan culture (1992) (two key works on whose shoulders this essay stands, if only as inspiration), we have come to understand the importance of attending to people's everyday experiences of popular culture, and in particular what they tell us about how people experience themselves, what Simon Frith has called 'the experience of [the] *self-in-process*' (2007, 294; original emphasis).

I am primarily interested in how the published discourse of fans contributes to our understanding of this self-in-process. This essay focuses on what was, from 1994 to 2000, the only Fall fanzine in the UK, *The Biggest Library Yet*. What can it tell us about how personal and critical accounts of popular music connect to social experience and to the formation of a critical community of fans? How does the communication of these experiences connect (if it does at all) to the perceived culture and ideology of The Fall's music and in particular to the group's leader, Mark E. Smith?

Before turning to the specific practices and discourses of *The Biggest Library Yet*, I shall make some general observations about the ideological nature of fanzines and how this ideology has been understood in terms of cultural politics.

[1]   I would like to thank Ken Sproat for generously agreeing to answer my questions, and for his patience. Ken also made valuable suggestions on an earlier draft of this essay. The final version benefited greatly from the perceptive comments of Sue Jarvis.

The Ideology and Cultural Politics of Fanzines

The fanzine challenges critical orthodoxy: it often arises because its contributors believe that 'their' culture is marginalized or misrepresented by mainstream tastes. They are less interested in reaching out to broader audiences, preferring to cultivate and consolidate a specialist audience. Seen in this way, the fanzine has a clear, ideological foundation. Frith has in fact termed them 'ideological magazines' and has argued that they are extremely effective spaces for establishing 'ideological musical communities' (2002, 240). It is in these spaces that a 'democratic conversation [takes place] between music lovers, a social celebration of a particular kind of musical attention and commitment' (Frith 2002, 241). This conversation becomes possible because, as Frith argues, 'critics of popular forms (TV, film and to some extent pop) need know nothing about such forms except as consumers; their skill is to be able to write about ordinary experience' (1996, 38, n. 40).

The conversation is 'democratic' because the knowledge and authority on which it is based come not from formal education or professional training but primarily from autodidactic, amateur enthusiasm. This untutored enthusiasm is common to fanzine writers and professional rock critics (however different the texts they produce might be, however different their motives and their audiences), which makes possible the frequent movement of fanzine writers to the professional music press, particularly in Britain (Gudmundsson et al. 2002; Lindberg et al. 2005). Professional rock journalists are fans too; the roots of their profession lie in the 1960s, with the fanzines and specialist music magazines of the US and the underground press of the UK, where many writers began as amateurs and non-professionals. Those that became professional journalists 'posit[ed] themselves as enlightened fans' (Gudmundsson et al. 2002, 60).

This theorization suggests a kind of 'social realism' in fanzine discourse that connects the music to its experience by an audience. It further suggests a symbolic fit between the experiences of the audience and those represented by the music itself, which might include an identification by the audience with aspects of the musicians' own experiences, or at least with interpretations of those experiences. The ways in which these two sets of experiences are brought together in fan discourse can involve the construction of identity and explorations of the personal by writers, as well as direct addresses to readers (and, if fanzines are a kind of conversation, the opportunity for those readers to reply, thus becoming writers; Atton 2002). Taken together, the construction of identity and the building of community constitute the dominant features of fanzine discourse (Duncombe 1997).

Fanzines and Homology

The argument that fans of popular music make sense of music and its creators by establishing a symbolic fit between their own cultural experiences and positions (their cultural politics) and those that they hear in the music and the statements of musicians (in interviews or sleeve notes) is an ideological argument. It assumes that there is a structural relationship – homology – between the music and the people (Willis 1978). The argument is used to explain the relationship between music-making and the social and cultural situations of musicians, as well as the relationship between the music and the situations of listeners.

Homology has been most frequently applied to the study of subcultures. Equally, there has been an emphasis on theorizing the fanzine in subcultural terms, in other words as an expression of a culture that emerges from and is in opposition to a parent culture, typically a working-class culture. Dick Hebdige argued that the punk fanzine can be seen as 'homologous with punk's subterranean and anarchic style' (1979, 112) through what have since been considered as the 'classic' features of fanzine production: stencilled lettering or Letraset type for headlines; primitive cut-and-paste page layouts based on typewritten (not typeset) copy and articles photocopied from newspapers and magazines; photocopied photographs (rather than half-tone reproductions); and the use of handwritten copy amid a variety of typefaces. The homological argument finds in these features a reaction against professionalism and a refusal to accord to the conventions of magazine layout and design. It assumes a symbolic fit between the fanzine and the lifestyle and experiences of its producers.

The form and the production values of the punk fanzine have endured as stereotypical of the fanzine. More significantly, though, in terms of fanzine practices, its 'anti-design' aesthetic has become the norm, regardless of the subcultural origins of the music, its musicians and its fans.[2]

Cultural Homology and the Demographics of Fanzines

The homological approach was developed through the early work in the British cultural studies tradition (for example, Hall et al. 1976) and emphasized the working-class basis of subcultural production. The fanzine, therefore, would tend to be produced by unskilled (in a conventional sense), working-class youth. In the case of punk this often seems to have been the case, but the assumption does not withstand close scrutiny. For example, while *Sniffin' Glue* was edited and written by a working-class Londoner (Mark Perry), Scotland's first punk fanzine (*Hanging Around*) was put together by middle-class students at the University of Edinburgh. The post-punk fanzine *Stabmental* was produced by pupils of Oundle School, an English public school (Atton 2006a). The special pleading for punk as the progenitor of late twentieth-century fanzine production also makes it difficult to consider – and seems to exclude – those people who produced fanzines that

---

[2]   There are exceptions: progressive rock fanzines seem to favour tidy, professional-like layouts that permit the reader to read through them – rather than against them – to their subject matter (see Atton 2001a).

dealt with other musical forms, whose publications were more clearly professional or which had relationships with the mainstream that are not straightforwardly 'oppositional'.

Nevertheless, because the fanzine does not require professional experience of either journalism or publishing, or any advanced educational attainment, it does make it amenable – in principle, at least – to a far wider range of people than we would expect to see as professional critics. In practice, though, this range is quite restricted: it is young, white males who seem to be responsible for most music fanzines. Some of the most significant fanzines in the history of rock writing fall into this category, such as Paul Williams's *Crawdaddy!* (founded in 1966 and not only the first rock fanzine but arguably the first rock magazine) and Greg Shaw's *Who Put the Bomp!* (1970), Paul Morley's *Out There* and *Girl Trouble*, and Jon Savage's *London's Outrage* (Atton 2003). There are exceptions: Sarah Champion published her first fanzine, *Alarm*, when she was a 14-year-old schoolgirl. She went on to produce *Scam* and *Bop City*, two influential publications in the British post-punk and dance scenes of the late 1980s (Dickinson 1997). The prominence of men reflects the gendered nature of much of the popular culture under discussion in fanzines. For example, women are not entirely absent from football fanzines, but they comprise a very small minority of contributors (Atton 2006b); by contrast, feminist cultures produce fanzines that are wholly edited and written by women (such as *Riot Grrrl*; Duncombe 1997, Ch. 7).

Homology and *The Biggest Library Yet*

How far does homology advance our understanding of *The Biggest Library Yet* (*TBLY*)? Superficially, *TBLY* resembled a punk fanzine; it exhibited the stereotypical design characteristics of the punk fanzine. But just as it is inadequate (or simply wrong) to consider The Fall as a punk group, so we cannot consider *TBLY* as a punk fanzine. By the time of its first issue, the formal presentation it adopted was, if not de rigueur, at least the dominant practice for fanzine editors. This is not necessarily the result of homology between subcultural values and their expression in print culture; neither is it explained by complacency or as a matter of choosing the most obvious fanzine 'style' to emulate. The rough cut-and-paste of the publication serves a number of purposes. First, there is the banal, but pressing, matter of producing a periodical in one's spare time (Atton 2001b). What could be more efficient than to reproduce submitted articles in whatever format they are received? Second, the photo-reproduction of published articles from other sources, mostly from the commercial music press, and from national and local newspapers, lends authenticity to the sources (reproducing the act of reading the original source); in the case of 'archive' stories it also affords an historical – and at times nostalgic – perspective on the content (by reproducing the form of the original the reader moves closer to the original content).

Issue 16 of *TBLY* (undated, but published in 1999) is representative of this approach. (The examples given here are all drawn from this single issue. I have chosen it because it seems *intensely* representative of the fanzine's complete run of 19 issues in its distillation of the diversity of styles, approaches and content that we find throughout the six years of *TBLY*'s publication). In issue 16 there are, not unexpectedly, numerous articles reprinted from other sources. What is surprising, particularly for theorists of homology, is the extent to which those sources do not suggest the expected 'subcultural choices'. There is a reprinted article from another fanzine (*City Fun*), but we also find articles from national newspapers across the political spectrum (*The Guardian* and *Telegraph Magazine*) as well as local papers (*Luton/Dunstable on Sunday*). Some of these are retyped; the range of sources and their original publication dates (from 1981 to 1999) attest to the assiduousness of the fanzine's contributors.

Assiduousness (or obsessiveness) is also present in a lengthy tour diary over six pages (part two of a series), where editor Rob Waite recounts gigs, travelling to gigs, 'selling merchandise' and meeting Mark E. Smith. The tour diary is typical of many fanzines, particularly those whose subjects are working outside the mainstream. The proximity and familiarity the writers often have with the artists pre-gig does not prevent them from engaging as devoted fan-at-a-distance during the gig itself (I have found a similar approach in *Pilgrims*, a fanzine for Peter Hammill and Van Der Graaf Generator; see Atton 2001a). At the same time, Rob Waite is quite aware that devotion to a single artist or group leads to an obsession with trivia. In his editorial 'Short Fall' he amiably describes Ian Ewart, the author of a piece on bootleg recordings of The Fall as '*TBLY*'s resident anorak'. Ewart's ongoing bootleg series sits alongside a continuing series that lists The Fall's radio and TV appearances and recordings, as well as a list of songs covered by The Fall. Ewart also contributes a think piece that muses on the pointlessness of some fan activities, in particular an attempt to qualitatively compare different periods of The Fall.[3]

The practices of bricolage and collage that Hebdige found in the punk subculture are present in this issue, where they can be interpreted as resembling the creative practices of The Fall's music, as well as its packaging in album sleeves. We can think of the album sleeves, particularly those that incorporate fragments of Mark E. Smith's handwriting (as Paul Wilson shows elsewhere in this collection); the songs and compositions constructed from disparate elements, including found sounds and recordings of Mark E. Smith's voice on cassettes (what Robert Walker terms 'dictaphonics', also in this collection) in songs such as 'Bonkers in Phoenix' and 'Putta Block'. Here homology seems to lie less in the content of the fanzine than in its practices. There is another explanation, however. We can think of this agglomeration of diverse sources as a practice of redaction. John Hartley (2000)

---

[3]   Ken Sproat pointed out to me that 'Ian Ewart' was a pseudonym used by Rob Waite. In this light Waite/Ewart's comments become self-reflexive, making the observations even sharper, I think.

Figure 14.1   Front cover of *The Biggest Library Yet*, no. 16

Figure 14.2   Front cover of *The Biggest Library Yet*, no. 17

The Fall Fanzine   **£1.50**

The Biggest Library Yet #17

THE PRESENT-DAY CIG SMOKER REFUSES TO KNUCKLE UNDER

has pointed out that public communication is becoming increasingly redactional. There is an emphasis on reduction, revision, preparation, editing and publishing; journalism as original writing becomes less prominent. Hartley defines redaction as 'the creative *editorial* practice of bringing existing materials together to make new texts and meanings' (Hartley 2004, 136). As other chapters in this collection suggest (for example, that by Janice Kearns and Dean Lockwood), we might also think of the working practices of Mark E. Smith and The Fall as redactional, to some extent.

   TBLY itself is redactional to the extent that it reprints – and thereby resituates – already-published writing. Moreover, its light (even haphazard) editorial touch suggests redaction of another kind, where the ungoverned collision of different styles of writing from different perspectives (and in different typefaces) can be understood not as a discourse of anarchy, but as the discourse of a 'demotic avant-garde' (Atton 2002, 30). This discourse blends elements of dominant popular culture with a kaleidoscope of fragments taken from more marginal cultures. When we turn to original contributions in the fanzine we find stronger evidence of these restless, multi-focused pursuits, and a particular interest in examining these marginal and out-of-the-way ('outsider') cultures. At this point, then, we must consider the fan not merely as redactor but as critic and expert, as someone who engages with the experience of music and its contexts. These contexts include, significantly in the case of *TBLY*, the man 'behind the music', Mark E. Smith.

Mark E. Smith and Cultural Politics

As amateur publications dedicated to the accumulation of detailed information and the display of knowledge, fanzines are always the product of autodidacts. As we have already seen, the expert culture of the fanzine does not depend on formal education or professional training. Fanzine writers (despite sharing their amateur enthusiasm with professional writers on popular culture) can therefore be seen as outsiders, as mavericks. It is tempting to make a homological point here, for Mark E. Smith too has frequently been cast in a similar way, celebrated as a maverick, self-educated intellectual (Tony Herrington's 1999 interview with him in *The Wire*, itself a 'maverick' publication, is headlined 'The Outsider').

   Though it is accurate enough to cast Mark E. Smith as an autodidact intellectual, this is both to state the obvious and to understate his interests and expertise. It is obvious in the sense that, in the history of rock, this portrayal is common enough (think of Dylan and Lennon; of Mark E. Smith's generation we can include people as diverse as Green Gartside of Scritti Politti, Billy Bragg and Mark Stewart of the Pop Group. The list goes on …). The history of rock reveals few formally trained intellectuals who have applied that training to their music (even the progressive rock groups of the 1970s, so often criticized for their intellectualization of rock, often have roots not in the conservatoires but in the British pop and rhythm and blues scenes of the 1960s). What sets Mark E. Smith apart from many other autodidacts in rock is what some might see as a contradiction in his cultural values and experiences. He lives 'within walking distance of the place of his birth', near his mother, and places value on being the only man in his family – it is necessary for him to be there to support her and the other female members of his family (as reported in Herrington's 1999 interview with Smith, but still the case today). These stereotypical working-class values (the value of community, the man as guardian of the family) might seem inconsistent with Smith's interest in the occult, in the music of Schoenberg and Stockhausen, and in writers such as M.R. James, Arthur Machen and Algernon Blackwood (all cited as interests in Herrington's interview), subjects that seem – equally stereotypically – the province of the middle class and the university-educated (Smith left formal education in his mid-teens). Smith's scepticism and suspicion of academics is well known, as is his antipathy towards most professional music writers; as if to emphasize this, in interviews he has often drawn attention to the approbation he and The Fall receive from working-class fans.

The Biggest Library Yet and Cultural Politics

Given the almost exclusive focus of a fanzine such as *TBLY* on the work of single group and its leader, we can expect Smith's interests to be reflected, at least through exploration by its contributors (by exploration I mean that the interests are not necessarily shared interests, rather that contributors are seeking to inform themselves about – and make sense of – those interests). This is the case in issue 16, which contains a summary of the life of the medium Helen Duncan ('ESP Medium Discord'). Smith's fascination with and personal experience of psychic phenomena is well known to his fans. The back cover of the issue is an illustrated page from the H.P. Lovecraft fanzine *Strange Aeons* (Lovecraft is another of Smith's favourite writers). It seems unlikely that these features would be present were it not for the fans' fascination with the intellectual interests of Smith himself. While these are the only contributions to have any direct fit with Smith's cultural interests, others are suggestive of a more subtle relationship between writer and artist.

   The work of Ken Sproat is of particular interest here. Sproat's involvement in fanzines began in the mid-1990s as a contributor to the football fanzine *When Saturday Comes* (*WSC*). He had been a Fall fan for some time and 'had nearly twenty years of thoughts and theories stored up – lots to say and learn'.[4] Meeting a fellow *WSC* contributor who was also a contributor to *TBLY* prompted Ken to write about The Fall.[5] Sproat's main reason for writing in *TBLY* echoes Frith's

---

   [4]   Email correspondence with the author, September 2008; all subsequent quotes by Sproat are from this source, if not otherwise noted.
   [5]   The editor of *WSC* was also a Fall fan. Shaw (1989) has shown a strong connection between football fanzines and music fanzines of the 1970s, though he argues that fans move

description of the fanzine as a democratic conversation between fans: 'like many I tried to analyse the words and music, only with me I had no one to talk it over with … the pleasure is not in self-aggrandisement'.

Two of Sproat's articles in *TBLY* 16 stand out for me. The first of these, 'The Outsiders', is titled after Smith's initial choice of name of The Fall (it also echoes the title of Herrington's article in *The Wire*). Rather than merely reproducing the Romantic myth of the artist as outsider, Sproat compares Smith's cultural position to the political position of Leon Trotsky. He argues that there is a parallel between Trotsky's notion of permanent revolution and Smith's work with The Fall. What they share is not a political perspective, but a methodology: both embody 'a critique of a critique' in their relationship with a proximate culture (for Trotsky this was the Communist Party; for Smith it was the punk/alternative music scene of the late 1970s and early 1980s):

> While Marxist parallels may be generally annoying to him, Smith has indeed general similarities with one of history's genuine outsiders – Leon Trotsky – largely due to the fact he is the embodiment of a critique of a critique. Communism was meant to cure all ills but it went wrong – Trotsky spent twenty years of his life alerting the world to this and trying to show what was possible. Punk's existence seemed to be in order to sort out the music business but it went wrong – The Fall alerted anyone who would listen and in doing so were forced to create an alternative universe of sound. (Sproat 1999a, 7)

I think this argument is illuminating for two reasons. Firstly, because it critically engages with the notion of Smith as outsider by arguing that to portray him as a malcontent or 'grumpy old man' (as many professional journalists do) is to miss the point: Smith uses his music (and his interviews at times) to develop a continuous critique of the worlds (musical, social, political and economic) in which he finds himself. The permanent revolution of Smith's critique is played out in his restlessness, whether this is in recorded musical experiments or the experimental nature of The Fall's line-up (an inevitable result of his continuous hiring and firing of group members). Secondly, the article avoids trying to essentialize Smith in terms of specific interests – instead it emphasizes Smith's work as a process.[6] Sproat puts his theory into practice in the second of his articles. Its title reads like that of an academic paper: 'The Aural and Social Effects of Permanent Construction, Deconstruction and Reconstruction of Music'. Is this parody, reflecting Smith's own attitude towards academics? Is it pretension? The title sits above what seems like a conventional concert review of The Fall (conventional in its list of songs

---

from writing about music to writing about football. Jary, Horne and Bucke note that *WSC* 'emerged as an off-shoot of a music fanzine, *Snipe!*' (1991, 584).

[6]   Despite its serious point, the article is also genuinely witty: however noble might have been the revolutionary aims of 'a certain, relatively well known Marxist political organisation', its members 'had an appalling taste in music'.

performed and its survey of the audience; no high theory in evidence here). Sproat told me that his title was deliberately chosen to highlight the nature of the concert: 'it was when Mark put his first "granny on bongos" line-up together'. This refers to an apocryphal statement to the effect that 'it's still The Fall, even if it's just Mark E. Smith and your granny on bongos'. The concert under review comprised an entirely new line-up of 'unknown' musicians – Smith's permanent revolution in action:

> The current line-up are good enough to be in a position where they can add an extra bass, more guitar, keyboards or whatever and instead of making things just louder or chunkier it will truly enhance, develop and twist the sound … As I surveyed Mark meandering around the stage it is apparent that he is reborn. He is not at the end of his career, he is only halfway through. (Sproat 1999b, 33)

Taken with the previous article, Sproat's title draws the reader's attention to the mutability of The Fall, at the same time as Smith remains at its heart. This position is reinforced elsewhere in this issue of *TBLY*, where another contributor reminds us of John Peel's assessment of the group: 'always different, always the same'.

We have already seen how the terrain of *TBLY* as a site for obsession and trivia is knowingly negotiated by other contributors. Sproat also achieves this, by contributing articles that are mischievously conceived. His 'Hey! Lisa Riley' article claims to be excerpted from an interview published in 'Woman on Top – The Magazine for the Enabled Woman' with the Emmerdale soap star, and is premised on her being Marc Riley's sister (Riley is a former member of The Fall). It is no such thing: neither the relationship nor the magazine exists. Elsewhere, Sproat has contributed an article that claims to be a translation of a Bulgarian review of a Fall album: again, it is no such thing. There is deliberateness here, not merely capriciousness: 'I don't like formulaic writing; things like *Q* magazine are anathema to me.'

I don't intend to suggest that Sproat's contributions define the content of this issue of *TBLY*, even less that of the entire run of 19 issues. What they do tell us, though, along with the other contributions I have discussed, is that *TBLY*'s blend of fan trivia, historical comparison, musical analysis and autobiographical account is not untypical of a fanzine. Yet its pages are no place for unswerving reverence; we find robust and insightful critique alongside playful fiction masquerading as fact. Arguments do not simply reduce to 'top ten lists'; they are interested in how to listen to The Fall. There are arguments about musical development and notions of progress; there is an acknowledgement of the marginality of the music and at the same time its centrality to fans' own social experience. In this democratic conversation there is no attempt at consensus. The discourse of *TBLY* is provisional; it offers a space for continuing discussion without seeking agreement. *TBLY* is no place for establishing a canon.

Conclusions

The homological approach to fan discourse – as a search for cultural politics – rests on the assumption that we can read back from the music to a particular representation of the social experience of fans, and that we can understand the structuring of social identity by attending to the structuring of the music. In the case of the fanzine, the homology model further assumes that we will be able to read off social identity by attending to the 'democratic conversation between music lovers' that takes place within its pages. In the case of *TBLY*, however, homological analysis seems inadequate. It essentializes the relationship between the experiences of the audience and those represented by the music (which, as I noted at the beginning of this essay and we have seen in the preceding analysis, can include those of the musicians).

What is important here is that this relationship is not fixed: it is unstable and not all predictable. As Ken Sproat's contributions to *TBLY* have shown, this relationship can be complex and continuous. That is to say, where homology seems to expect a more or less static fit between sets of experiences and values that results in a fixed notion of cultural identity, we have seen instead, as Frith has argued, that 'identity is *mobile*, a process not a thing' (2007, 294; original emphasis). When Ken Sproat first wrote to me he suggested that 'the only link between Fall fans away from the music is a willingness to be contrarian'. If there is any homology at work here at all, it is that the fan's 'self-in-process' resembles that of The Fall (and Mark E. Smith): the continuous development of their accounts of experiences and their efforts – Sproat's critique of a critique – to make sense of those experiences are central to the creativity of the fanzine and the music that is its subject.

Chapter Fifteen
'As if we didn't know who he was': Mark E. Smith's Untimeliness

Janice Kearns and Dean Lockwood

Mark E. Smith's lyrics for The Fall weirdly dislocate the present, populating it with characters, events and elliptical narratives in ways that push us to find ourselves at variance with the times (and indeed, with the very notion of 'the times'). Even the interviews he gives can demonstrate this untimely power. However, the broadsheet press marks Smith chiefly as an acerbic and comical reminder of a prole-art rebellion now on the whole put safely to bed. Smith opens his recently published self-portrait, *Renegade* (Smith 2008a), with the pronouncement 'All is as all shouldn't be', but, as filtered through the prism of *The Guardian* or *The Independent*, his objection to the present comes to seem quaintly stranded in a less politically correct era.

In what follows we will discuss Smith's importance in terms of the Deleuzo-Guattarian notion of the 'minoritarian'. The minoritarian constitutes an experimental, fluid force within majoritarian culture – the 'official' shared culture which, we are encouraged to believe, rests upon already given and settled forms of being. This force foments the transformative expression and becoming of multiplicitous identity. Minor art offers a form of resistance to those culturally and politically marginalized which does not flee into an oppositional strategy, taking up a position outside and against the dominant, but rather seeks to move and work from within the dominant. In their study of Kafka, in which they worked out this notion of the minor, Deleuze and Guattari (1986) show how Kafka, marginalized as a Jew in Prague, chose not to retreat into the Czech language to write, but preferred to attempt to awaken a power of difference within the official German language and literary tradition, to speak it differently, to speak in such a way as to disturb and subvert, 'stuttering' in order to do new things, create new affects, stir and move readers in new ways.[1] Claire Colebrook, drawing on Deleuze, argues that we must make of Shakespeare a 'minor' author, to find Shakespeare's stutter, as it were, recognizing 'the potential in his work to be read as if we didn't know who he was' (2002, 105). We will put a case for approaching Smith similarly, arguing for an analysis that is suspicious of any attempt to bind him into the physiognomy of popular culture, to definitively capture the *disturbance* that he is.

---

[1] For useful discussion and clarification of Deleuze and Guattari's idea of the minor, we recommend Bogue (2005).

A Licensed Fool?

Press coverage of Smith intensified in the months leading up to the 'Messing up the Paintwork' conference (May 2008) due to the publication of Smith's autobiography, *Renegade*, and the release of the new Fall album, *Imperial Wax Solvent*. Articles and reviews of the book and the album graced the pages of broadsheet newspapers, signalling an attempt to legitimize Smith and his work within the cultural mainstream. They regurgitated the Smith persona forged in his previous encounters with music journalists and cast him as taciturn and outlandish in his behaviour, an 'idiot savant' who produces work of merit in spite of himself. This image of Smith – grumpy, gurning and unyielding – has become familiar to readers and constitutes what Paige Baty (1995) terms a 'mediapheme'.

Baty describes the mediapheme as an essential building block of an icon. In order for a subject to become an icon (her example is Marilyn Monroe) he or she must first be compressed into a mediapheme. The mediapheme simplifies the subject into a recognizable stereotype which can then be commodified and sold through a variety of different media. It 'ricochets through the channels of mass mediation with ease' (Baty 1995, 60). Thus the shorthand persona of Smith as a belligerent drunk travels from the music press through to broadsheets and on to television. The composition of this mediapheme draws on mainstream 'establishment' values and, in particular, class values.

The nature of the media and the class position of its commentators ensure that mediaphemes are created from a middle-class perspective. Subjects deemed to fall outside of a narrow definition of acceptability are typically represented as in some way lacking. Traditional categorizations of class have broken down to some extent, but have not been superseded by a classless society as expounded by British Conservative Prime Minister John Major in the 1990s and by his Labour successor Tony Blair. Class relations now revolve around lifestyle choices. People are judged not on their occupation but on how they furnish their homes, what they eat and what they wear. Class is performed and conferred through consumer choice and what Bev Skeggs terms 'compulsory individuality' (2005, 973). Individuals demonstrate their cultural, educational and symbolic capital through conforming to (or diverging from) a middle-class ideal.

> It is up to the individual to 'choose' their repertoire of the self. If they do not have access to the range of narratives and discourses for the production of the ethical self they may be held responsible for choosing badly, an irresponsible production of themselves. (Skeggs 2005, 973)

Thus the moral impetus is placed upon the subject to present a self that conforms to the middle-class ideal. Working-class subjects do not have sufficient cultural capital to achieve this and so display a lack for which they are deemed responsible. This lack is seen as evidence of insufficient will or self-control. The media pathologizes the working classes, representing them as grotesque figures of disgust (for example 'Chavs'). Class and moral authority is tied to taste and the ability to discriminate correctly according to the codes of taste. This has given rise to legions of experts who advise the consumer on how to present and package the self. Reality television parades a grotesquerie of hapless ill-displayed subjects ripe for a makeover of their body, their clothing or their lifestyle.

However, Skeggs notes that disgust is double-edged: along with the repulsion comes a sense of fascination. The middle classes are fascinated by the rawness of working-class life. Tyler (2008) discusses how middle-class students hold Chav parties, taking on the role temporarily in order to explore behaviours that, in other circumstances, would be deemed unacceptable. In doing this they are not only vicariously experiencing working-class pleasures but also rendering the threat of the working class impotent. In a similar way, Skeggs notes that working-class entertainment has long focused on the sending up of the 'stuffy' middle classes. Bursting the pretensions of the middle class gives the impression of some small exercise of power for the working-class subjects. The mediapheme assigned to Smith in the broadsheet press inflicts a little bit of danger and rawness on a middle-class readership. Journalists simultaneously relish and fear interview encounters, pointing to Smith's legendary temper and taciturn nature while recognizing his increasing status as a 'godlike genius' (NME Brat music awards 1998). The record of the encounter is often gladiatorial with journalists testing themselves against Smith as if he were a sparring partner. Building up the mediapheme is an essential element in displaying their open-mindedness and well-honed sense of irony.

Smith is invariably late for the interview – this is portrayed as evidence of his maverick nature. We are always told what he is wearing and his appearance is summed up as grotesque; this is usually accompanied by a photograph of Smith gurning to evidence the fact. For example, Sean O'Hagan in *The Observer* notes that his 'smart black-woollen jacket and white shirt only accentuate his scarecrow-thin frame' and goes on to describe Smith as looking like a 'malevolent goblin' (2005, 6). We are told what he is drinking and how much ('he orders a pint of lager, sinks half of it, declares it piss poor and replaces it with two bottles of cider'), when he lights a cigarette, when he swears and even when he coughs. O'Hagan again: 'The combination of the fag and the cackle produces a rattling cough, which he deals with by hawking up and gobbing in the ashtray' (2005, 6). This imagery clearly thrills the interviewer. Smith himself refuses to acknowledge that his behavioural and image misdemeanours represent any kind of 'lack'. He does not modify his behaviour to conform to the expected majoritarian values, nor does he acknowledge his mediapheme. However he does not entirely escape its effects.

Fred Johnson, discussing U2, sees the mediapheme as akin to Baudrillard's simulacrum. He states that the 'mediapheme, as an easy encapsulation also strips away the vicissitudes of the real. It takes a complex person, group, event or message and reduces it to the simplest, clearest, most immediate terms. It "deters" the real subject by substituting it with its "operational double"' (Johnson 2004, 88). Johnson sees the process of producing mediaphemes as reductionist and exploitative while at the same time enabling celebrity culture to flourish by providing a network of publicity outlets for celebrities and their products. However, this publicity has a price, and the trap of the simulacral mediapheme is that it hollows out, simplifies and disambiguates the media persona.

In his review of *Renegade* for *The Wire*, Mark Fisher writes that 'Smith's art used to be to channel voices, to schizophrenically fragment into a polyphony of selves. Then, the Mark E Smith interview persona was a deflection, a trap for unwary middle class journalists ... now the "clever prole in the pub" persona is a trap for Smith himself' (2008a, 70). In his Blog, Fisher adds that the book signals and underlines Smith's reduction to biographical entity, his art closed off around his persona ('See, we can explain it all now. True life tales. Nothing odd to see here'; Fisher, 2008b). Smith has been duped into believing his own myth, and as a consequence, or perhaps because of years of alcohol abuse, has lost his mediumistic channelling powers: 'Smith is a lapsed sorcerer turned celebrated cabaret star, licensed fool on the BBC, licensed prole in *The Guardian*' (Fisher, 2008b). On this view, Smith's capture by his mediapheme and entry into the culture supplements has reduced him to a mere frisson. The cackling goblin invoked by broadsheet journalists has for many years had a strong whiff of the carnivalesque, and here, Fisher's references to Smith's jestering as thoroughly sanctioned by the middle classes invoke a frequent critique of this celebrated Bakhtinian notion.

For Bakhtin ([1965] 1984), the carnival of the Middle Ages, revivified by Rabelais, can be characterized by its seriously playful ambivalence. The carnival, ringing with laughter, was a contradictory affair, mingling joy and horror, fun and danger, affirmation and negation. The laughter was collective, participatory, directed everywhere and excessive. It resonated with the grotesque bodies the carnival presented, public bodies which penetrated and were penetrated by the world, built for connectivity (sending out protuberances, opening up orifices). Carnivalized speech made a mockery of language, foregrounding the ugliest vocabulary, wordplay and nonsense. Above all, the carnival was subversive and counter-hegemonic, inimical to the identitarian order crucial to the official culture of the ruling classes. However, for Bakhtin, carnival was not merely oppositional. It lacked a programme, it was 'the true feast of time, the feast of becoming, change, and renewal' and it lacked an essential meaning (Bakhtin [1965] 1984, 10). Nevertheless, the concept has been frequently criticized by those who argue that it is prone to easy recuperation. The carnival, acting as a form of catharsis or safety valve, allows a release of tension, a letting off of steam which, once the festivities are over, actually serves to sustain the prevailing order. The carnival is, all too often, a mechanism for social control and institutional capture. The Smith mediapheme could be understood as a carnivalesque interval, punctuating and sustaining the majority view.

Mediaphemes are essentially hegemonic and are constricted and narrow in the narrative templates that they support. Celebrities often attempt to reinvent their mediapheme and 'set the record straight' about their lives through autobiography. In this way they can present their 'true' selves for public scrutiny; to embrace or deny their mediapheme. There was some expectation by reviewers of *Renegade* that Smith would seize the opportunity of autobiography to publicly claim his place in the cultural pantheon. For example, D.J. Taylor bemoaned the book's failure to capture Smith as a figure of 'dazzling sociological import'. The book is a 'brain-dump', a mere 'rock memoir' rather than a 'proper autobiography'. Smith, he complains, has thrown away an opportunity to give a 'precise cultural underpinning' to the 'whole question of articulate, alienated teenage boys abandoned by the educational system who opt to forge some kind of career in music (Lydon, Weller, Morrissey et al)' (Taylor 2008, 35). Taylor believes the highest aspiration of such a book is to establish a transparent critical context, with discernible origins and determinations. It is an approach that would chastise Smith for failing to account for, and narrate, himself in a lucid and timely fashion. It advocates a form of biography which perpetuates what Deleuze and Guattari identify as an arborescent logic, fixated on essentialized identities taking clear historically accountable paths through their contexts and times.[2] According to the principles of rhizomatic thought, however, identity is a transformative multiplicity, comprising nothing other than the 'lines' with which it connects and is connected to the heterogeneous elements of its world.

Renegade does not reveal a great deal about Smith's personal life; in fact Smith states 'I think you've got to make a stand against this attitude that everybody's life is common knowledge: when it isn't' (Smith 2008a, 53). It is in many senses an anti-autobiography, which refuses to yield to the conventions of the form. Instead of answering questions the book obfuscates the revelatory nature of autobiography in both the method of its production and its content. Why did Smith – a writer – elect to have his memoirs ghosted? In effect, the sense that they emerge from what is essentially a series of chats to a more or less anonymous fellow in a pub distances the book from a dominant authorial point of view. The structure of the book is not a conventional chronological account of a life, but a series of interviews in which Smith spins yarns about his background, his family and his band, interspersed with chapters called 'Voices' which read like nonsensical streams of consciousness or 'Word salads'(Smith 2008a, 127). These are multivocal segments that appear almost like the literary equivalent of a cubist painting, simultaneously giving different facets and viewpoints while skipping unsignalled between literal description and metaphor. The origin of these sections is unclear, and throughout the book there is no indication of how the ghosting process impacts on the material. We don't know if we are reading verbatim transcriptions from interviews, or whether these have been authored by Austin Collings.

---

[2]   According to Deleuze and Guattari, the dominant logic of the West can be conceived as arborescent, or tree-like, predisposing us to privilege origin and causality in a linear and hierarchical manner, akin to the tree's origin in the seed and branching from a central trunk. In contrast, the rhizome, an acentred root system growing horizontally by means of sending out shoots from multiple nodes, suggests a non-linear, non-hierarchical model for thought (see Deleuze and Guattari 1988, 3–28).

The book in no way seeks to break down the mythologies of Smith but adds layers to them. It neither rejects nor embraces the mediapheme. This is not a consistent and explanatory record of a life which presents an 'authentic' and coherent first person account. The authenticity is deliberately undermined by the intervention of a ghost writer, the inclusion of pub style rants that imply a less reliable state of consciousness and the constant spinning of yarns to illustrate points. Note Smith's admiration for Orson Welles who, he claims, 'saw life as a story' (Smith 2008a, 240): 'He was in another zone. Telling stories on stories until in the end he himself is a story ... it's like heightened awareness, similar to when you don't eat for a few days or you've been on a bit of a bender – you see things differently. And not always in an obvious way' (Smith 2008a, 241). *Renegade*'s 'lives and tales' (multiple and equivalent) fall in with his regard for Wellesian perspectivalism which respects contingency and becoming by *quoting* identity, generating stories *about* story-creation, and about characters fabulating new and experimental identities for themselves (see Sutton and Martin-Jones, 2008, 55–6). Welles, in such films as *Citizen Kane* and *F for Fake*, can be seen as refusing an authoritarian, definitive approach to narrative identity which locks it down, pre-empting further elaboration. His more modernist approach suggests we can never definitively have done with narrative identity, that it is always potentially open to new directions and becomings from new points of view. Here we anticipate one of the key characteristics of minor aesthetic practice, which is that 'everything in it is political' (Deleuze and Guattari 1986, 17). It is open and engaged; it connects up aspects of life in the search for escape routes, ways out of intolerable situations. As Smith puts it in reflecting upon his work: 'I wanted to write *out* of the song ... I wanted to explore, to put a twist on the normal. People think of themselves too much as one person – they don't know what to do with the other people that enter their heads' (Smith 2008a, 84).

Universal Solvent

> We think too much in terms of history, whether personal or universal. Becomings belong to geography, they are orientations, directions, entries and exits. (Deleuze and Parnet 2006, 2)

Much of what can be described as carnivalesque can be detected in punk. Punk shared the carnival's affinity for the marginal and the oppressed. It foregrounded the excessive corporeality of grotesque bodies and the suspension of boundaries between inside and outside: 'In the protean and spectacular punk body, the apparently impervious façade of the classical or disciplined consumer body which underpins ideals of unity, control and autonomy are countered by a fragmented *bricolage* aesthetic and a carnivalesque double movement of penetration and profusion' (P. Jones 2002). Punk foregrounded a technique of the cut-up and the crudely stitched together. The most astute participants recognized that there was no transcendental outside, no pre-existing authentic real which punk could unleash. Punk's resistance was immanent, possible only by virtue of the existence of what the mainstream had already othered. As Sara Thornton (1995) has shown, resistant subcultures don't exist prior to their capture within the mediascape, only then to be represented. There is no untrammelled space of the subcultural real before or behind the mediascape.

Although Smith disavows the influence of punk, citing its proclivity for sloganeering and instant generalizations (Smith 2008a, 44), the carnivalesque prole aesthetic informing it is a key inspiration for the minor practice and politics of The Fall. The lesson to take forward here is that transgression must be from within, involving creative recombination of torn away elements which constitute openings. Becoming minor, for Deleuze and Guattari, is about loosening the elements of a relatively settled major language or territory against itself, to render it fluid and stir it into motion, to tear it away from its programmed sense or trajectory. It is conceived as a 'stuttering' or 'stammering', speaking one's language as if it was foreign, as if we were strangers (Deleuze and Guattari 1986, 26). It is processual – on the one hand a break with what exists, but on the other, a putting to work of the given – it stands both 'inside and outside the major, in the world but not quite of it' (O'Sullivan 2006, 76).

If, for Deleuze and Guattari, the world is conceived as 'machinic assemblage', Smith, (post-)punk *bricoleur* as minor artist, unplugs himself from the machinery and re-plugs, re-maps the assemblage with ripped-out components from the debris. Art must bear witness to the event, which is the untimely, the irruption of the new, a becoming which is not part of history. In the words of Castoriadis: 'true time, the time of otherness-alteration is a time of bursting, emerging, creating. The *present*, the *nun* is here explosion, split, rupture – the rupture of what is as such. This present exists as originating, as immanent transcendence, as source, as the surging forth of ontological genesis' (1987, 201). The role of minor artists is to estrange us experimentally from the present, to put its insertion into a known trajectory into question, opening up a cartography of the 'not yet', a time that is not pre-organized and controlled. Their work is untimely because it refuses a 'representative response' to our context (Colebrook 2002, 62). It throws out hooks to snag in new places, embracing the affect of time as becoming, a time in which one seizes one's own singular story. An identity is created as a rhizome is created with the world with the connections to be found.

In Episode 23 of the first TV season of *Batman* (1966), entitled 'The Ring of Wax', the Riddler plans to hold the USA to ransom with his Universal Wax Solvent, capable of dissolving anything, which he smuggles into the country concealed within a waxwork statue of Batman. The idea of such a substance informs The Fall's most recent album at the time of writing, *Imperial Wax Solvent* (2008). The lyrics of the song 'Exploding Chimney', specifically, convey the pronouncement of an irredeemable Pied Piper-type figure that he is blowing his stack: 'Got rat poison in my workshop.../Listen to me now, kids/A Universal Wax Solvent/Is exploding'. The album as a whole could be said to deal with boundaries and their untimely carnivalesque dissolution, with the breakdown of identity, and the breakdown of language. It is diagnostic and exploratory, imagining anew a smeared present.

This England is a hideous media fun park, offspring of a 'lad's mag' and BBC culture show. Moreover, it is a spatio-temporal scramble. Has the protagonist of 'Strangetown' dwelt there for two years, 23 years or two weeks? It's like the fairy tale temporal distortion of the intertitles in Buñuel and Dali's *Un Chien Andalou*. Useless codes, place names and labels abound ('Bury zero seven seven/Fifty-eight/Driver B'). Characters are unstable, threatening to blur into their surroundings ('Mr J. Archer as he separated everywhere'). The album seems to take age as its theme, the carnival of the generations from the perspective, in part, of the now middle-aged Smith. Characters are neglected children ('Latch Key Kid'), kids 'watching vids' ('I've Been Duped'), and infantilized adults ('Wolf Kidult Man'). *Imperial Wax Solvent* rolls out at street level, among the kids, a fabulatory flaneurism around the streets of strange towns, or familiar towns rendered labyrinthine (as in '50 Year Old Man': 'Go down Manchester Town/Can't navigate it'). This is not detached modernist flaneurism, however, but rather the overwhelming affect of the 'schizo's stroll', interpenetrated by the world, which Deleuze and Guattari have in mind in the opening pages of *Anti-Oedipus* (2004; and see O'Sullivan 2006, 139). *Imperial Wax Solvent* is a dissolute singer's fantasy of dissolving England, for the sake, perhaps, of a new youth to come. Like Walter Benjamin's 'destructive character' (1985), Smith, rejuvenated by the path-clearing effects of his solvent, 'I got a three foot rock hard on/But I'm too busy to use it/I'm a fifty year old man.../And I like it', pursues no vision other than that of an empty space: 'Someone is sure to be found who needs this space without it being filled' (Benjamin 1985, 158).

None of this is simply the point of view of Mark E. Smith. Fragments of speech, psychotic notions, noises, colours, speeds, images and events do not have the coherent organization of a fully rounded psychology and biographically situated character. Smith says his talent is for putting himself in other people's shoes. He puts them on and takes 'flight on a line of nonsense' (Deleuze and Guattari 1986, 21). The solvent – his writing – eats into his own subjectivity and persona. As Polan comments, 'Deleuze and Guattari don't see writing as a solution to the interiorised problems of an individual psychology. Rather, writing stands against psychology, against interiority, by giving an author a possibility of becoming more than his or her nominal self, of trading the insistent solidity of the family tree for the whole field of desire and history' (1986, xxiii). Deleuze has celebrated writing which adopts the character of 'a schizoid flow, drawing in all sorts of things', advising that 'it's not a matter of escaping "personally" from oneself, but of allowing something to escape, like bursting a pipe or a boil. Opening up flows beneath the social codes that seek to channel and block them' (Deleuze 1995, 19).

Smith's lyrics should not be approached as a matter of meaning or representation. As he has said: 'I hate the way other people imagine their lyrics to be utterly complex. Who's interested? Who can be bothered working it out? It's the same with Lennon – all those concealed meanings. I always thought he was the biggest spaz of all!' (Wilde 1984, 26–7). There is no call to read behind or decode these words – nothing is concealed, there are only fragments set out on a surface, all there to see (Colebrook 2002, 139). In fact, the words are *already* the world torn away from its moorings. Hence the sentences are short, clipped, ripped from the fabric of experience. Stories are told, but plot information is missing. They show the world in its partiality, a world dissolving in its unleashed, interrupted and scrambled flows. It is the world that fragments around us and refuses to fix. The universal solvent is already at large in the world. This is not metaphor – we are not called to discover what things mean but rather to apprehend *how things work*, or how things melt, fuse and defuse. As Colebrook says, in analysing a poem by Sylvia Plath, we are not simply dealing with 'a speaker who is judging some outside world. The poem collects objects, proper names, using words as though they were found objects rather than expressions' (Colebrook 2002, 138). Smith's lyrics tap into the schizoid processes of the world, the freed up desire of the world of late capitalist deterritorialization. It is the precise nature of this 'freeing-up' that is problematic. The rhizome has the potential to send out new shoots at any node, new lines of flight, which open up and destabilize – that is, 'deterritorialize' – the 'territory' the root system has already established. Capitalism constitutes a constant, all-pervasive deterritorialization which, at the limit, threatens to destabilize everything and everyone, to plunge us into schizophrenia: 'We're saying there's a schizoid process, of decoding and deterritorializing, which only revolutionary activity can stop turning into the production of schizophrenia' (Deleuze 1995, 23–4).

We could join Lyotard in pointing out the strange collusion between capitalism and avant-garde art. Capitalism constitutes a sublime destructive force which destabilizes reality and dissolves the subject into the 'calculation of profitability' and the instantaneity that comes with increasing informationalization, all of which 'encourages among artists a mistrust of established rules and a willingness to experiment with means of expression, with styles, with ever-new materials' (Lyotard 1989, 209). With information, '"nothing happens" by definition' and this is easily confused with the 'Is it happening?' of the avant-garde sublime. However, capitalism cynically defuses the intensity of the sublime through mere innovation, which 'means to behave as though lots of things happened, and to make them happen' (Lyotard 1989, 210): 'Through innovation, the will affirms its hegemony over time. It thus conforms to the metaphysics of capitalism, which is a technology of time. The innovation "works". The question mark of the "Is it happening?" stops' (Lyotard 1989, 211). Informationalization and innovation must not be permitted to dissolve the 'enigma of the "Is it happening?"' Art's ethical role is to continue to undo, or deterritorialize, the 'presumption of the mind with respect to time' (Lyotard 1989, 210–11). Out of the melted ruins of the 'Alton Towers' which is our England, *Imperial Wax Solvent* invokes true time: 'The town is anti-life/Time to change back/Time to change back/Turn the radio off' ('Can Can Summer').

The Present Day Proletariat Refuses to Knuckle Under

Imperial Wax Solvent and Mark E. Smith's writing generally, intimates and comprises a blueprint for a new militancy, some new proletarian refusal to 'knuckle under'. This brings us to a further determining characteristic of Deleuze and Guattari's conception of minoritarian culture, which is that 'in it everything takes on a collective value' (Deleuze and Guattari 1986, 17). Minor artists 'express another possible community' and forge 'the means for another consciousness and another sensibility' (Deleuze and Guattari 1986, 17). The very name of Smith's group – The Fall – is indicative of a futural and prophetic (again, untimely) function of the music, its ability to call forth connections between people, to summon an 'audience' into being. The band name evokes the biblical 'Original Sin' of disobedience, and the fall of a humanity severed from a divine model. Hardt and Negri (2005) use the concept of the 'multitude' to name this mutant community-to-come, conceiving the proletariat in terms of a gathering of singularities outside of any established political model or agenda. As Simon O'Sullivan puts it:

> If there is an affirmation of a new community, it is precisely of the always already excluded, a bastard community of the sick and the frail, a mutant community always in progress, always open to any and everyone. If there is a gathering of the new people, then what they will have in common is their stuttering and stammering, their failure (intentional or otherwise) to 'live up' to the models offered (in fact forced upon them) by the major. (2006, 78)

The fabulations of minor writers and artists break with dominant signification to follow lines of flight: 'We might say that it is the traitor who follows his or her line of flight, makes his or her own myths, and produces his or her own reality' (O'Sullivan 2006, 150). As the old society dissolves, 'we need a new Rabelais' to keep the way open for 'alternative networks of affection and social organization' (Hardt and Negri 2005, 194, 193). We need the examples of those who, like Smith, treacherously outpace the presumptions of their deterrent mediaphemes: 'I'm a fifty year old man/What you gonna do about it?'

Bibliography

'100 Rarest Records: The Ultimate UK Collectables' (2004), *Record Collector* 304, 69–91.

Adorno, T.W. (1992), *Quasi una Fantasia: Essays on Modern Music*, trans. Rodney Livingstone (London and New York: Verso).

Ahmed, S. (2000), *Strange Encounters: Embodied Others in Post-Coloniality* (London: Routledge).

Andreotti, L. and Costa, X. (eds) (1996), *Theory of the Dérive and Other Situationist Writings on the City* (Barcelona: Museu d'Art Contemporanai de Barcelona).

APB (1988), Border Television [YouTube video clip; 6 September 2006: 00:06:41].

Armitage, S. (2008), *Gig: The Life and Times of a Rock-star Fantasist* (London: Viking).

Atton, C. (2001a), '"Living in the Past"? Value Discourses in Progressive Rock Fanzines', *Popular Music* 20 (1), 29–46.

Atton, C. (2001b), 'The Mundane and its Reproduction in Alternative Media', *Journal of Mundane Behavior* 2 (1), February, available at http://www.mundanebehavior.org/index.htm

Atton, C. (2002), *Alternative Media* (London: Sage).

Atton, C. (2003), 'Fanzines', in J. Shepherd et al. (eds) *The Continuum Encyclopedia of Popular Music of the World*, vol. 1: *Media, Industry and Society* (London: Continuum), pp. 226–8.

Atton, C. (2006a), 'Sociologie de la Presse Musicale Alternative en Grande Bretagne', *Copyright Volume! Autour des Musiques Populaires* 5(1), 7–25.

Atton, C. (2006b), 'Football Fanzines as Local News', in B. Franklin (ed.) *Local Journalism and Local Media: Making the Local News* (London: Routledge), pp. 280–89.

Auslander, P. (2006), *Performing Glam Rock: Gender & Theatricality in Popular Music* (Michigan: University of Michigan).

Auster, P. (1988), *The New York Trilogy* (London: Faber and Faber).

Badiou, A. (2001), *Ethics*, trans. P. Hallward (London: Verso).

Bailey, D. (1992) *Improvisation: Its Nature and Practice in Music*, 2nd edn (New York: Da Capo Press).

Bakhtin, M. ([1965] 1984), *Rabelais and his World*, trans. H. Iswolsky (Bloomington and Indianopolis: Indiana University Press).

Bakhtin, M. ([1973] 1990), *The Dialogical Imagination: Four Essays by M.M. Bakhtin*, ed. M. Holquist, trans. C. Emerson and Michael Holquist (Austin: University of Texas Press).

Barfe, L. (2004), *Where Have all the Good Times Gone: The Rise and Fall of the Record Industry* (London: Atlantic Books).

Barker, H. and Taylor, Y. (2007), *Faking It: The Quest for Authenticity in Popular Music* (London: Faber and Faber).

Barnard, S. (1989), *On the Radio: Music Radio in Britain* (Milton Keynes and Philadelphia: Open University Press).

Barnes, M. (2000) *Captain Beefheart* (London: Omnibus Press).

Barthes, R. (1990), *S/Z*, trans. Richard Miller (Oxford: Basil Blackwell).

Barthes, R. (1991), *The Grain of the Voice: Interviews 1962–1980*, trans. Linda Coverdale (Berkley and Los Angeles: University of California Press).

Baty, S.P. (1995), *American Monroe: The Making of a Body Politic* (Berkeley: University of California Press).

Baudrillard, J. (1983), 'The Ecstasy of Communication', in H. Foster (ed.), *The Anti-Aesthetic: Essays on Postmodern Culture* (Port Townsend: Washington Bay Press), pp. 126–35.

Bauman, Z. (1991) *Modernity and Ambivalence* (Cambridge: Polity).

Bauman, Z. (1997) 'The Making and Unmaking of Strangers', in P. Werbner and T. Modood (eds), *Debating Cultural Hybridity* (London: Zed Books), pp. 46–57.

Bell, D. and Hollows, J. (eds) (2005), *Ordinary Lifestyles: Popular Media, Consumption and Taste* (Maidenhead: Open University Press).

Bell, M. (1977), 'Collect These Pages', *New Musical Express*, 3 September, pp. 23, 26.

Benjamin, A. (ed.) (1989), *The Lyotard Reader* (Oxford: Blackwell).

Benjamin, W. (1985), 'The Destructive Character', in *One Way Street and other Writings*, trans. E. Jephcott and K. Shorter (London: Verso), pp. 157–9.

Blanchot, M. (1997), *Friendship*, trans. E. Rottenberg (Stanford, Calif.: Stanford University Press).

Blincoe, N. (2008), 'Mark E Smith: Wonder and Frightening', *Daily Telegraph*, 26 April.

Bogue, R. (2005), 'The Minor', in C.J. Stivale (ed.), *Gilles Deleuze: Key Concepts* (Chesham: Acumen), pp. 110–20.

Booth, S. (1991), *Rythm Oil* (London: Vintage).

Bourdieu, P. ([1979] 1984), *Distinction: A Social Critique of the Judgment of Taste*, trans. R. Nice (London: Routledge).

Boyd-Barrett, O. and Braham, P. (eds) (1990), *Media, Knowledge and Power* (London: Routledge).

Bracewell, M. (1997), *England is Mine* (London: Flamingo).

Bradley, L. (2000), *Bass Culture: When Reggae was King* (London: Viking).

Brown, J. and O'Hagan, S. (1989), 'The Three Horsemen of the Apocalypse', *NME*, 25 February, available at http://www.visi.com/fall/gigography/89feb25.html

Buchler, P. and Lingwood, J. (eds) (1990), *Jiří Kolář: The End of Words* (London: ICA).

Burchill, J. and Parsons, T. (1978), *The Boy Looked at Johnny – the Obituary of Rock'n'Roll* (London: Pluto).

Burroughs, W.S. (1968) 'The Invisible Generation', in *The Ticket That Exploded* (New York: Grove Press), pp. 205–17.

Cage, J. (1968) *Silence* (London: Marion Boyars).

Camus, A. (1957), *The Fall*, trans. J. O'Brien (Harmondsworth: Penguin).

Cardew, C. (1971,) 'Towards an Ethic of Improvisation', in *Treatise Handbook* (London, Frankfurt and New York: Edition Peters), pp. xvii–xxi.

Carlyle, T. ([1832] 2000), *Sartor Resartus: The Life and Opinions of Herr Teufelsdröckh in Three Books* (Berkeley: University of California Press).

Castoriadis, C. (1987), *The Imaginary Institution of Society*, trans. K. Blamey (Cambridge: Polity Press).

Champion, S. (1990), *And God Created Manchester* (Manchester: Wordsmith).

Chapman, R. (1992), *Selling the Sixties: The Pirates and Popular Music Radio* (London and New York: Routledge).

Chion, M. (1994), *Audio-Vision: Sound on Screen*, trans. and ed. Claudia Gorbman (New York: Columbia University Press).

Chtcheglov, I. (1996), 'Formulary for a New Urbanism', trans. K. Knabb, in L. Andreotti and X. Costa (eds), *Theory of the Dérive and Other Situationist Writings on the City* (Barcelona: Museu d'Art Contemporanai de Barcelona), pp. 14–17.

Clegg, R. (2008), 'Mark E. Smith: We're not a Manchester Band', *Manchester Evening News* [website], (updated 2 May 2008).

Colebrook, C. (2002), *Gilles Deleuze* (London: Routledge).

Collins, A. (1990), 'Funky, Cold, Modernah', *NME*, 25 January, pp. 24–6.

Coppola, Francis Ford (dir.) (1974), *The Conversation* (Paramount).

Coverley, M. (2006), *Psychogeography* (Harpenden: Pocket Essentials).

Crisell, A. (1986), *Understanding Radio* (London and New York: Methuen).

Crystal, D. (1992), *The Cambridge Encyclopedia of Language* (Cambridge: Cambridge University Press).

Curtis, D. (1995) *Touching From a Distance: Ian Curtis and Joy Division* (London: Faber and Faber).

Debord, G. (1996), 'Introduction to a Critique of Urban Geography', trans. K. Knabb, in L. Andreotti and X. Costa (eds). *Theory of the Dérive and Other Situationist Writings on the City* (Barcelona: Museu d'Art Contemporanai de Barcelona), pp. 18–21.

Debord, G. (2003), *Complete Cinematic Works*, trans. K. Knabb (Oakland/Edinburgh: AK Press).

Debord, G. (2004), *Panegyric*, trans. A. Brook and J. McHale (London: Verso).

Deleuze, G. (1995), *Negotiations*, trans. M. Joughin (New York: Columbia University Press).

Deleuze, G. and Guattari, F. (1986), *Kafka: Toward a Minor Literature*, trans. D. Polan (Minneapolis: University of Minnesota Press).

Deleuze, G. and Guattari, F. (1988), *A Thousand Plateaus*, trans. B. Massumi (London: Athlone Press).

Deleuze, G. and Guattari, F. (2004), *Anti-Oedipus*, trans. R. Hurley, M. Seem and H. Lane (London: Continuum).

Deleuze, G. and Parnet, C. (2006), *Dialogues II*, trans. H. Tomlinson, B. Habberjam and E.R. Albert (London: Continuum).

Derrida, J. (1976), *Of Grammatology*, trans. G.C. Spivak (Baltimore and London: Johns Hopkins University Press).

Derrida, J. (1997), *The Politics of Friendship*, trans. G. Collins (London: Verso).

Devoy, A. (1989), 'Art for Art's Sake', *Q* 1 (31), April, 8–11.

Dickinson, R. (1997), *Imprinting the Sticks: The Alternative Press outside London* (Aldershot: Arena).

Disraeli, B. ([1848] 1948), *Coningsby, or the New Generation* (London: London Edition).

Duncombe, S. (1997), *Notes from Underground: Zines and the Politics of Alternative Culture* (London: Verso).

Easlea, D. (2005), 'Sleeve notes' for CD boxset, *The Fall: The Complete Peel Sessions, 1978–2004* (Sanctuary Records: CMXBX982).

Edge, B. (1989), *Paintwork: A Portrait of The Fall* (London: Omnibus Press).

Eliot, T.S. (1969), *The Complete Poems and Plays of T. S. Eliot* (London: Faber and Faber).

The Fall (1983), *Perverted by Language Bis*, VHS (Ikon: IKON 008).

The Fall: The Wonderful and Frightening World of Mark E. Smith (2005), BBC 4, first broadcast on 21 January 2005.

The Fall Lyrics Parade, *The Fall Online*, at http://fall.byethost13.com/lyrics.html

The Fall Online (formerly The Unofficial Fall Website and formerly The Official Fall Website), at www.visi.com/fall/index.html

Fisher, M. (2008a), 'Review of *Renegade: The Lives and Tales of Mark E Smith*', *The Wire: Adventures in Modern Music*, 293: 70.

Fisher, M. (2008b), 'The Place I Made the Purchase No Longer Exists', k-punk, available at http://k-punk.abstractdynamics.org/archives/010367.html (accessed 17/09/08).

Ford, S. (2002), 'Primal Scenes', *The Wire*, 219, May, 28–33.

Ford, S. (2003), *Hip Priest: The Story of Mark E. Smith and The Fall* (London: Quartet Books).

Ford, S. (2005), *The Situationist International: A User's Guide* (London: Black Dog Publishing).

Foucault, M. (1972), *The Archaeology of Knowledge and the Discourse on Language*, trans. A.M. Sheridan (New York: Pantheon).

Foucault, M. (2004), *Madness and Civilisation* (London: Routledge).

Franklin, B. (ed.) (2006), *Local Journalism and Local Media: Making the Local News* (London: Routledge).

Freud, S. ([1919] 1990), 'The Uncanny', trans. David McLintock, *Penguin Freud Library*, 14 (London: Penguin).

Frith, S. (1988), *Music For Pleasure: Essays in the Sociology of Pop* (Oxford: Polity Press).

Frith, S. (1996), *Performing Rites: Evaluating Popular Music* (Oxford: Oxford University Press).

Frith, S. (2002), 'Fragments of a Sociology of Rock Criticism', in S. Jones (ed.), *Pop Music and the Press* (Philadelphia: Temple University Press), pp. 235–46.

Frith, S. (2007), *Taking Popular Music Seriously: Selected Essays* (Aldershot: Ashgate).

Garner, K. (1993), *In Session Tonight: The Complete Radio 1 Recordings* (London: BBC Books).

Garner. K. (2007), *The Peel Sessions: A Story of Teenage Dreams and One Man's Love of New Music* (London: BBC Books).

Genette, G. (1997), *Paratexts: Thresholds of Interpretation*, trans. J. Lewin (Cambridge: Cambridge University Press).

Gill, A. (1981), 'The Wit and Wisdom of Mark Smith', *NME*, 10 January, available at http://www.visi.com/fall/news/pics/81jan10_nme/81jan10_nme-gill.html

Gramsci, A. ([1929–35] 1971), 'Americanism and Fordism', *Selections from the Prison Notebooks*, ed. G.N. Smith (London: Lawrence and Wishart), pp. 277–318.

Gudmundsson, G., Lindberg, U., Michelsen, M. and Weisethaunet, H. (2002), 'Brit Crit: Turning Points in British Rock Criticism, 1960–1990', in S. Jones (ed.), *Pop Music and the Press* (Philadelphia: Temple University Press), pp. 41–64.

Guignon, C. (2004), *On Being Authentic* (London and New York: Routledge).

Hall, S., Clarke, J., Jefferson, T. and Roberts, B. (eds) (1976), *Resistance Through Rituals* (London: Hutchinson).

Hardt, M. and Negri, A. (2005), *Multitude* (London: Penguin).

Harris, J. (2004), *Britpop! Cool Britannia and the Spectacular Demise of English Rock* (Cambridge, Mass.: Da Capo Press) (published in the UK as *The Last Party: Britpop, Blair and the Demise of English Rock*, London: Fourth Estate, 2004).

Hartley, J. (2000), 'Communicative Democracy in a Redactional Society: The Future of Journalism Studies', *Journalism: Theory, Practice and Criticism* 1 (1), 39–48.

Hartley, J. (2004), 'The "Value Chain of Meaning" and the New Economy', *International Journal of Cultural Studies* 7 (1), 129–41.

Haslam, D. (2003), 'The History of the Haçienda', *Pride of Manchester,* June, available at http://www.prideofmanchester.com/music/hacienda.htm

Heatley, M. (2005), *John Peel: A Life in Music* (London: Michael O'Mara).

Hebdige, D. (1979), *Subculture: The Meaning of Style* (London: Methuen).

Hebdige, D. (1987), *Cut 'n' Mix: Culture, Identity and Caribbean Music* (London: Comedia).

Hendy, D. (2000), *Radio in the Global Age* (Cambridge: Polity Press).

Hennion, A. (2001), 'Music Lovers: Taste as Performance', *Theory, Culture and Society* 18 (5), 1–22.

Herrington, T. (1996), 'Mancunian Candidate', *The Wire* 151, 26–31, available at http://www.pipeline.com/~biv/FallNet/articles/wire_interview.html.

Herrington, T. (1999), 'The Outsider: Mark E. Smith', *The Wire* 183, 32–8.

Hetherington, K. (2007), 'Manchester's URBIS', *Cultural Studies* 21 (4–5), September, 630–49.

Heylin, C. (2007), *Babylon's Burning: From Punk to Grunge* (London: Viking).

HMSO (1995), *Manchester, Fifty Years of Change: Post-War Planning in Manchester* (London: Her Majesty's Stationery Office).

Irwin, C. (1981), 'The Decline and Fall in Iceland', *Melody Maker*, 26 September.

James, M.R. (2005), *Count Magnus and Other Ghost Stories: The Complete Ghost Stories of M.R. James,* vol. 1 (Harmondsworth: Penguin).

Jarry, A. ([1896] 2003) *Ubu Roi*, trans. Beverly Keith and Gershon Legman (Mineola, NY: Dover).

Jary, D., Horne, J. and Bucke, T. (1991), 'Football "Fanzines" and Football Culture: A Case of Successful "Cultural Contestation"', *Sociological Review* 39 (3), 581–97.

Jenkins, H. (1992), *Textual Poachers* (New York and London: Routledge).

Johnson, F. (2004) 'U2, Mythology, and Mass-mediated Survival', *Popular Music and Society* 27 (1), 79–99.

Jones, G. (2006), 'Collector's Corner: Vinyl Could Make You Record Returns', *The Independent*, 22 April 2006, available at http://www.independent.co.uk/

Jones, P. (2002), 'Anarchy in the UK: '70s British Punk as Bakhtinian Carnival', *Studies in Popular Culture* 24 (3), available at http://pcasacas.org/SPC/spcissues/24.3/Jones.htm (accessed 17/09/08).

Jones, S. (ed.) (2002), *Pop Music and the Press* (Philadelphia: Temple University Press).

Joshi, S.T. (2005), Introduction to M.R. James, *Count Magnus* (Harmondsworth: Penguin).

Kent, N. (1985), 'Dreamer in the Real World', *The Face,* May.

Kessler, T. (1993), 'Mark E. Smith: Heroes & Villains', NME, 11 December.

Khatib, A. (1996), 'Attempt at a Psychogeographical Description of Les Halles', trans. P. Hammond, in L. Andreotti and X. Costa (eds), *Theory of the Dérive and Other Situationist Writings on the City* (Barcelona: Museu d'Art Contemporanai de Barcelona).

Langridge, D. (1970), *Your Jazz Collection* (London: Clive Bingley).

Lester, P. (1990), 'Prole Art Threat', *Melody Maker,* 1 September, 42–3.

Lewis, W. (ed.) ([1914] 2009), *Blast 1* (London: Thames and Hudson).

Lindberg, U., Gudmundsson, G., Michelsen, M. and Weisethaunet, H. (2005), *Rock Criticism from the Beginning: Amusers, Bruisers, and Cool-headed Cruisers* (New York: Peter Lang).

Long, P. (2006), 'The Primary Code: The Meanings of John Peel, Radio and Popular Music', *Radio Journal – International Studies in Broadcast and Audio Media* 4 (1/3), 25–48.

Lovecraft, H.P. (1964), 'Cool Air' (1928), in *The Lurking Fear and Other Stories* (London: Panther Books).

Lovecraft, H.P. (1985), *Omnibus 2: Dagon and Other Macabre Tales* (London: Harper Collins).

Lovecraft, H.P. (1999), *The Call of Cthulhu and Other Weird Stories* (Harmondsworth: Penguin).

Lowenstein, O. (1978), 'A New Career in a New Town', *NME*, 18 November, p. 43.

Lowry, M. ([1947] 1967), *Under the Volcano* (London: Jonathan Cape).

Lowry, M. (1968), *Lunar Caustic* (London: Jonathan Cape) (first published *Paris Review* 29, 1963).

Lowry, M. (1985a), 'Letter to James Stern (May, 1940)', in H. Breit and M. Bonner Lowry (eds), *Selected Letters of Malcolm Lowry* (Harmondsworth: Penguin), pp. 27–31.

Lowry, M. (1985b), 'Letter to Jonathan Cape (January, 1946)', in H. Breit and M. Bonner Lowry (eds), *Selected Letters of Malcolm Lowry* (Harmondsworth: Penguin), pp. 57–88.

Lyotard, J.-F. (1989), 'The Sublime and the Avant-Gard', trans. L. Liebmann, in A. Benjamin (ed.), *The Lyotard Reader* (Oxford: Blackwell), pp. 196–211.

McCullough, D. (1978), 'The Last Great Band Not in Captivity', *Sounds*, 4 November, 14–15.

MacDonald, I. ([1994] 1997), *Revolution in the Head: The Beatles' Records and the Sixties*, revised edn (London: Pimlico).

Machen, A. (1918), *War and the Christian Faith* (London: Skeffington and Son).

Machen, A. (1946a), 'The Cosy Room' (1929), in *Holy Terrors* (Harmondsworth: Penguin).

Machen, A. (1946b), 'The Happy Children' (1925), in *Holy Terrors* (Harmondsworth: Penguin).

McKay, G. (1996), *Senseless Acts of Beauty: Cultures of Resistance Since the Sixties* (London: Verso).

McLuhan, M. (2002), *The Mechanical Bride* (Berkeley, Calif.: Gingko Press).

Major, M. 'The Fall Press Kit', at http://www.visi.com/fall/presskit.html

Mann, T. (1968), Doctor Faustus, trans. H.T. Lowe-Porter (Harmondsworth: Penguin).

Markson, D. (1978), *Malcolm Lowry's Volcano: Myth, Symbol, Meaning* (New York: Times Books).

Marvin, J.N. (1981), 'Everything We Do Has an Unexpected Impact', unpublished interview [July], available at http://www.jneomarvin.com/words/thefall1.htm (accessed 1/5/2008).

Marwick, A. (1982), *British Society Since 1945* (London: Allen Lane).

Marx, K. (1946), *Capital: A Critical Analysis of Capitalist Production*, trans. Ben Fowkes (London: Allen and Unwin).

Middles, M. (2002), *From Joy Division to New Order: The True Story of Anthony H. Wilson and Factory Records* (London: Virgin).

Middles, M. and Reade, L. (2007) *Torn Apart: The Life of Ian Curtis* (London: Omnibus).

Middles, M. and Smith, M.E. (2003), *The Fall* (London: Omnibus).

Middleton, R. (2006), 'In the Groove or Blowing Your Mind? The Pleasures of Musical Repetition', in Andy Bennett et al. (eds), *The Popular Music Studies Reader* (London and New York: Routledge), pp. 15–20.

Moorcock, M. (1973), *The Final Programme* (Frogmore, St Albans: Mayflower Books).

Morley, P. (1978), 'These are the Mancunian Mancunians', *NME,* 1 September, p. 25.

Morley, P. (2008), *Joy Division: Piece By Piece* (London: Plexus).

Neal, C. (1987), *Tape Delay* (Harrow: SAF).

Negus, K. (1996), *Popular Music in Theory: An Introduction* (Cambridge: Polity Press).

Nolan, D. (2006), *I Swear I Was There: The Gig that Changed the World* (Church Stretton, Shropshire: Independent Music Press).

Nolan, D. (2007) *Bernard Sumner: Confusion: Joy Division, Electronic and New Order versus the World* (Church Stretton, Shropshire: IMP).

Noys, B. (2005), 'Lovecraft the Sinthome' (unpublished paper given at the Gothic Remains: Symptoms of the Modern conference, hosted by The Centre For Modernist Studies at Sussex University, 3 December).

O'Hagan, S. (2005), 'He's still the Fall Guy', *Observer Review*, 16 January, p. 6.

O'Hagan, S. (2007), 'Wear Your Heart on Your Sleeves', *The Observer,* 28 January, 8–9.

O'Sullivan, S. (2006), *Art Encounters Deleuze and Guattari: Thought Beyond Representation* (Basingstoke: Palgrave Macmillan).

Ouspensky, P.D. (1981), *Tertium Organum: The Third Cannon of Thought/A Key to the Enigmas of the World*, trans. N. Bessaraboff and C. Bragdon (London: Routledge).

Papaelias, A. (2004), 'Personal/Standard: Cultural Implications of Handwriting and Handwriting Fonts', available at http://www.typetalkfonts.com (accessed 5/5/2008).

Parrinder, P. (1984), *James Joyce* (Cambridge: Cambridge University Press).

Peart, A. (1990), 'Badmouth Strikes Again', *Sounds*, 8 December.

Peel, J. and Ravenscroft, S. (2005), *Margrave of the Marshes* (London: Bantam).

Penman, I. (1980), 'The Fall: All Fall Down', *NME,* 5 January, available at http://www.rocksbackpages.com

Polan, D. (1986), 'Translator's Introduction', in G. Deleuze and F. Guattari (1986), *Kafka: Toward a Minor Literature*, trans. D. Polan (Minneapolis: University of Minnesota Press), pp. xxii–xxix.

Poyner, R. (1999), 'Typographica', *Eye: the International Review of Graphic Design* 31 (8), 64–73.

Radway, J. ([1984] 1991), *Reading the Romance: Women, Patriarchy, and Popular Literature* (Chapel Hill and London: University of North Carolina Press).

Reynolds, S. (2005), *Rip it Up and Start Again: Post Punk 1978–1984* (London: Faber and Faber).

Reynolds, S. (2009), *Totally Wired: Post-Punk Interviews and Overviews* (London: Faber and Faber).

Riddell, A. (ed.) (1975), 'The Image in the Machine', in A. Riddell (ed.), *Typewriter Art* (London: London Magazine Editions), pp. 10–15.

Rilke, R.M. (1997), *Diaries of a Young Poet*, trans. E. Snow and M. Winkler (New York: W.W. Norton & Co.).

Rimmer, D. (1986), 'Why is He Still in the Job?', *Q* 1 (3), December, 63–9.

Robertson, S. (1982), 'Hex Education', *Sounds*, 8 May.

Rom, R. (1986), 'Semi-Detached Suburban Mr. Smith', *Sounds*, 19 July.

Rose, J. (2001), *The Intellectual History of the British Working Classes* (London: Yale University Press).

Rothenbuhler, E.W. and McCourt, T. (1992), 'Commercial Radio and Popular Music', in J. Lull (ed.), *Popular Music and Communication*, 2nd edn (London: Sage), pp. 101–15.

Savage, J. (1991), *England's Dreaming: The Sex Pistols and Punk Rock* (London: Faber and Faber).

Savage, J. (2008), 'The Things That Aren't There Anymore', *Critical Quarterly* 50 (1–2), 180–97.

Segal, D. (1989), 'Hip Priest in Motown', *You Can't Hide Your Love Forever* 3, Winter, 2, 3, 32, available at http://www.visi.com/fall/gigography/89ychylf.html

Shapely, P. (2006), 'Tenants Arise! Consumerism, Tenants and the Challenge to Council Authority in Manchester, 1968–92', *Social History* 31 (1), 60–78.

Sharp, Colin (2007) *Who Killed Martin Hannett? The Story of Factory Records' Musical Magician* (London: Aurum Press).

Shaw, P. (1989), *Whose Game is it Anyway? The Book of Football Fanzines* (Hemel Hempstead: Argus).

Shaw, W. (1986), 'The Fall/Adult Net. Who?', *Smash Hits* 8–21 October, 48–9.

Shepherd, J. et al. (eds) (2003), *The Continuum Encyclopedia of Popular Music of the World*, vol. 1: *Media, Industry and Society* (London: Continuum).

Shirley, I. (2006), *Record Collector: Rare Record Price Guide 2008* (London: Diamond).

Shuker, R. (1998), *Key Concepts in Popular Music* (London: Routledge).

Simmel, G. (1971) *On Individuality and Social Forms*, ed. D.N. Levine (Chicago: University of Chicago Press).

Simpson, D. (2008), *The Fallen: Searching for the Missing Members of The Fall* (Edinburgh: Canongate Books).

Sinker, M. (1986), 'Watching the City Hobgoblins', *The Wire*, August, available at http://www.rocksbackpages.com

Sinker, M. (1988), 'England: Look Back in Anguish', *NME*, 2 January, available at http://www.rocksbackpages.com

Skeggs, B. (2005), 'The Making of Class and Gender through Visualizing Moral Subject Formation', *Sociology* 39 (5), 965–82.

Smith, M.E. (1985), *The Fall Lyrics* (English and German) (Berlin: Lough Press).

Smith, M.E. (2008a), *Renegade: The Lives and Tales of Mark E. Smith* (London: Viking).

Smith, M.E. (2008b) *vII* (Berlin: The Lough Press).

Smith, M.E. as Totale, R. (1980), 'Call Yourselves Bloody Professionals?' (sleeve notes to The Fall, *Totale's Turns*, Rough Trade, ROUGH10).

Smith, R.T. (2003) *The Hollow Log Lounge* (Champaign: University of Illinois Press).

Sproat, K. (1999a), 'The Outsiders', *The Biggest Library Yet* 16, 6–7.

Sproat, K. (1999b), 'The Aural and Social Effects of Permanent Construction, Deconstruction and Reconstruction of Music', *The Biggest Library Yet* 16, 33.

Stallybrass, Peter and White, Allon (1986) *The Politics and Poetics of Transgression* (Ithaca: Cornell University Press).

Stephanson, Anders (1988) 'Regarding Postmodernism – A Conversation with Fredric Jameson', in A. Ross (ed.), *Universal Abandon? The Politics of Postmodernism* (Minneapolis: University of Minnesota Press), pp. 3–30.

Sullivan, C. (2004) 'How I Became a Girl Aloud', *The Guardian*, 17 September.

Sutton, D. and Martin-Jones, D. (2008), *Deleuze Reframed* (London: I.B. Tauris).

Taylor, D.J. (2008), '"Mein Kampf" for Generation "Hollyoaks"', *Independent on Sunday*, 27 April, pp. 34–5.

Taylor, F.W. (1998), *Principles of Scientific Management* (New York: Dover).

Taylor, L. (2005), 'It was Beautiful Before You Changed It All: Class, Taste and the Transformative Aesthetics of the Garden Lifestyle Media', in D. Bell and J. Hollows (eds), *Ordinary Lifestyles: Popular Media, Consumption and Taste* (Maidenhead: Open University Press), pp. 113–27.

Tessler, H. (2006), 'Dialect and Dialectic: John Peel's "Stylised Scouseness" and Contested Contexts of Englishness in Broadcast Radio', *Radio Journal – International Studies in Broadcast and Audio Media* 4 (1/3), 49–67.

Thompson, B. (2001), *Ways of Hearing: A User's Guide to the Pop Psyche, from Elvis to Eminem* (London: Orion).

Thompson, D. (2003), *A User's Guide to The Fall* (London: Helter Skelter).

Thomson, P. (1972), *The Grotesque*, Critical Idiom Series (London: Methuen).

Thornton, S. (1995), *Club Cultures: Music, Media and Subcultural Capital* (Cambridge: Polity Press).

Thornton, T.P. (1996) *Handwriting in America: A Cultural History* (New Haven: Yale University Press).

Tickell, A. and Peck, J. (1996), 'The Return of the Manchester Men: Men's Words and Men's Deeds in the Remaking of the Local State', *Transactions of the Institute of British Geographers* 21 (4), 595–616.

Time Out editors (2008), *Time Out – London Calling: High Art and Low Life in the Capital Since 1968* (London: Ebury Publishing).

Tyler, I. (2008), 'Chav Mum Chav Scum', *Feminist Media Studies* 8 (1), 17–34.

Valentine, M. (1987), *Town of a Magic Dream: Arthur Machen in Whitby* (Southampton: Caerman).

Walker, S. (2001), *Typography and Language in Everyday Life: Prescriptions and Practices* (Harlow: Longman).

Wall, M. (2004), *John Peel: A Tribute to the Much-loved DJ and Broadcaster* (London: Orion).

Wall, T. (2003), *Studying Popular Music Culture* (London: Arnold).

Ward, K. (2003), 'Entrepreneurial Urbanism', *Area* 35 (2), 116–27.

Watson, B. (2004), *Derek Bailey and the Story of Free Improvisation* (London and New York: Verso).

Weingart, W. (2000), *Typography: My Way to Typography*, trans. K. Wolff and C. Schelbert (Baden: Lars Müller).

Wilde, J. (1984), 'The Frightening World of The Fall', *Jamming!* 22, 26–8.

Williams, G. (2003), *The Enterprising City Centre: Manchester's Development Challenge* (London: Taylor & Francis).

Williams, R. (1973), 'Base and Superstructure in Marxist Cultural Theory', *New Left Review* 82, 5–16.

Willis, P. (1978), *Profane Culture* (London: Routledge and Kegan Paul).

Wilson, A. (2002), *24 Hour Party People: What the Sleeve Notes Never Tell You* (London: Channel 4 Books).

Wilson, C. (1956), *The Outsider* (London: Victor Gollancz).

Winterbottom, M. (dir.) (2002), *24 Hour Party People* (London: Baby Cow Productions).

Select Discography of The Fall

The following is a discography of selected recordings of The Fall referred to in this volume. It includes all the major studio LPs along with some significant singles, live albums and compilations. For an annotated discography up until 2002, see D. Thompson (2003), *A User's Guide to The Fall* (London: Helter Skelter) and for a full up-to-date discography see The Fall Online, 'Discography' at http://www.visi.com/fall/discography.html, compiled by Conway Paton, on which this discography is based.

References are to LPs up until 1999 and CDs from 2000.

(1978), 'Bingo-Master's Break-Out!/'Repetition' (Step Forward: SF 7).
(1979), *Live at the Witch Trials* (Step Forward: SFLP1).
(1979), *Dragnet* (Step Forward: SFLP4).
(1979), 'Rowche Rumble'/'In My Area' (Step Forward: SF11).
(1980), *Totale's Turns (Its Now or Never)* (Rough Trade: RT 10).
(1980), *Grotesque (After the Gramme)* (Rough Trade: RT 18).
(1980), 'Fiery Jack'/'2nd Dark Age'/'Psychic Dancehall 2' (Step Forward: SF13).
(1980), 'How I Wrote "Elastic Man"'/'City Hobgoblins' (Rough Trade: RT 48).
(1980), 'Totally Wired'/'Putta Block' (Rough Trade: RT 56).
(1981), *Slates* (10 inch EP) (Rough Trade: RT 71).
(1982) *Hex Enduction Hour* (Kamera Records: KAM 005).
(1982), *Room to Live* (Kamera: KAM011).
(1982), *A Part of America Therein* (Cottage: LP1).
(1982), 'Look Know'/'I'm Into C.B.' (Kamera: ERA004).
(1983) *Perverted by Language* (Rough Trade: RT 62).
(1983), 'The Man Whose Head Expanded' (Rough Trade: RT 133).
(1983), 'Kicker Conspiracy'/'Wings' (Rough Trade Records: RT 143).
(1983), *Hip Priests and Kamerads* (Situation 2: SITU 13).
(1984), *The Wonderful and Frightening World of The Fall* (Beggars Banquet: BEGA 58).
(1985), *This Nation's Saving Grace* (Beggars Banquet: BEGA 67).
(1986), *Bend Sinister* (Beggars Banquet: BEGA 86).
(1988), *The Frenz Experiment* (Beggars Banquet: BEGA 91).
(1988), *I am Curious Oranj* (Beggars Banquet: BEGA 96).
(1988), 'Jerusalem'/'Big New Prinz' (Beggars Banquet: FALL2B).
(1990), *Extricate* (Cog Sinister/Fontana: LP 842.204-1).
(1991), *Shift-Work* (Cog Sinister/Fontana: LP 848.594-1).
(1992), *Code: Selfish* (Cog Sinister/Fontana: LP 512.162-1).
(1993), *The Infotainment Scan* (Cog Sinister/Permanent: PERMLP 12).

(1994), *Middle Class Revolt* (Cog Sinister/Permanent: PERMLP 16).

(1995), *Cerebral Caustic* (Cog Sinister/Permanent: PERMLP 30).

(1995), *The Twenty Seven Points* (Cog Sinister/Permanent: PERMLP36).

(1996), *The Light User Syndrome* (Jet Records: JETLP 1012).

(1997), *Levitate* (Artful Records: ARTFULLP 9).

(1999), *The Marshall Suite* (Artful Records: ARTFULLP 17).

(2000), *The Unutterable* (Eagle Records: EAGCD 164).

(2002), *Are You Are Missing Winner* (Cog Sinister/Voiceprint: COGVP131CD).

(2003), *The Real New Fall LP Formerly 'Country on the Click'* (Action Records: TAKE 041).

(2003), *It's The New Thing! The Step Forward Years* (Castle/Sanctuary Records: CMQCD697).

(2004), *Interim* (Hip Priest/Voiceprint: HIPP004CD).

(2005), *Fall Heads Roll* (Slogan Records/Sanctuary: SLOCD003).

(2005), *The Complete Peel Sessions 1978–2004* (Castle/Sanctuary: CMXB982).

(2007), *Reformation Post TLC* (Slogan Records/Sanctuary: SLOCD007).

(2008), *Imperial Wax Solvent* (Sanctuary, Universal: CD: 1765729).

(2009), *Last Night at the Palais* (Sanctuary, Universal: CD and DVD: 2713432).

Video

(1983), *Perverted by Language Bis* (Ikon Videos: IKON 8).

Index